Wondrous
Contrivances

Research for this book was made possible by a grant
from the Alfred P. Sloan Foundation

Wondrous Contrivances

TECHNOLOGY AT THE THRESHOLD

* * *

by Merritt Ierley

CLARKSON POTTER / PUBLISHERS
NEW YORK

Published by Clarkson Potter / Publishers, New York, New York.
Member of the Crown Publishing Group, a division of Random House, Inc.

www.randomhouse.com

CLARKSON N. POTTER is a trademark and POTTER and colophon are
registered trademarks of Random House, Inc.

Printed in the United States of America

Design by Caitlin Daniels Israel

Library of Congress Cataloging-in-Publication Data
Ierley, Merritt.
Wondrous contrivances : technology at the threshold / Merritt Ierley.—1st ed.
Includes bibliographical references and index.
1. Technology—Social aspects—United States—History.   I. Title.

T14.5 .I36 2002

609.73—dc21   2001035957

ISBN 0-609-60836-3

10 9 8 7 6 5 4 3 2 1

First Edition

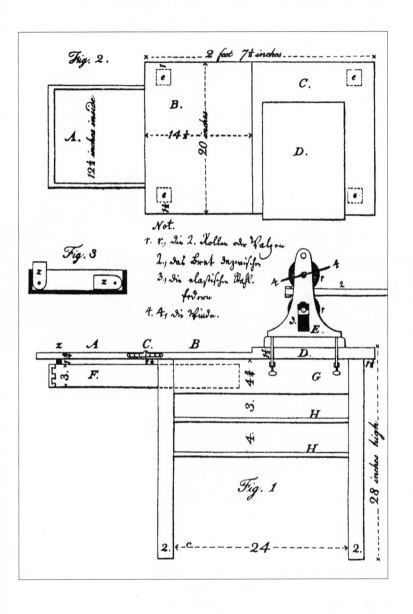

Fig. 2.

2 feet 7⅛ inches

A.

12⅞ inches inside

B.

C.

e

e

D.

14⅞

20 inches

Not.

r. r., die 2. Rollen oder Walzen

2., das Brot dazwischen

3., die elastische Stahl-
feder

4. 4, die Winden.

Fig. 3

z   z

z   A   C   B

4

4   r

2

3   r

E

z   3.   F

D

H

4⅞

G

3.   H

4.   H

Fig. 1

28 inches high

2.   c   24   2.

CONTENTS

PART 2: COMMUNICATIONS

PART 3: ENTERTAINMENT

ACKNOWLEDGMENTS

UNIQUELY APPROPRIATE as a primary resource for this work was the Smithsonian Institution, and I am enormously grateful for all the support and cooperation that was provided. My thanks in particular to the following, both for their suggestions and for reading and critiquing all or parts of the manuscript: Air and Space Museum: F. Robert van der Linden, curator of air transportation; Computer Technology: Jon Eklund, curator emeritus of information technology, and Alicia Cutler, museum specialist, computer collections; Electrical Collections: Dr. Bernard S. Finn, curator; Elliot Sivowitch, museum specialist emeritus, and Hal Wallace, museum specialist; History of Technology: William E. Worthington Jr., assistant curator; Photographic History Collections: Shannon Perich, museum specialist; Division of Social History: Anne M. Serio, assistant curator; and Transportation Collections: William L. Withuhn, senior curator; Roger B. White, museum specialist, and Albert S. Eggerton, consultant on railroads.

For reading and most capably critiquing the manuscript, my sincerest thanks also go to two longtime, close friends: John L. McKnight, professor emeritus of physics, College of William and Mary, Williamsburg, Virginia, and William A. Molineux, Williamsburg, Virginia, recently retired editorial page editor and book review editor, the *Daily Press,* Newport News, Virginia.

The New York Public Library has been a vital resource to me throughout my writing career. In particular I wish to thank for their help (past projects as well as this one): Elizabeth Diefendorf, chief librarian for general research; and Madeleine Cohen, head of information services, and Jacqueline Gold, librarian, Science, Industry and Business Library, a division of the New York Public Library.

I wish to thank the American Antiquarian Society, Worcester, Massachusetts, and especially Laura E. Wasowicz, reference specialist for children's literature and graphic arts; the Museum of the City of New York, Amy A. Weinstein, curator, and Elizabeth Ellis, senior cataloguer/collections access associate; the National Archives, Still Pictures Branch, Mary Ilario, archives specialist; and the Strong Museum, Rochester, New York, Patricia Hogan, curator.

My thanks to Paul Van Eeckhoven, Net Access Technology, Newton, New Jersey, who has kept the author's computer running through several books and, in the process, provided much appreciated insight into the practical side of how computers work.

My sincere thanks also to my editors at Clarkson Potter, Roy Finamore, special projects editor, and Lance Troxel and Martin Patmos, editorial assistants, and my agent, Faith Hamlin, and her associate, Sean McCormick, of Sanford J. Greenburger Associates, for their unique contributions.

Last, but most important, I wish to acknowledge with profoundest thanks the support of the Alfred P. Sloan Foundation, and in particular, Doron Weber, program director. It was a grant from the Foundation, under its Public Understanding of Science and Technology Program, that made the writing of this book possible.

GLORY TO GOD ON HIGH

AND ON EARTH PEACE GOODWILL TOWARDS MEN

TRINITY CHURCH, NEW YORK,
SEPTEMBER 1, 1858
Frank Leslie's Illustrated Newspaper, September 18, 1858

PROLOGUE

THERE WAS ONCE a time when people never talked to each other except in each other's company . . . when not a note of music was ever heard except in the performer's presence . . . when only the dwindling dimness of memory sufficed for remembering some special occasion.

Communicating with one another was changed forever by the telegraph (1844) and then with transmission of the human voice by telephone (1876); with the latter, one could converse at great distance with all the immediacy and much of the intimacy of being in the other's presence. With the phonograph (1877), that performer whose presence had been the sine qua non of listening to music was now a cylinder of wax that could be listened to anytime, almost anywhere. And with photography (the mid– to late nineteenth century) a moment in time that was heretofore just a fleeting memory became a photographic image preserved for posterity.

This was technology at the threshold. This is what the technology revolution was like at the front lines.

Today the telegraph and telephone, the phonograph and the camera, are so taken for granted as barely to be thought of as modern inventions. It is almost as if talking on the telephone and listening to recorded music are things people have always done. Yet these were extraordinary changes in modern life. Did people recognize them as such, right from the start? Did they appreciate the significance? Were they comfortable with how things changed?

For the most part, there was not only early recognition but often wide-eyed wonder that has never been equaled. Perhaps the most extraordinary outpouring of tribute to new technology took place in the late summer of 1858: an "irrepressible outburst of enthusiastic joy in all parts of the country" (quoting the *New York Times*) . . . the firing of guns and ringing of bells . . . flags and banners in the streets. "Everybody all agog," wrote a diarist in the city; while in the country sixteen-year-old Caroline Cowles Richards observed that in just her little, rural village, "Guns were fired and church bells rung and flags were waving everywhere. In the evening there was a torchlight procession and the town was all lighted up."

In New York City, the official celebration of "the wondrous event of a wondrous age" was on September 1, 1858: "a display such as even New York has never witnessed" with parades and fireworks, stores and hotels decked out with banners and bunting, and even a "Reception of the Heroes" at the Battery and a parade up Broadway to City Hall. At Trinity Church—then the tallest structure in the city's slowly rising skyline—what happened is especially noteworthy because no one today expects to find a house of worship the focus of a celebration of technology. Yet what happened there, according to *Frank Leslie's Illustrated News,* was "probably the most impressive service that has ever been performed in this country." Thousands who wanted to be a part of it had to settle for standing on the sidewalks outside. Those who got in were astounded by the magnificent decorations: three lofty Gothic arches of wood covered with flowers—literally thousands and thousands of roses and lilies, gladioli and asters, and so on "in infinite profusion," highlighted by a floral inscription reading "Glory to God on High."

All this, in veneration of the first transatlantic telegraph cable.

The more the wonders, though, the less wondrous they seem to be. Surely no one of the present era doubts the ingeniousness of the times. If anything, the present seems preeminent for the sheer show of what technology can do. No church bells, though. No torchlight parades. No gathering of worshipers to praise God on High for the newest miracle of computer science.

So times have changed. And yet the drawing of conclusions can be risky. Are we simply a more blasé age? Or are there just too many wonders to celebrate?

It is not essential in looking back at technology at the threshold to draw moralistic conclusions. What we are seeking is a deeper historical perspective against which to appreciate better what is on the threshold today, and whatever may come along tomorrow.

Going back to what was new in communications, transportation, and entertainment—and continuing through to the personal computer, Internet, and e-mail—let us see: how people first became aware of what was new and sometimes startling; what they first learned about it; how they reacted; what they liked or didn't like; whether they were bewildered or skeptical; what skills they had to learn (skills often taken for granted today); how fast new technology was assimilated into everyday life.

The emphasis in these pages will be on the original impact of technology. We will generally not attempt to follow the development of new devices and systems except to the extent that some particular development is significant to our basic perspective. Nor, by any means, will we attempt to include everything that might be considered a wondrous contrivance. The focus will be in three areas where technology impacts directly on everyday life. Specifically not included is household technology (heating, plumbing, lighting, major appliances) since the evolution of household comfort and convenience was the subject of my previous book.

We will be looking for parallels between one emerging form of technology and another. Some interesting overlaps emerge. Take the following two quotations, for example:

> The *computer* has become a necessity of modern civilization. The age is one of intense concentration and specialization. It is tremendously exacting. Everything must be done in the quickest time and in the best way.

> My boys talk *computers* all day—and dream them all night, I guess. . . . They certainly get a lot of amusement and good, sound and useful knowledge out of their work. Their *computer* is the best investment I ever made.

Each quotation would seem to be a quintessential comment on the computer age—except that neither was written about computers. The first is from *Education* magazine, June 1892. Substitute *typewriter* and it reads as originally written. The second is from a 1922 book, *The Wireless in the Home*. Substitute radio.

The typewriter and the home computer rose to popularity in remarkable parallels almost exactly a century apart. The first typewriter, for all practical purposes, was Christopher Sholes's Remington Model No. 1, which had its public introduction in 1876. It was slow to catch on, in part because it was expensive. The typewriter represented a new technology and an entirely new way of doing something that had been done in only one way since the dawn of literacy—writing by hand, with stylus or pen, in prescribed patterns of lines and circles. In using the typewriter, one had to adapt to a strange new way of accomplishing the same end. It was not until the 1890s that the typewriter began to soar in popularity.

The personal computer—and vastly more sweeping change—arrived almost exactly a century after the Remington Model No. 1. The first successful one was the Altair 8800, which was introduced late in 1975. Other home computers, more sophisticated and practical, appeared in the following years, but use of computers in the home remained relatively limited for the time being. It was not until the 1990s that the computer began to soar in acceptance, following precisely the same trajectory as had the typewriter in the 1870s through the 1890s.

Going back and observing this parallel, and then in ampler detail seeing how the typewriter came into use, and how it developed in response to reaction to it, we may then reflect: Without the typewriter having been so thoroughly assimilated into everyday life, would the personal computer—a more complex form of technology than anything yet faced by the consumer—look and work anything like it does? Would it have come into use relatively so quickly? Would it have come into use at all?

Home computers might be entirely different. The 1975 Altair actually had toggle switches instead of a keyboard and mouse, and data printout in place of a monitor—a configuration quickly abandoned by home computer makers in favor of a typewriter-like device. How we use the home computer and how we communicate with its inner workings generally mirror our experience with the typewriter right down to the very posture we have in using the computer. In each case we sit in front of a keyboard and watch our progress on an interface immediately in back of it—in the case of the computer, a screen; on a typewriter, a platen and sheet of paper.

How much more significant, now, that 1892 reaction to the typewriter: It "has become a necessity of modern civilization."

Gauging contemporary reaction is our goal here, and we must be rather imaginative, but this often provides unique insight. For example, one means of gauging assimilation of technology into everyday life will be to see when a new device shows up in the form of toys for children. Or as games, or in children's literature. Sources such as this amplify our appreciation of just how quickly and deeply certain technologies have impacted on American life.

Consider the telegraph, for example. It is essential to know that only one day after Samuel F. B. Morse's 1844 demonstration of the "Electro Magnetic Telegraph" at the United States Capitol, the *Baltimore Patriot* declared it a "truly astonishing contrivance. . . . This is indeed the annihilation of space." But is it not also significant to learn that in *Little Charley's Christmas Amusements,* published in Philadelphia in 1852, there is already talk about children playing with "electric toys"?

That was a very fast response. Little Charley's playthings weren't electric trains or anything of that sort, to be sure. Electricity still had very limited application. Arc lighting would not come into practical use until the late 1850s, and then only for lighthouses. The word *electric* was still barely used in everyday conversation; it was largely limited to the lexicon of scientists. Morse's invention, commonly identified as the "electro-magnetic" telegraph, began changing that. Fast. What Little Charley had were magnetic devices of some kind, possibly also playthings using static electricity. But the point is that the modern concept of electricity was coming into public consciousness. We can also look to a children's story of the early 1850s for evidence of this:

George and Thomas Bates had often expressed a desire to visit the telegraph office. They had heard of the strange doings of this wonderful machine, and had often stood and looked at the wires stretched along from one high post to another, seeming like cobwebs in the air. One day . . . George asked Thomas how it could be that on those wires unseen messages were passing to and fro. "I don't know how it is," replied Thomas; "father says it is by means of electricity, and lightning is electricity, and that is the reason news travels so quickly by the magnetic telegraph." One day, after school, these boys went into their father's store . . . and asked him if he would be so kind as to take them to see this wonderful invention.

In toys as well as literature, we are looking for evidence of impact. But there is a curious, one-of-a-kind twist to this—a toy *cre-*

ating the impact. It was the toy "helicopter" Bishop Milton Wright took home with him from a church trip in 1878 for sons Wilbur and Orville. As Orville later recalled: "Our first interest [in flying] began when we were children. Father brought home to us a small toy actuated by a rubber spring which would lift itself into the air. We built a number of copies of this toy, which flew successfully."

There is insight also in looking at owner's manuals. What they emphasize tends to indicate what the new owner needs to know about that new technology (or to put it the other way around, what it's assumed he or she doesn't know yet). From time to time, this will be done in the form of a sidebar quoting from an owner's manual or some other learning tool.

And there are traditional sources like newspapers, magazines, professional journals, and trade publications. Especially helpful were *Scientific American,* which was founded in 1845, and *Popular Science,* 1872. Both were there to help unravel the secrets of a host of new inventions.

Sometimes, as we will see, reaction to incoming technology triggered imaginative conceptions of entirely new technology that would only come to pass decades, or even a century, later. The telephone (1876) had a particular proclivity for this. In chapter 10, "Doing What Came Naturally: The Home Computer," will be found a short section considering how a series of improvisations on the early telephone—some merely imaginative ideas; others, like the Telephone Herald, that actually went into limited use— presaged elements of what eventually became the Internet in the late twentieth century. Drawings by Albert Robida dating to c. 1883 (page 177) show his imaginative *téléphonoscope* being used— on-line, in a rudimentary sense—to pick out clothes and take a course in mathematics at home. A classic drawing by George Dumaurier in the British magazine *Punch* (page 248) portrays a family watching "television" in 1879. In effect, these were responses to the coming of the telephone. Similarly, early radio gave rise to an imaginative device called the "Wireless Type- writer," demonstrated by Norwegian scientist Hans Knudsen, as reported in *Scientific American* in 1908.

As we look back, we will find aspects of original impact that tend to appear and reappear, offering much for us to reflect on as we encounter technological innovation coming now and still to come. Points to ponder include the following.

HIGH EXPECTATIONS

Sometimes the euphoria of newness prompts expectations that are patently unrealistic. It was once thought, for example, that the telegraph might do away with the postal system:

> In fact, we believe that the magnetic telegraph is going to produce a greater change in some of the social institutions of the country than any one now imagines. We do believe that it will supersede entirely the Post Office Department. (*New York Herald,* October 24, 1845)

As for the phonograph:

> When the phonograph first made its appearance, in 1878, it took a remarkably strong hold on the imagination both of scientific men and of the general public. It was prophesied at the time that . . . letters would be spoken instead of written. (*Scientific American,* March 9, 1901)

TECHNOLOGY AND THE PACE OF LIFE

A marked effect of technological evolution, albeit one often forgotten, has been to quicken, indeed greatly accelerate, the pace of life. Transportation timetables. Instant communication by cell phone. Nightly television schedules. Life governed by the clock, whereas long ago there was only light and darkness by which to divide one's day. All these have resulted in the quickened pace of modern life.

THE NEED FOR SPEED

A corollary to the pace of life will be most evident in transportation, but it overlaps into communications and entertainment. We have an insatiable need to go places and do things at an ever faster pace. The first railroad passengers were breathtaken. "We flew on the wings of the wind at the varied speed of fifteen to twenty-five miles an hour, annihilating time and space," proclaimed a passenger in South Carolina's *Charleston Courier* in 1830. And by the turn of a new century: "The sentiment which influenced the managers of these through lines to introduce these extremely fast trains is the desire for racing, common to all animals, and most thoroughly developed in human beings," said Angus Sinclair, publisher of *Railway and Locomotive Engineering,* in 1905, commenting on the New York Central's new Twentieth Century Limited that would run from New York to Chicago in eighteen hours, at an average speed of 53 miles per hour.

TECHNOLOGY IS WHAT WE MAKE OF IT

As fast and effortless as it is today, communication is still only what is being communicated. Does speed and facility improve or diminish the essential quality of thought that is transferred from one mind to another? That seems to be what one early observer was thinking, at the time of one of those really great explosions of technological advancement—the establishing of nearly instantaneous communication between America and Europe by transatlantic cable:

> A successful Atlantic telegraph will not, in itself, be so monstrous an advance in the art of far-writing. Its significance is in the importance of the two parties who talk through it. (*Galaxy,* September 1, 1866)

Ralph Waldo Emerson, on hearing that the cable might eventually enable someone in London to talk by telephone with someone in New York, is said to have wondered, "But will he have anything to say?" Such skepticism may be contrasted with the admission of a self-confessed "radio maniac" of the 1920s:

> It is not the *substance* of communication without wires, but the *fact* of it that enthralls.

Prior to e-mail, the fax machine seemed to revolutionize correspondence. But was it necessarily better to be faster? Complained *New York Times* columnist Russell Baker in 1991 with typical wry humor: "For centuries whenever people had felt an urge to send a message, they sat down and wrote a letter [and] the act of thinking about it usually showed it wasn't worth the price of a stamp. Thus were perhaps billions of superfluous messages happily aborted between the impulse and transmission. . . . With a fax machine whenever you felt a message coming on you could drop it immediately on the target. Bingo! Bombo! Message delivered."

THE CONQUERING OF COMPLEXITY

The early automobile was probably the most complex piece of consumer-operated machinery anyone had confronted to date. The relatively quick acceptance of the automobile, its intricacies of operation notwithstanding, was part of a process of conquering complexity that made possible the relatively easy assimilation of a host of consumer-operated devices in the twentieth century. As Hiram Percy Maxim wrote in his recollections of the early motor car:

> One of the major difficulties in 1897 and 1898 was getting the average person to operate properly the gear shift of a gasoline-carriage. . . . At the time of which I write, few people believed that the general public would ever be able to coördinate the clutch pedal and the gear-shift lever. That the authorities were absolutely wrong and that the public did learn the complex manipulations necessary to shift gears is very significant.

The mastering of complexity has been a cumulative process. Before the early nineteenth century there was barely anything that could be described as consumer technology—a few copying machines, a few water closets, a few Rumford ovens, for example. As consumer technology evolved—at first, mostly in the form of household conveniences—manufacturers took it for granted that even seemingly simple devices would take some getting used to. With Terriff's Perfect Washer, c. 1850, came a pasted-on printed notice advising: "Don't put too many garments in the machine until you get used to operating it; about three shirts at a time is sufficient. Do not get discouraged if you do not learn to run the machine thoroughly the first time. Use for at least three washings." And this was basically just a tub full of suds with a handle to turn it.

When the Edison phonograph was coming on the market in

1878, *Popular Science Monthly* was as much impressed with its seeming simplicity as with its technological significance: This "acoustical marvel of the century" is "as simple as a grindstone . . . as simple as a coffee-mill. . . . By the simple turning of the crank, the machine talks, sings, shouts, laughs, whistles, and coughs, so naturally and distinctly, that the listener can hardly believe his senses."

By the time the automobile came on the scene, people at least had the experience of turning the cranks of washers and phonographs as a prelude to cranking engines. Even so, the early automobile was not an easy device to master. Just starting the engine was a complex procedure, something like preparing a small plane for flight today. It's a wonder enough people persevered in the very early days to make motoring eventually something for everyone.

But people did persevere, and the explanation is analogous to what has happened in athletics, where records for speed, endurance, and distance are continually broken. Running (assuming footwear to be a negligible factor) is perhaps the purest example of what the human body has adapted itself to do. In 1886, a mile in 4:12.3 was the world record and lasted the better part of half a century. When it was broken in 1923, by two seconds, a mile in four minutes still seemed beyond human capability. Yet that was accomplished in 1954, and as of 2000 the record stood at 3:43.1– almost half a minute faster than the record of 1886.

What one person can do, why can't another do? What one can learn, why can't the next person learn?

Collective experience helps to account for assimilation of consumer technology that would have been totally unfathomable to someone pondering instructions about washing three shirts at a time. The collective conquering of complexity goes a long way in explaining how the personal computer–arguably the most complex consumer technology of all–was being used by more than 80 million Americans at the turn of the twenty-first century.

A FEELING OF MASTERY

Finally, there is that quality of technology that often bestows on **10** its user, subtly or not, a sense of power, almost of omnipotence. It was a quality that was recognized right at the beginning of the automobile age. *Motor World* magazine put its finger on it in 1901:

> To take control of this materialized energy, to draw the reins over this monster with its steel muscles and fiery heart—there is something in the idea which appeals to an almost universal sense, the love of power.

That was a steel monster of just a few horsepower. How much greater the sense of power sitting behind the steering wheel today. Yet the automobile is only one facet of daily living. How greater still the sense of mastery sitting behind the keyboard of a personal computer linked to the Internet. Surely much of the rapture is the sense of being in the center of things, of having the world at one's fingertips.

RIVER IN THE CATSKILLS, THOMAS COLE, 1843
Courtesy Museum of Fine Arts, Boston. Gift of Martha C. Karolik for the M. and M. Karolik
Collection of American Paintings.

PART I

TRANSPORTATION

FOR SOME, AS FOR THOMAS COLE, whose painting *River in the Catskills* (1843) is the frontispiece to Part 1, new technology was intrusive. A naturalist and poet as well as a painter, Cole abhorred even the buzz of sawmills and the smell of tanneries in his beloved Catskill Mountains. How much worse the ruination when the Canajoharie and Catskill Rail Road rumbled into his wilderness in the mid-1830s. Cole pressed for a public debate: "Are railroads and canals favorable or unfavorable to the morality and happiness of . . . the United States?" When the debate was put to the tip of his brush, however, Cole subtly allowed the inevitability of progress. His painting, showing the Catskills in all their splendor, admits the railroad as a wisp of smoke (center left on page 12) that divulges a train making its way across a trestle.

That Cole's hostility was tempered by a sense of inevitability is apparent from a curious sidelight. *River in the Catskills* was painted in 1843. In March 1840 the Canajoharie and Catskill suffered a devastating accident: A trestle over the Catskill Creek gave way, sending a train hurtling into the river. The line's only passenger cars were destroyed and its one locomotive damaged; the mishap effectively put the railroad out of business. Cole might have painted a scene of mangled cars lying in the Catskill Creek and called *that* his River in the Catskills. Instead, this first great American landscape painter—in this first representation of the railroad in American art—allowed his hallowed landscape to illustrate a point: What no clock can turn back ought to be accepted with equanimity.

We generally find an overwhelmingly positive reaction to new technology. As the British novelist Anthony Trollope wrote in 1862 after visiting America, "The great glory of the Americans is in their wondrous contrivances." But it has never been a one-way street. Transportation, in particular, has often imposed heavy hardship through dislodgment and a disquieting presence. Railroads, in the early days, were notorious for running roughshod in laying out routes. Highways, airport runways, even aircraft approach routes have all dislocated in various ways. The noise factor in modern transportation is vastly beyond the buzz that Cole dreaded.

Yet whatever the negatives, Americans have gloried in their wondrous devices from the start, and railroads provided the first real savor of speed.

The automobile combined speed with another American trait—a zest for personal mobility. When it came to taking to the air, Americans were more cautious. Even in 1927, according to a major magazine of the day, it was thought to be a case of "Air-Shy America . . . The United States, except for its flyers, is air-shy. It quickly made an industry of the movies and the automobile; but of the airplane it made only a stunt performer, never considering it seriously as a vehicle for the civilian." That would change with the coming of scheduled airline travel. As in that valley in the Catskills, the clock turns only clockwise.

CHAPTER ONE

ANNIHILATING TIME AND SPACE

THE RAILROADS

We flew on the wings of the wind at the varied speed of fifteen to twenty-five miles an hour, annihilating time and space.

—*Charleston Courier,* December 29, 1830

IN ALL THE AGES OF HUMAN HISTORY, from the confines of the cave dweller to the post-Napoleonic world of steam power, the general pace of travel had never progressed much beyond what could be done with one's own two feet. Most people had to settle for walking, usually never far from home.

At more than 15 miles an hour, the first run of the first scheduled railroad train in America, on Christmas Day, 1830, seemed as fast as the wind to a passenger who told all about it in the *Charleston Courier.* That kind of travel, at a speed the equivalent of a brisk breeze, was faster than humankind was used to moving. For most people in 1830, a walking pace of 2 to 3 miles an hour was as fast as the scenery ever went by.

Steamboats plying the Hudson River between New York and Albany could traverse the 150 or so miles in roughly ten hours in the early 1830s. That was 15 miles an hour, but only a relative few could afford that kind of travel or even lived in proximity to steamboats. Otherwise travel on water was considerably slower: by canal boat, anywhere from 1½ to 5 miles per hour; and interruptions in service—ice in winter, floods or drought in summer—were a constant problem. Sailing packets depended on the wind. At the turn of the nineteenth century, those on the Hudson River took anywhere from two days to two weeks, depending on the wind and the direction of travel, to get from New York to Albany.

The fastest land travel, before the age of railroads, was the stagecoach, which on a good road averaged perhaps 6 to 8 miles an hour. On that critical route between New York and Philadelphia, sharp competition forced maximum effort by drivers and horses, upping average speed to roughly 11 miles an hour, but that was exceptionally fast travel over land.

No wonder travelers were so awed by what the railroad accomplished. The redoubtable Davy Crockett, a few years later, had his own way of reckoning it: "I can only judge of the speed by putting my head out to spit, which I did, and overtook it so quick, that it hit me smack in the face." So great became an obsession with speed that it tended to distort reality. When a Baltimore and Ohio train was late leaving Cumberland, Maryland, in 1855, it tried to make up the time, its engine darting with "rocket-like impetuosity." "In vain," said passenger Charles Richard Weld, "was the conductor urged to slacken the excessive speed." There was a "terrific crash . . . heavings and collisions, terminating in deathlike silence." Whereupon, said Weld, survivors, instead of rebuking the conductor, praised him for his noble attempt to arrive on time.

But speed was more than physical sensation. It was also a redefinition of time and space. "To see more clearly the curtailing influence of these [rail]roads on space and time," said *Niles' Register* in 1831, projecting rail travel a few years hence, "let us suppose that at less speed *by a third* than in *this early stage* of locomotive experiment, has already been safely accomplished, a passenger [in Philadelphia] was to set out on a rail road toward the west. [He would] reach Lancaster in 2 hours, Pittsburg in 10 hours, New Orleans in less than 2 days, and return to Philadelphia within a week."

In the context of travel times in 1831, that was redefining time and space. A few years later, *Niles'* declared that "Science has conquered space. . . . The people of places 1,000 miles apart, are nearer neighbors. . . . As we have said before, distance will not be measured by *miles,* but by *hours* and *minutes.* 'It is ten hours to such a place, or 49 minutes to another.' "

"Neighbors," though a thousand miles apart? Distance measured not in miles but in minutes? These were expectations of a new order—one that seemed to some even to challenge the proportions of the technological revolution that was the coming of steam power in the eighteenth century. As the telegraph would do a decade later in eliminating time, so also were the railroads seen to be annihilating space. In this redefining of time and space, predicted *Niles' Register* in 1831, "rail roads, we think, associated with steam power, are about to accomplish a much greater revolution in the future affairs of men and nations, than steam, itself, has yet about in the present condition of things."

Such far-reaching effect was only barely sensed in the original "rail" roads that began operating in the early 1800s using horse-drawn conveyances for moving coal or quarry stone on primitive forms of track. The Baltimore & Ohio Railroad first used horse-drawn cars on its opening 13-mile stretch between Baltimore and Ellicott's Mills, Maryland. But the locomotive *Tom Thumb*, first used in the summer of 1830, pointed the way to the future (see illustration, below). The South Carolina Canal and Railroad Company used the steam locomotive *Best Friend of Charleston* to inaugurate the first scheduled railroad service in America on Christmas Day, 1830. Steam power quickly became synonymous with railroads and remained so until superseded by diesel power in the mid–twentieth century.

One of the earliest records of a railroad journey was kept by Annapolis lawyer Alexander Randall of a trip on the Baltimore & Ohio Railroad in May 1831. Said Randall: "I again travelled on the Rail Road & was delighted with the ride. We went at about the rate of 12 miles an hour." John M. Gordon, a young Baltimore lawyer and banker traveling to Michigan to invest in land, used the railroad where possible instead of the Erie Canal while traveling through New York. Between Schenectady and Utica, he took the just-opened Utica and Schenectady Railroad: "[Thursday, September 23, 1836]. We left Albany in the cars for Utica at 7½ A.M. . . . At Schenectady, we got into another train of cars by which we were whirled to Utica at the rate of 20 miles per hour, (i.e. ⅓ of a mile per minute) as observed by the watch. . . . There are two [trains] running in each direction daily, making 4 trips."

Others had less favorable reactions—for example, John W. Baker of Philadelphia one morning in June 1838: "6 A.M. left home

On the Baltimore and Ohio Railroad in 1830, the passing of a horse-drawn car by the locomotive Tom Thumb, a race the horse is said eventually to have won when the locomotive lost a fanbelt. It is one of the best known stories in railroad history, but may well be apocryphal; there is no known documentary evidence such a race actually took place. Whatever the case, Tom Thumb had the last word; it was steam power, not horse power, that was quickly established as the driving force of railroads. (William H. Brown, *The History of the First Locomotives in America*, 1874)

The interior of a railroad car, mid–nineteenth century. It was said to show
"the attention paid to the comfort of travelers by the railway companies of America."
(*London Illustrated News,* April 10, 1852)

in the Cars for Pittsburgh. . . . We had a good number of passengers but was not crowded . . . passed through several small towns &
at 11 A.M. arrived at the City of Lancaster stopped about 15 min. &
then proceeded on . . . & arrived in Harrisburg at 3 P.M. . . . we now
took the Packet [boat] on Pens Canal. . . . The change from the
noisey jarring Rail Road to the smooth & easy canal was very grate-
full to me for I had by this time a considerable head ache."

Headaches, however, were hardly new to traveling. Stagecoach
travelers got them as well. There was Matilda Houstoun, for example, in western Maryland, 1847: "It was impossible, for one moment,
to lose sight of the absolute necessity for holding on, without being
punished for our temporary negligence in a most signal manner. The
great object was to prevent our heads coming in contact with the
roof of the carriage. . . . I find no difficulty in believing all the stories of concussion of the brain and other frightful misadventures
connected with stage travelling across the mountains."

Early railroad travel, if generally less prone to producing
headaches, had its other woes. Dirt, sparks, and blowing cinders
were a common concern, as related by Frederica Sophia Broke,
wife of a British army officer stationed in Nova Scotia, touring
America with her family in 1834: "Wednesday–Augst. 20th–Being

the first time I ever travelled on a railroad, it was amusing for a few minutes; but after that, the noise, the smoke, & the particles of dirt became very annoying. The [railroad] was in its infancy, so there were many stoppages, and though we did at times make a mile in 3 minutes, & once went 5 miles in ¼ of an hour, yet owing to these, which occupied altogether nearly an hour & ¾, we did not accomplish our journey—37 miles—till almost seven o'clock!"

There were other perils. The first rails (before the T-shaped rail that is still standard today) were straps of iron that were not always securely strapped to wooden stringers. A bumpy ride was the lesser of consequences; more to be feared was a strap, popularly known as a "snakehead," uncoiling and slashing through the floor of a coach. Derailments were common, owing both to the weather (snow and ice dislocating a rail, mud in the spring covering the tracks) as well as to improperly laid and/or unballasted track. The first coaches were inherently uncomfortable and provided little protection from the elements, and their primitive chain-or-bar couplings meant frequent banging.

THE THRILL OF RIDING INTO THE FUTURE

But trains were exciting. There was no shortage of riders willing to put up with the danger and discomfort just to be riding into the future. Something of this spirit was caught by William H. Brown, who was among those on board the first run of the Mohawk & Hudson Railroad on August 9, 1831. The third steam railroad in America, linking Albany and Schenectady, it provided a 17-mile alternative to an all-day, 40-mile trip through the locks of the Erie Canal. The inaugural run was hauled by the locomotive *DeWitt Clinton*. Wrote Brown:

> This locomotive, the "De Witt Clinton," stood upon the track already fired up, and with a train of some five or six passenger-coaches attached to it. These passenger-coaches were of the old-fashioned stage-coach pattern, with a driver's seat or box upon either end outside. . . . The cars were crowded inside and outside; not an available position was unoccupied. Two persons stood ready for every place where one could be accommodated, and the train started on its route, leaving hundreds of the disappointed standing around.

Along with all their benefits railroads brought man-made devastation as never before known. Here, a wreck of the Lancaster Express on the Pennsylvania Central Railroad in 1864. (*Harper's Weekly.* Library of Congress)

But how shall we describe that start, my readers? It was not that quiet, imperceptible motion which characterizes the first impulsive movements of the passenger-engines of the present day. Not so. There came a sudden jerk, that bounded the sitters from their places, to the great detriment of their high-top fashionable beavers, from the close proximity to the roofs of the cars. This first jerk being over, the engine proceeded on its route with considerable velocity for those times, when compared with stage coaches, until it arrived at a water-station, when it suddenly brought up with jerk No. 2, to the further amusement of some of the excursionists. . . .

As there were no coverings or awnings to protect the deck-passengers upon the tops of the cars from the sun, the smoke, and the sparks, and as it was in the hot season of the year, the com-bustible nature of their garments, summer coats, straw hats, and umbrellas, soon became apparent, and a ludicrous scene was enacted among the outside excursionists before the train had run the first two miles. . . .

In a short time the engine (after frightening the horses attached to all sorts of vehicles filled with the people from the surrounding country, or congregated all along at every available position near the road, to get a view of the singular-looking machine and its long train of cars; after causing thus innumerable capsizes and smash-ups of the vehicles and the tumbling of the spectators in every direction to the right and left) arrived . . . at Schenectady, amid the cheers and welcomes of thousands.

On the whole, said Brown, "The passengers were pleased with the adventures of the day, and no rueful countenances were to be seen, excepting occasionally when one encountered in his walks in the city a former driver of the horse-cars, who saw that the grave had that day been dug, and the end of horse-power was at hand."

It was the cheers, and especially the welcome of the thousands, not the sparks and capsizes, that came to characterize the impact of the railroad on American life. When its import was realized, the railroad's arrival in once isolated towns and cities across America prompted much the same response as in Binghamton, New York, one snowy evening late in December 1848. This was the newest stop on the Erie. The railroad was laying track steadily westward from New York, and it was already the longest railroad (at 200 miles) in the United States. The first arrival in Binghamton was a trainload of dignitaries, scheduled to reach town at dinnertime that night of Wednesday the 27th. In honor of the event, a great feast was laid out. But dinnertime came and went with no train in sight, and the feast was growing cold by seven, and colder still at eight, with still no word. Many in the crowd went home. Finally . . .

> Midnight, the sound of a distant whistle came booming down the line. Bang! Bang! went the cannon and suddenly all was excitement. Many who had gone home and retired to rest arose and repaired to the depot grounds. The cooks and waiters set themselves to the final arrangements at the long tables. The firing of cannon continued. The whistle sounded nearer and louder and the long pent-up hurrahs of the crowd, becoming more enthusiastic, altogether marred the usual midnight stillness of our quiet village. At this moment the stately train, drawn by the panting locomotives, approached and halted at the car house where the refreshments were in waiting. From 300 to 400 passengers alighted and entered the car-house and began at once the discussion of the merits and bounties of the table.

The merits and bounties, not of the feast but of the railroad, came more and more to dominate American life. There was something magical, something mystical, something captivating about railroads. Although he acknowledged the significance of other applications of steam power, a writer in the *American Railroad Journal* in

24

1841 was chiefly referring to railroads when he commented, "The transforming power of steam seems like the work of a master Magician. . . . The mere introduction, as an agent of power, of the vapor which fumes up from the spout of the tea kettle, has produced an entire revolution in the affairs of men." How awesome, now, was that agent of power as the driving force of an iron horse, snorting and chugging, bellowing smoke, its whistle shrieking and bell clanging, hauling the country into a new age when distant corners became neighborhoods and miles turned into minutes.

Some of the magic of railroading was later captured in the model trains that were virtually a staple of every boy's (and many a girl's) childhood through much of the twentieth century—indeed well past the golden age of railroading. These were chiefly electric trains, but simple wood or tin toys appeared soon after the earliest railroads. The first known self-propelled toy locomotive was a windup produced by a Connecticut clock manufacturer in 1856. It did not run on rails but had a small pivoting wheel at the rear that could be set to contain the locomotive in a circle. From the 1880s through the 1920s steam-powered toy locomotives were popular, although cheap versions apparently left much to be desired. Track was still not generally used; and of one model it was

Are kids too prone to violence today? One of the best-selling products of Milton Bradley & Co. in the 1870s was this puzzle titled *The Smashed-Up Locomotive*. Its jumble of pieces, once assembled, gave a gruesome picture of a smashed and mangled railroad engine. Of course, kids loved it. So successful was it that Bradley followed up with a grotesque sequel called *The Blown-Up Steamer*, which proved just as popular. (Milton Bradley & Co., *Catalogue.* Springfield, Mass., 1872)

said that "the blow-off catch could be turned on and off only with much labor and burning of fingers." An "Electric Railroad" could be found by 1892 in the catalog of Marshall Field & Company, but it consisted only of a single electric street car that was battery-operated on a circular track a little less than 2 feet in diameter. The real electric trains of the twentieth century made their appearance in 1901 with the first offering from Lionel—a 12-inch-long loco-motive that ran on a track of 2⅞-inch gauge. Lionel's first catalog appeared in 1903 and included such additional equipment as a derrick car, a switch, and a suspension bridge.

The magical allure of railroads for children also showed itself in children's books. A particularly good one, *Forrester's Pictorial Miscellany for Boys and Girls,* published in Boston in 1854, caught much of the excitement of the times:

> The progress of railroad building in New England, since it com-menced, has been astonishing, almost beyond belief. The first train of cars ever run by a locomotive [in New England] was on the seven-teenth of April 1834; less than fifteen years ago. Now there are more than three thousand miles of road in operation in New England. It is almost incredible that people twenty years since were contented with the slow tumbling of old stages; but so it is. The destiny of civiliza-tion is onward, higher improvement; and a few years hence we shall look back upon some of our present customs and habits with as much wonder as we now do upon the days of Uncle Sam's fast [horse-drawn] "Mail Coaches."

Not everyone agreed that the railroad represented a higher level of civilization. Snarled Henry David Thoreau: "We do not ride on the railroad; it rides on us." On another occasion Thoreau wrote tartly, "When I hear the iron horse make the halls echo with his snort-like thunder, shaking the earth with his feet, and breathing fire and smoke from his nostrils . . . it seems as if the earth had got a race now worthy to inhabit it." Others also saw dragons. James Lanman in 1840 wrote in *Hunt's Merchants' Magazine* of "dragons of a mightier power, with iron muscles that never tire, breathing smoke and flame through their blackened lungs"; and trains "leaping forward like some black monster, upon its iron path, by the light of the fire and smoke which it vomits forth."

To the extent the monster was literally annihilating space—displacing whomever and whatever was in the way of its iron road—there was often some substance to the complaints. Yet the metaphor of the tamed beast also worked the other way around, as Ezra Dean showed in writing in 1869 about all the wondrous

But the greatest of works astonishing me,

Above any other in Rail Roads I see!

Nor rivers nor mountains can hinder their course,

Or stop for a moment, the huge Iron Horse!

He challenges lightning to run him a race,

No other conveyance with him can keep pace;

His lungs made of iron, his sinews of steel,

His limbs never falter, nor weariness feel!

The railroads established mass transportation essentially as we know it today, down to the custom of reading while riding, something that was never feasible with stagecoach travel. Nathaniel Hawthorne noticed it on a train ride out of Boston in 1850: "Four or five long cars, each perhaps with fifty people in it, reading newspapers, reading pamphlet novels, chattering, sleeping; all this vision of passing life!" J. Henry Clark, a physician, also remarked about it in 1856: "Observe the passengers in the train, on any of our public routes. A shelf of popular novels is passed before the eyes of every individual; next, a pile of popular magazines, then, illustrated newspapers, while advertisements, guidebooks, newspa-

One of the principal effects of the railroad was facilitating the opening of the west, as portrayed in this allegorical rendering, "Across the Continent," by Currier & Ives in 1868.

pers with long, narrow, closely printed columns are distributed or purchased, until all tastes are suited."

These books, newspapers, magazines, and other forms of reading material also were finding faster and wider distribution around the country by way of the railroads. Once-isolated towns and villages were becoming part of the mainstream, resulting in a more homogenous national cultural life.

Writing letters also increased markedly at mid–nineteenth century, for no other apparent reason than that the mail was now going by rail instead of stagecoach or horseback. The numbers are dramatic. Domestic letters carried by the postal service totaled some 27 million in 1840; in 1860, nearly 162 million. Per capita correspondence rose from 1.61 letters in 1840 to 5.15 in 1860.

In these and other ways was the impact of the railroad felt on life in America. Suffice it to add one other because it is uniquely relevant: Railroads facilitated the growth of such industries as iron and steel that in turn made possible the development of other technologies. Virtually all–from typewriters to television–are indebted in some way to the railroads.

TIME MINUS NINE-THIRTY-TWO

At 12 o'clock noon yesterday, or rather at nine minutes thirty-two seconds after 12 o'clock, Chicago time, the railroads put into effect the new Central standard time.

—Chicago Tribune, November 19, 1883

Even as they were annihilating time, the railroads were also having a profound effect on how it was kept. Before railroads had really permeated society, there was Harriet Martineau writing in *Society in America* (London, 1837) that Americans were "very imaginative . . . in respect of the hour"–meaning very loose and flexible. A few years later there was Thoreau, still scorning the fire-breathing monster but conceding it had some positive effect. The trains, he said, "come and go with such regularity and precision, and their whistles can be heard so far, that the farmers set their clocks by them. . . . Have not men improved in punctuality since the railroad was invented?"

Some measure of the influence of railroads on American life in the later nineteenth century is evident in that they, not Congress, established standard time for the country. That was the substance of what happened November 18, 1883, when Chicago wound its clocks back nine minutes and thirty-two seconds while other cities and towns were winding theirs ahead, or back, by varying ticks of the clock in order to conform with one another.

The Standard Time Act, passed by Congress in 1918 at the height of World War I, has been the statutory basis of national timekeeping ever since. But for all practical purposes, standard time owes its existence to the General Time Convention of 1883, when a consortium of railroad officials from throughout the country met in Chicago and voted to adopt a new standard time for railroads. It went into effect at noon on Sunday, November 18, 1883.

It was a standard that cut across society. As the *New York Herald* reported on November 18, standard time was being "generally adopted by the community through the action of various official and corporate bodies as an obvious convenience in all social and business matters."

Nonetheless, some in Washington thought so sweeping a change ought only to come by federal action. Six days before the change went into effect, the United States attorney general wrote to the heads of all departments of the federal government, giving his opinion that "the proposed change is open to grave objections, and cannot be properly effected except by Congressional action." The following Sunday, when the attorney general went to catch a train to Philadelphia, he confidently used the old time. He was eight minutes late.

Before the era of the railroads, the "correct" time was almost anything approximating the hour of the day. In small towns and villages, and especially in the country, one's daily events were scheduled by the sun. Sunup began the day and sundown ended it, a day that was obviously lengthened and shortened by the seasons. Most activities—working, farming, doing household chores—were not dependent on starting or stopping at a certain time. And an activity that was so dictated—say, going to church—could be time-coordinated for all involved by the ringing of a bell. Even in cities where there was a somewhat more rigid fabric to society, time was relative to what city one was in, or even what part of what city.

Before the coming of the railroads this mattered little. But railroad travel, at then unheard-of speeds, made "correct" time more and more important. This resulted in calculating local time, or "sun time," based on the transit of the sun across the meridian. But since this was relative both to the latitude and the season, there were almost as many local times as there were localities.

And any number of ways of establishing the accurate hour. The Pennsylvania Railroad used Philadelphia time, which was five minutes slower than New York and five minutes faster than Baltimore. Trains running west and south from Chicago followed Chicago time, which produced some confusion since when it was exactly noon in Chicago it was (all "correct" times) 11:27 in Omaha, 11:39 in St. Paul, 11:48 in Dubuque, 11:50 in St. Louis, 12:07 in Indianapolis, 12:09 in Louisville, 12:13 in Cincinnati, 12:17 in Toledo, 12:24 in Cleveland, and 12:31 in Pittsburgh. The faster trains traveled, the more critical these variations became.

Furthermore there was disparity as to what clock one looked at. In the railroad station at Buffalo there were three—one clock for the New York Central (set to New York City time), one for the Lake Shore and Michigan Southern Railroad (Columbus time), and one set to local time for railroads serving the Buffalo area. And there was not necessarily even an official clock. An advertisement of the Rock Island Railroad published in the *Chicago Tribune* in 1853, during the building of Chicago's La Salle Street station, advised travelers that "the clock in Sherwood and Waiteley's store, at the corner of Lake and Dearborn streets, is at present the adopted standard time [and] the trains will arrive and depart promptly at the time stated, and as indicated by that clock."

Pending adoption of standard time, a partial solution was found in the 1870s in disseminating time signals from observatories. The most common way of providing a free public display of a signal was with a time ball, a now-forgotten part of daily life. A vestige remains in the ball that descends at midnight on New Year's Eve in New York's Times Square. Time balls, sometimes 3 or 4 feet in diameter so as to be seen at a considerable distance, **30** were lowered on poles at the tops of towers or tall buildings, usually at noontime. When the ball reached the bottom of the pole, it was exactly noon, and clocks and watches could be checked accordingly.

Accurate though this might be, it did not solve the problem of what to do about train schedules with the unheard-of speeds that trains were now attaining. The solution adopted by the General Time Convention of the railroads was to divide the earth into 24 (for the hours of the day) time zones, each representing 15 degrees of longitude (24 times 15 equals 360 degrees), counting from the meridian at which was located the Greenwich Observatory in London. This meant five time zones within the United States, including one that embraced only the northeastern tip of Maine. The four main zones were designated Eastern, Central, Mountain, and Pacific time, just as they remain today. Maine has since been entirely included in Eastern time.

Thus did the railroads, joined by countless local jurisdictions, make four broad squares out of a vast checkerboard of fifty—the fifty-some separate time zones that railroads had to cope with, by one contemporary estimate. In standardizing time, the railroads not only facilitated schedule-making but made cross-country journeying feasible for the traveler. *Real* cross-country travel had arrived.

THE RAILROAD AND THE TELEGRAPH

The earliest telegraph lines frequently paralleled railroad tracks as they spread throughout the country, and indeed the early development of these two major technologies have always seemed inseparably linked. Yet curiously the usefulness of the telegraph to the railroad was not immediately appreciated. The railroads made no attempt to use telegraphy for dispatching trains until 1851, and then almost as an afterthought.

The first use was on the Erie. The practice there, as on all other lines, was for trains going in one direction (in the case of the Erie, eastbound) to have the right of way and those going in the other direction to proceed only so far as regularly designated stops. There they switched to a sidetrack and waited until the train with the right-of-way passed by. The wait-order was immutable. No matter how long it might take, the westbound could not proceed. If the eastbound was broken down and it might take hours to get it going, the westbound had to sit and wait.

One who learned the frustration of this firsthand was the Erie's general superintendent, Charles Minot, who happened to be on board a train westbound out of New York City on September 22, 1851. From a designated stop, where the train had been waiting for some time, Minot telegraphed to Point Jervis, New York, and learned that the eastbound had not even reached that point yet. When it arrives, hold it there, he ordered the agent in Port Jervis; and then he had his own train proceed. Telegraphing ahead from station to station, Minot coordinated the progress of the two trains, avoiding unnecessary delay and proving the expediency of dispatching by telegraph. As a result, Minot put a telegraph dispatcher in charge of train operation in each division; and other railroads quickly followed. The telegraph quickly became indispensable to fast and safe railroad travel.

CHAPTER TWO

TRAVELING, NOT BEING TRAVELED

THE BICYCLE

You are traveling, not being traveled. You look upon horse machines with contempt, and even your old acquaintance, the pedestrian, with pity. . . . With the wind singing in your ears, and the mind as well as body in a higher plane, there is an ecstasy of triumph over inertia, gravitation.

—*Boston Advertiser,* December 27, 1878

FROM THAT FIRST "flying on the wings of the wind" in 1830 through the grand age of railroading in the late nineteenth and early twentieth centuries, the railroad was the idealization of fast transportation. The railroad got America hooked on speed.

But fast transportation was also mass transportation: "being traveled." What an ecstasy of triumph, then, a fast machine for traveling oneself—the modern bicycle. Speed? It was no more than 18 miles an hour at best, but it seemed like escaping the bounds of gravitation. Mobility! It was no more than roving tens of miles from home, but it seemed like traveling the globe.

Just as the railroad had signaled a new age of speed and convenience in public transportation, the bicycle of 1878 was the threshold of a new age of fast, *personal* mobility. Here was that first savor of what it was like to go fast on one's own—a sensation that became an American obsession.

Fast, of course, is relative. From a later perspective, it is hard to gauge how swift it seemed to be going 10 or 15 miles an hour, on one's own, for hour after hour. Yet from a contemporary standpoint it was remarkable.

What were the alternatives? The railroad was the fastest form of transportation yet devised, but one was beholden to those times and routes the railroad went. And how much faster was it, really, in the 1870s? The most rapid train between Washington and New York took 7 hours 35 minutes. Given a distance of 228 miles, that represented an average speed of just over 30 miles per hour. Other New York-to-Washington trains were as slow as 9 hours 25 minutes, or roughly 24 miles per hour. The New York Central's "New York Express" took 12 hours and 15 minutes to cover the 298 miles between Albany and Buffalo—an average speed also of about 24 miles per hour. A steamboat on the Mississippi, meanwhile, was described by one contemporary source as "ploughing along at the rate of twelve miles an hour."

Personal transportation usually meant on foot. One could go
one's own route at one's own times, but at 2 or 3 miles an hour.

Or if one had the means, one could go by horseback or by horse and buggy, neither one of which was much faster than walking. A horse can sprint at relatively fast speeds, as in a race, but only for short distances. For travel purposes, a horse saves wear and tear on the human constitution but doesn't propel the human body much faster than the body can propel itself. And a horse is expensive, requiring considerable upkeep, including a stable, hay, oats, straw, and grooming.

The "modern" bicycle of the late 1870s was economical by comparison and could be stowed on the back porch. And it was surely a convenient means of personal mobility. But it was more. It was an exhilarating triumph over distance. As the *Boston Advertiser* explained in 1878:

> Mounted on his 52-inch wheel, with the wind humming in the spokes and the mile-stones flitting behind him, the bicyclist appropriates the aesthetic meaning of the "winged heel" with which the ancients endowed the messenger of the gods. The prophetic myth of the wise and athletic Greeks has become a modern reality.
>
> To get over the ground and through the water in the quickest manner is the goal for which ardent spirits in all ages have put forth their best endeavors. The bicycle ranks among those gifts of science to man, by which he is enabled to supplement his own puny powers with the exhaustless forces around him. He sits in the saddle, and all nature is but a four-footed beast to do his bidding. Why should he go a-foot when he can ride a mustang of steel who knows his rider and never needs a lasso? . . .
>
> . . . Though there are difficulties to be overcome, we claim that any one of ordinary patience and pluck can learn to ride a bicycle satisfactorily. The feat is somewhat gyroscopic and less than it looks to be. Once learned it is an elegant and healthful accomplishment, worth all the time and money it costs. . . . As to safety in general, the bicycle, being a machine, is safer than a horse, for the latter has a will of its own to be consulted and controlled.

"Mounted on his 52-inch wheel . . ." Here was the key. Here is what made the bicycle modern, and fast. The bicycle of 1878—commonly known then as the Ordinary and later as a high-wheeler—was a considerable improvement over its forerunner of only a decade earlier, the so-called velocipede, and a vast improvement over a scattering of two-wheeled contrivances that began appearing early in the century. Though quickly superseded, the velocipede of the late 1860s—a wood and iron two-wheeler with pedals on the front wheel—was the first mechanical contrivance for personal transportation to catch on. It arrived at a time of new expectations as to what mechanization could do. And although it was something entirely new ("There is no man living who can say he was born a velocipedist," said one observer) and was hardly inexpensive (new velocipedes sold for between $65 and $125, even the lesser being a considerable sum), velocipede riding quickly caught the public's curiosity. In New York City, it was considered a rage by early 1869. And since people had not been born veloci-pedists, riding schools sprang open to teach them. New York had several such schools, yet those open by January 1869 were thought "too limited to accommodate the hundreds of persons who are desirous of learning the use of this new means of locomotion." According to the same newspaper account:

> The rooms of Messrs. Monod, Wood, Pearsall Bros., and Hanlon are open from early morning till late at night, where beginners are con-stantly practicing, and still they cannot all be accommodated. Mr. Sommerville is converting his art gallery in Fifth-avenue into a velocipede riding school, and still another enthusiast is arranging to open a large hall in the vicinity of Forty-seventh street and Broadway. The great difficulty encountered thus far is in getting the velocipedes. There are four manufacturers in this City, all of whom are over-whelmed with orders, who cannot, with their present facilities, sup-ply the demand. The enthusiastic velocipedist who desires to obtain a machine of his own, cannot possibly obtain it from the manufac-turers now under a month's time. . . . It is estimated that there are now in New-York and vicinity 5,000 persons who either know how to ride the velocipede or are learning, and that fully half this number will be mounted next Summer. While it will be impossible for them to navigate successfully in the crowded thoroughfares, they will break out in side streets and in the parks to an alarming extent.

Yet though the "Rinks and schools multiplied [and] carriage makers hurried to produce . . . the mania ended suddenly, and soon the machines disappeared: they went to the lumber-room or were broken up." Their inherent failing, said *Lippincott's* magazine, was that "the speed they gave was attained at a cost of labor and fatigue which only children are willing to incur."

When the short-lived velocipede craze arrived in the 1860s, almost no one knew anything about riding a bicycle. Hence, as reported by *Lippincott's* magazine, "Rinks and schools multiplied." This 1869 illustration of a riding school suggests that help was sorely needed. (*The New York Coach-Makers Magazine,* vol. 10, 1869)

THE "MODERN" MACHINE

A machine that adults could enjoy was also coming on the scene, superseding the velocipede in name as well as design. As reported by a correspondent for the *New York Times* in 1874: "A form of amusement which appears to be becoming very popular in England is what is called 'bicycling.' "

In 1877, said *Lippincott's,* several Bostonians who had learned to appreciate the "modern bicycle" in Europe imported several English machines and started the new popularity in cycling. "Being free from the objections which proved fatal to the wooden machine of 1869, the bicycle is coming into use [1879], and in all probability is coming to stay."

The velocipede looked more or less like a later bicycle but had a frame mostly of wood or wrought iron, with wheels of wood and tires that were bands of iron; and it weighed anywhere from 80 to 100 pounds. The modern bicycle of the late 1870s, on the other hand, had a frame and wheels mostly of lighter-weight steel and tires of solid rubber and weighed as little as 20 pounds (though usually closer to 60). Most important, its front wheel—the pedaling wheel—could now be considerably larger because lighter materials went into its construction. As compared with the velocipede's 30 to 40 inches, the new version was 40 to 60 inches. There was yet no gearshift, so "high gear" was equivalent to the diameter of the front, or driving wheel: the greater the circumference, the greater the distance the wheel traveled with one revolution of the pedals, and thus the higher the speed that could be obtained. This also explains its strange design, a very large wheel in front and a much smaller one in back. The rider had to sit over top in order to reach the pedals at the hub. The second wheel was simply for balance.

This was the technological advance—a new design utilizing lighter-weight materials—that made the bicycle fast enough and practical enough to become popular in America for the first time. And in so doing, it set America on the road to that predilection

The first national meet of American bicyclists, at Newport, Rhode Island, 1880. The high-wheeled Ordinary looks quaint, indeed almost whimsical, from a later perspective. In fact, it represented technological advance that made speed an element of personal transportation for the first time. Its front wheel was made of relatively lightweight steel, with a tire of rubber, as opposed to the wood and iron of a velocipede wheel. Being lighter, the wheel could be made larger. And before use of gears became common, being larger—frequently 50 to 60 inches in diameter—meant covering a greater distance with one revolution of the pedals. Speed. (*Frank Leslie's Illustrated Newspaper,* June 19, 1880)

The evolution of the bicycle: a velocipede, 1868 (top), an Ordinary, 1878 (center), and a Safety of the 1890s (bottom), essentially the modern bicycle. (Byrn, *Progress of Invention*, top and bottom; Pratt, *American Bicycler*, center)

for fast personal transportation that is so much a part of American society today.

As to the bicycle's exhilarating speed: In Boston, the hub of early cycling popularity, the best time in the City Races on July 4, 1878, was a mile in 3 minutes 33 seconds, or roughly 17 miles per hour. The fastest time yet recorded in America, as of November 1879, was a mile in 3 minutes 21½ seconds, nominally faster at approximately 18 miles an hour. These were championship speeds; lesser riders had to settle for a lesser pace—say, 10 to 12 miles an hour. But what made the bicycle such an awesome advance in transportation was that a rider of reasonably good stamina could keep going like that for 30, 40, or more miles. A horse could go much faster, but only for short distances. Now there was a machine by which humankind not only could go *fast,* by all contemporary measure, but go whenever and wherever it suited. A giant stride!

Some measure of the bicycle's quick popularity in the wake of this technological refinement is evident in the many cycling clubs that sprang up around the country in the 1870s and 1880s. Still another sign of popularity is the range of accessories that became available almost overnight. They represent virtually the same assortment that is standard today. In 1879 they included: a small padlock and chain ("a very useful device for securing the machine from mischievous or impertinent use in the absence of the owner"); a bicycle stand; a bicycle bell (or whistles, which were considered better); saddlebags and pouches; wrenches; an odometer, or cyclometer as it was called then, for recording distance traveled; and headlights and lamps ("desirable for night riding when it is not moonlight, and outside the domain of street-lamps"; the usual was a small oil lantern with a reflector and circular plate-glass lens).

Accessories aside, the Ordinary, by virtue of those qualities that made it speedier than its predecessors, tended also to be less safe and less easy to ride than the machines that preceded it. The great disparity in size between the huge front wheel and the tiny back wheel combined with the inordinately high position of the rider tended to make the Ordinary a tricky thing to ride—or at least seem so. Some mastered it easily; others shied from even trying lest they "take a header" over the handlebars.

A bicycle that *looked* safe and promised to go even faster than the "wind singing in your ears" ought then to have been the promise of the future. And was. The first commercially successful example was devised in England in the mid-1880s by J. K. Starley. Known almost from the first as the "Safety," the new version of the bicycle was essentially what it has remained to the present day: two wheels of equal size pedaled by a crank mechanism located between them, attached by a chain to a sprocket on the rear. Within a few years, pneumatic rubber tires, coaster brakes, and adjustable handlebars arrived.

The Safety popularized cycling. By the early 1890s, one in every sixteen men, women and children had a bicycle—roughly 4 million cyclists for an 1890 population of 63 million. Most were first-timers, some improbable. One such was Frances Willard, founder of the Woman's Christian Temperance Union. She was fifty-three when she decided to take up riding the bicycle—"the most remarkable, ingenious, and inspiring motor ever yet devised upon this planet"—partly to prove *to everyone* that she wasn't too old and partly to demonstrate *to men* that riding was better for the soul than walking to the local saloon. "I found a whole philosophy of

Frances Willard and "Gladys" along with some helping hands in 1895. The bicycle, said social reformer Willard, once she got the knack of riding one, is "the most remarkable, ingenious, and inspiring motor ever yet devised upon this planet." (Willard, *A Wheel Within a Wheel*, 1895)

life . . . in my bicycle," she wrote. "In many particulars, the bicycle is like the world. When it had thrown me painfully once, and more especially when it threw one of my dearest friends, then for a time Gladys [as she called her bicycle] had some gladsome ways for me no longer, but seemed the embodiment of misfortune and dread. Even so the world has often seemed in hours of darkness and despondency; its iron mechanism, its pitiless grind, its on-rolling gait have oppressed to melancholy. I finally concluded that all failure was from a wobbling will rather than a wobbling wheel. I felt that indeed that will is the wheel of the mind—its perpetual motion having been learned when the morning stars sang together. When the wheel of the mind went well then the rubber wheel hummed merrily."

Actually of greater social significance than its inducement to moral virtue was, as Willard put it:

> the impetus that this uncompromising but fascinating and illimitably capable machine would give to that blessed "woman question." We saw that the physical development of humanity's mother-half would be wonderfully advanced by that universal introduction of the bicycle sure to come about within the next few years, because it is for the interest of great commercial monopolies that this should be so, since if women patronize the wheel the numbers of buyers will be twice as large. If women ride they must, when riding, dress more rationally than they have been wont to do. If they do this many prejudices as to what they may be allowed to wear will melt away. Reason will gain upon precedent, and ere long the comfortable, sensible, and artistic wardrobe of the rider will make the conventional style of woman's dress absurd to the eye and unendurable to the understanding. . . . the graceful and becoming costume of woman on the bicycle will convince the world that has brushed aside the theories, no matter how well constructed, and the arguments, no matter how logical, of dress-reformers.

Another effect of the bicycle was literally to pave the way for the automobile. Whereas the bicycle was the forerunner of the automobile as fast personal transportation, so too was it a precursor of the roads they run on. Most roads of the 1890s were what we would call "unimproved" today. Mapmaker Rand, McNally classified the majority as being "good dirt roads" or "ordinary dirt roads." Where roads were improved—usually in cities or from city to major suburb—pavement was in the form of bricks or paving blocks or of macadam.

Cyclists around the country pressured not only for improvements to existing roads but creation of new ones, especially paths that would be set aside for the exclusive use of bicycles. In Brooklyn, New York, in 1895, twin cycle paths were opened between Prospect Park and Coney Island. On weekends, the bicycle traffic was said to be tire-to-tire.

Five years later came the prototype of Los Angeles's famed freeway system—but still for cycles only. It was the Pasadena and Los Angeles Cycleway. A partly elevated road stretching 9 miles between the two cities, it quickly became as popular for **42** Californians as the Coney Island cycle path was for New Yorkers.

Writing in *Scientific American* in 1900, Charles F. Holder called it "a perfect road . . . the only one of its kind in the world." Perfect, indeed. Virtually peering into the future without realizing it, Holder wrote:

> Whether this is true has not been given out, but a few days ago an automobile owned by a resident of Pasadena, was run out upon the cycleway and went speeding toward Los Angeles under the most perfect conditions; and it was evident that if the road permitted an automobile to run upon it, it would soon become very popular as a literal sky route to Los Angeles for these vehicles.

Automobiles, of course, were very few and even farther between in 1900. That changed dramatically in the first decade of the twentieth century—so much so that bicycle-mania came to a screeching halt. Bicycle production in the United States tumbled from well over a million in 1899 to fewer than 200,000 a decade later, a decline of roughly 80 percent.

It was not until the 1960s that the popularity of bicycling staged a comeback that still prevails. And largely for one reason. Cycling is a uniquely good form of recreation and a wonderful way to stay physically fit.

Among adult riders, that is. No resurgence was needed for youngsters. Among children, bicycles have always been that first set of wheels with which to have one's own freedom—be it only to go down the block and around the corner—while awaiting that magical age for getting a driver's license.

In much the same sense, the bicycle was society's first set of wheels.

CHAPTER THREE

LOVE AT FIRST SIGHT

THE AUTOMOBILE

To take control of this materialized energy, to draw the reins over this monster with its steel muscles and fiery heart—there is something in the idea which appeals to an almost universal sense, the love of power.

—*Motor World,* 1901

IF IT IS TRUE (and who doubts it?) that America has long had a love affair with the automobile, then looking back it can only be called love at first sight.

Well, almost at first sight. The hand-built horseless carriages that began showing up in the mid-1890s—literally as horseless buggies and carriages, for horsed and horseless conveyances were virtually indistinguishable—were clattery, cantankerous contraptions, and smelly to boot; and their threat to life and limb was all too obvious. People who weren't convinced that this was progress in transportation had plenty to point to, and did. Their best hope was that the horseless carriage would prove to be just another novelty, a curiosity that would pass as quickly from the scene as it appeared.

But these amazing new buggies and wagons that were neither pulled nor pushed—that could go all by themselves, without any visible means of propulsion—were too wondrous for that.

The year 1900 was pivotal. If the horseless carriage could make a strong run into the new century, many were convinced its momentum would keep it rolling on forever. The pivotal factor was what Cleveland Moffett singled out in *Review of Reviews* in 1900: The automobile had to be something for "the average man," not just the rich one; and of late, said Moffett, the average man "has been stirred to a different kind of interest in this horseless invasion—a personal interest; for scarcely can he go forth of a Sunday afternoon but he meets his friend Jones or his friend Smith (and a lady) rolling complacently down the avenue on some trim, swift-moving contrivance that buzzes and flashes past to the general admiration. He wonders where Jones or Smith got that thing from; speculates on its cost and advantages; thinks he would like to try one himself; presently has a chance to try one, and presto! the seed is sown. By the fact that he has marveled and yearned, this average man has joined the swelling army of those who would fain possess an automobile—nay more, who propose to possess one as soon as may be."

The year 1900 also brought with it the first car show in the United States—the New York Automobile Show, sponsored by the Automobile Club of America at New York's Madison Square Garden. For the Joneses and Smiths (and their ladies) it was a whole week, not just a Sunday afternoon, to marvel and yearn. And by the thousands—more than 12,000 the last afternoon and evening alone—marvel they did.

> Nearly every man, woman, and child that visited the show yesterday seemed to want the experience of riding in the vehicles that go without being either pulled or pushed, and to all requests, whether timid or clamorous, the obliging attendants at the various exhibits replied that they were present for the very purpose of gratifying such desires [on a wooden track constructed inside the Garden]. . . . in phaetons, and in runabouts all applicants were whirled in their turn once about the oval. One little girl, with red frock and yellow hair streaming out under a big red bonnet, caught the attention of the whole Garden last night by her squeals of delight as she was spun around the track in a trim little runabout. The child clung to the big purple-coated cha[u]ffeur and refused to be taken from the wagon when the circuit of the track was completed. She was whirled about a second time.

A toy version of the automobile appeared on the scene quickly in part because the auto became so popular so fast and in part because of the precedent of making toy wagons. Probably the earliest toy auto was made c. 1895, but it looked like a cross between an auto and a Hansom cab. This one was a bit more realistic. Its tiny electric motor, powered by two small dry cells, turned the rear wheels through reduction gears visible underneath the carriage. The small tiller on the seat actually steered the front wheels. When this advertisement appeared in 1900, there were still only some 8,000 motor vehicles in the United States. (Hiscox, *Horseless Vehicles, Automobiles, Motor Cycles,* New York, 1900)

Love in bloom. Yet the remarkable, indeed extraordinary thing, looking back, is that it sprang from so few blossoms. In that pivotal year of 1900, there only *seemed* to be as many cars as Cleveland Moffett suggested. In fact, in all of America—on all of its roads and lanes, in all of its stables-turned-garages—there were only as many autos as might be found today at the country's largest mall at two-thirds of capacity. Mall of America in Bloomington, Minnesota, has on-site parking space for 12,750 cars; in 1900 there were 8,000 registered vehicles in the entire country. But they were getting attention as if they were 8 million.

It would have been no surprise to Thomas A. Edison, who in 1895 had given his opinion, in an interview with the *New York World,* that it was only a matter of time until "the carriages and trucks in every large city will be run with motors [albeit electric]." A few years later, Frank Munsey, writing in *Munsey's Magazine* in 1903, said the auto "is certain to supplant the horse for general road use, and the sooner we accept it, and the more gracefully we accept it, the better." *Outing* magazine that same year saw automobile travel as increasing "appreciation of the joys of living, of the beauties of nature, the hallowings of history."

In 1903, horses still vastly outnumbered motor vehicles. Some people thought they always would. As recently as 1899 a writer in *Harper's Weekly* had predicted confidently that the age of the horse would go on forever: "As the companion of man, he [the horse] would be fit to be cherished even if there were no work left for him to do; but there is, and always will be." Nor was the horse forgotten even at that historic first automobile show. A reporter covering the show pointed out that the site was the hallowed home of the annual New York Horse Show, and he certainly had man's old companion in mind as he wrote:

> It is the Horse Show, indeed, to which perhaps, nine out of every ten visitors at the Garden during the past week have more or less unconsciously compared the array of motor vehicles and their performances. The sleek, graceful machines with their suggestion in repose of energy and speed have aroused an interest akin to that felt in the living machines of speed and power that hold the centre of the stage during the Horse Show.

But love is fickle. Although the number of horses in use (for farming as well as transportation) continued to be relatively constant the first two decades of the twentieth century, a sharp decline began in the 1920s. With the coming of the automobile, the horse was never again to be cherished as once he was. His successor rolled all the right virtues into just the right product at just the right time. America, as we have seen, had already caught a craving for speed. Its appetite was awakened by that 1830 train that could fly on the wings of the wind at 15 to 25 miles an hour; and whetted by ever faster and more comfortable travel (trains *averaging* more than 50 miles an hour at the turn of the twentieth century). Meanwhile Americans also had gotten a taste of relatively fast personal transportation with the bicycle. Here now were speed and personal freedom stamped into one, to which was added a sense of personal power virtually unknown before. Barely into the age of the automobile, *Motor World* magazine recognized it in 1901:

> To take control of this materialized energy, to draw the reins over this monster with its steel muscles and fiery heart—there is something in the idea which appeals to an almost universal sense, the love of power.

SINGING ITS PRAISES

It was just what America wanted. That desire showed in what Americans heard, sang, and played. "In My Merry Oldsmobile" was an instant song hit in 1905. The Oldsmobile went into production in 1901 as the first assembly-line* gasoline-powered automobile (some 425 cars that first year). Its popularity was reflected in the music, which was one of the most sung songs of its time and surely the best remembered song about a car. So successful was it that the Olds Motor Works in Detroit presented a new Oldsmobile to the song's composer-lyricist team, Gus Edwards and Vincent Bryan. But they could not agree on which one should keep it and sold it, dividing the money. Between 1905 and 1907 alone well more than a hundred songs were published in celebration of the

---

*But not yet a *moving* assembly line, a faster process that began with the
Model T Ford in 1913.

 AL. JOLSON'S TERRIFIC HIT!

HE'D HAVE TO GET UNDER-
GET OUT AND GET UNDER
(TO FIX UP HIS AUTOMOBILE)

WORDS BY
GRANT CLARKE &
EDGAR LESLIE

MUSIC BY
MAURICE ABRAHAMS

MAURICE ABRAHAMS MUSIC CO.
1570 BROADWAY
NEW YORK

"In My Merry Oldsmobile," probably the best-known automobile song of all, became an instant success in 1905. Within two years, at least 120 pieces of music about the automobile were published. Romance and humor predominated. The title character of Al Jolson's "terrific hit" was "just dying to cuddle his queen [but] every minute, when he'd begin it, he'd have to get under, get out and get under . . . to fix up his automobile." (Library of Congress)

automobile's sudden new role in American life. On the stage, the auto—and especially the honk-honk sound effect of its horn—was the stuff of many a vaudeville act and many a musical comedy, beginning with *The Great Automobile Mystery* of 1904. Movies, likewise, came to appreciate the auto's star role quality.

Although newspaper editorialists did not hesitate to denounce the automobile's negatives—notably speeding, or what then was taken for speeding—the press, and magazines especially, realized how fascinated the public was with the automobile and provided readers with more than ample material. Even at the turn of the century, *Automobile* magazine proudly proclaimed that "the unprecedented and well nigh incredible rapidity with which the automobile industry has developed . . . is largely due to the fact that every detail of the subject has been popularized by the technical and daily press."

The press was there beginning with that famed first jaunt of

J. Frank Duryea in September 1893 on the outskirts of Springfield, Massachusetts. Although it was not the first gasoline-powered vehicle to be tried out, Duryea's is generally thought of as the first of the line since it was the first automobile to be manufactured in America, beginning in 1896. The morning after his first run on September 21, 1893, as Frank was tinkering with the car's balky transmission [his recollection]

> a reporter from the *Springfield Union* appeared and requested an interview. Clearly this reporter had but little knowledge of mechanics but his article was printed that evening in the *Springfield Union* on September 22, 1893.

It was not the *Evening Union*'s first automobile story, but it showed how much curiosity there was. A week earlier, on September 16, 1893, using information Frank Duryea had supplied, the *Union* announced:

NO USE FOR HORSES
Springfield Mechanics Devise a New Mode of Travel
Ingenious Wagon Now Being Made in This City
for Which the Makers Claim Great Things

> A new motor carriage when, if the preliminary tests prove successful as expected, will revolutionize the mode of travel on highways, and do away with the horse as a means of transportation, is being made in this city. It is quite provable that within a short time one may be able to see an ordinary carriage in almost every respect, running along the streets or climbing country hills without visible means of propulsion. The carriage is being built by J. F. Duryea, the designer and E. F. Markham, who have been at work on it for over a year. The vehicle was designed by C. E. Duryea, a bicycle manufacturer of Peoria, Ill., and he communicated the scheme to his brother, who is a practical mechanic in this city.

By the turn of the century countless stories about the automobile were appearing in newspapers and magazines around the country. There were also a number of new magazines and trade papers devoted to the automobile, beginning with *The Motocycle,* launched in Chicago in October 1895. (It was named for the winning entry in a *Chicago Times-Herald* contest for what to call the horseless carriage,

Charles Duryea and his automobile, c. 1894. (Library of Congress)

and obviously *motocycle* did not catch on, although *motorcycle*, for a different kind of conveyance, did.) A month later, the highly regarded *The Horseless Age* appeared in New York.

But where the popularity of the automobile was becoming most apparent to the most people was on the street. Production began to climb just after the turn of the century: from 4,000 cars in 1900 to more than 100,000 in 1909. As if confirming a judgment that "The automobile has become almost a necessity" (*Outlook* magazine, 1908), sales by 1916 had broken the million mark (in fact, they exceeded 1.5 million that year); and in 1929 reached 4.5 million, the high-water mark until after World War II. By 1929 there were more than 23 million registered automobiles on the road—one for every five of the 123 million men, women, and children counted in the census of 1930.

Yet as of its early years, this new necessity was arguably the most complex consumer-operated machine anyone had confronted to date. Even the simplest aspect of driving today—turning the steering wheel—was a wholly new technique to almost everyone in the early 1900s. Bicyclists had a head start in learning how, being used to steering with handlebars; and helmsmen of ships and yachts actually had experience turning wheels. But the vast majority of people who walked, rode a horse, took a train, or used the streetcar had never even seen a steering wheel. Thus steering an automobile for the first time was thought to be a sufficient challenge that new drivers were advised to pick a secluded road to practice on.

Gear shifting was another challenge some people thought was well nigh insurmountable for anyone without mechanical training. Inventor Hiram Percy Maxim, who was among the early developers of the automobile, said one of the major hurdles faced by manufacturers was convincing "the average person" that he or she could actually operate the gearshift of an early automobile. "At the time of which I write [1897 and 1898]," said Maxim, "few people believed that the general public would ever be able to coordinate the clutch pedal and the gear-shift lever." That they did learn is long since history, although it was not without a frequent and "indescribable gnashing and grinding of gear teeth," as Maxim also observed.

Another early authority on motoring, R. J. Mecredy, urged particular caution going downhill: "Steep hills should never be descended quickly. If the car once gets out of control the momentum acquired becomes so tremendous that it is nearly impossible to pull it up. The brakes, too, may go on fire, or suddenly become inoperative." Cornering could also be tricky, Mecredy wrote in 1903: "Corners constitute a very serious danger, especially to the beginner. Only judgment and experience can enable one to calculate speed to a nicety, and know if a corner can be taken at a certain pace. It is always better to err on the slow side. In taking a corner, too, it is advisable to take the clutch out of operation on the bend of the corner, and let it in again as the car straightens itself. This is especially so if the corner is greasy."

An early motorist, Alice Huyler Ramsey, described cranking the engine as "part of the motoring adventure . . . a clash with an unpredictable temperament; a gamble with a possible broken arm."

Sitting behind the wheel presented a different degree of complexity than in the modern turn-the-key-and-set-the-automatic-transmission car. Here is what confronted the early driver as

HOW TO START AN AUTOMOBILE (1904)

From the owner's manual for a 1904 Cadillac. Note that a handy cold-weather accessory was a handkerchief saturated with gasoline.

TO START THE MOTOR

First. Open the throttle. **Second.** Turn the switch. **Third.** Retard the spark lever. **Fourth.** See that controlling lever [gearshift] is in neutral. **Fifth.** Insert starting crank in end of shaft, turn crank (in direction indicated by arrow under fly wheel) until the compression is felt to resist further motion, then turn the engine quickly over compression once. If engine fails to start "prime it" by priming rod until gasoline flows. . . . In extreme cold weather . . . it may be necessary to saturate a handkerchief with gasoline and hold in the hands a few seconds, then place over the intake air pipe. This warms the mixture and aids in starting a cold motor on a zero morning.

A FEW DON'TS

Don't try to start without the switch turned on. **Don't** throw high speed lever forward before low speed lever is released or vice versa, or a broken crank shaft may result. **Don't** try to run without **oil, water and gasoline.**

Cadillac Motor Car Co., Instructions for Operation and Care of the Single Cylinder Cadillac (Detroit, [1904]); illustration: 1904 Cadillac Model B with single-cylinder 8¼-hp. engine.

described by Ramsey, who took forty-one days to drive cross-country in 1909 in a brand-new Maxwell 30 touring car:

> The driver occupied the right front seat, since the vehicle was then built with a right-hand drive, and controlled the gear shift and the emergency brake levers with the right hand. There were 4 gears arranged in progressive order: reverse (far forward), then neutral position, and three forward speeds. [This, of course, was a manual transmission operated with a foot clutch; no one had even dreamed of an automatic transmission.] Also at the right hand just beside the seat was the rubber bulb of the "honk-honk" horn. The presence of the spare tires on the right side precluded egress from the driver's seat. The spark and gasoline throttle levers were located beneath the steering wheel, on the steering post. On the dash was a non-vibrating coil, an odometer [speedometer] and a glass tube through which one could view the circulation of the oil. . . . The fuel tank was located under the front seat and its contents had to be approximated by measuring with a ruled stick. There was no gasoline gauge at that time.

On the left running board was a carbide generator with which to make illuminating gas for the headlights. To drive at night, Ramsey dropped carbide pellets into the generator and turned the cock to drip water on the carbide. Then, opening the front lenses of the large lamps, she "struck a match and applied the flame to the escape orifice. The odor of that gas was an indescribably acrid one."

All this must have bewildered a lot of people—certainly countless women, perhaps the vast majority, who were out of their element coping with carbide generators and magnetos. Alice Ramsey was an exception. "I was born mechanical," she explained, "an inheritance from my father. . . . My father, who had magic in his fingers, understood my interests and encouraged me."

Not that every man was born mechanical. The Model T Ford, produced from 1908 to 1927, was a mechanical leap over the first autos, Fords included, but was still notorious for its quirks, not least of all its balkiness in starting. The trick ("which you usually learned from another Ford owner"), wrote essayist E. B. White, was first to give it a couple of nonchalant upward lifts of the crank with the ignition *off*.

Although as C. O. Morris observed in *Country Life in America* in 1909, many Americans made their driving debuts by learning "through experience—sometimes disastrous," conscientious new drivers had recourse to private driving schools, some of which, at least by 1917, were using dual-control vehicles, as shown here.

Then, whistling as though thinking about something else, you would saunter back to the driver's cabin, turn the ignition on, return to the crank, and this time, catching it on the down stroke, give it a quick spin. . . . If this procedure was followed, the engine almost always responded—first with a few scattered explosions, then with a tumultuous gunfire, which you checked by racing around to the driver's seat and retarding the throttle. Often, if the emergency brake hadn't been pulled all the way back, the car advanced on you the instant the first explosion occurred, and you would hold it back by leaning your weight against it. I can still feel my old Ford nuzzling me at the curb, as though looking for an apple in my pocket.

Given the need for a wholly new kind of expertise (and even for a few tricks now and then), how did people learn to drive in the early days of the automobile? Many did not. Despite their inexperience and lack of knowledge, they simply got behind the wheel. Writing on "The Cause of Automobile Accidents" in *Country Life in America* in 1909, C. O. Morris observed that "new drivers are making their debut every day, and it is generally admitted that most of us will insist on gaining our knowledge through experience—sometimes disastrous."

The disasters weren't all in the form of accidents; they also showed up as bent axles and gear teeth that hinted strongly of "indescribable gnashing and grinding." *Scientific American* in 1906 reported that "manufacturers of popular cars have estimated that three-quarters of the troubles reported to them by automobile owners are the results of inefficient handling rather than of inherent defects in the machine." When repairs were necessary, the

LOVE AT FIRST SIGHT

55

experience bore a curious similarity to what many a modern-day motorist encounters. As *Horseless Age* magazine lamented in 1901: "the owner just sits down and trembles until the job is finished."

Whether to ward off costly repair bills or simply to ensure their own safety and convenience, many drivers took it upon themselves to learn how to operate an automobile properly. A few manufacturers offered training, but chiefly those of high-priced cars, and chiefly for chauffeurs. Locomobile had a factory school in operation in 1904, and after 1906 Pierce-Arrow offered two-week training sessions.

For owners of more moderately priced automobiles, there were courses of instruction furnished by various YMCAs (Young Men's Christian Association) in cooperation with the Automobile Club of America in major cities. Although the rationale was to provide useful training for young men to become chauffeurs and mechanics, car owners and their sons were also welcome. A basic course at the Boston YMCA—the first YMCA to establish a driving school, in the winter of 1903–1904—was specified for "owners, chauffeurs, and prospective purchasers," which took in pretty much everyone. By mid-1905, there were more than 2,000 people enrolled in YMCA driving schools. By late 1908, some 2,000 motorists, or would-be motorists, had taken courses just at New York City's West Side YMCA.

There were also private driving schools, some of which, at least by 1917, were using dual-control vehicles (see illustration, page 55). Driver education in the schools, the mainstay today, began in the mid-1930s, largely in cooperation with the American Automobile Association.

LAWS AND LICENSING

Meanwhile, there were safeguards coming in the form of ordinances and legislation at the local and state levels to impose at least minimal levels of safety. The first (and easiest) such measure to be implemented on a wide scale was the requirement for the vehicle itself to be registered. This allowed a minimum standard of safety in order for the vehicle to qualify for registration and also **56** provided a visible means of identification (a license plate) by which the owner could be traced in the event of not stopping after an accident. New York, in 1901, was the first state to require registration of all motor vehicles. Eight other states had done likewise by 1903, and by 1915 all states had registration laws.

Licensing of drivers in any meaningful form was slower to come about. Where there were licensing requirements they were often at first too lenient to ensure qualified drivers. A Milwaukee city ordinance of 1904, for example, merely required that the applicant be at least eighteen years old and have use of both arms. A Kansas City, Missouri, ordinance of 1902 nominally required examination of applicants, but only two or three had actually been checked out a year after the ordinance took effect. Until 1906 New Jersey only required that an automobile owner file a notarized declaration that he was competent to drive a car.

An early exception to leniency was Chicago, which in 1900 set forth fourteen questions (motor vehicle operation, responsibilities of drivers, and so on) that had to be answered for a license to be issued. This written examination was repeated annually as a condition of renewal. The initial license fee was three dollars, a renewal one dollar. A license could be revoked after a hearing.

By 1906 states were stepping up the prerequisites. New Jersey that year required an applicant to appear in person before a state examiner. And in 1907 Massachusetts began requiring an actual road test as well as a written examination—essentially what is the case everywhere today. Even so, by 1909 only twelve states and the District of Columbia required all drivers to obtain a license.

The result of mechanically primitive vehicles and inexperienced drivers—coupled with inevitable human carelessness—was the automobile accident. The first known mishap occurred in New York City on May 30, 1896, when a Duryea motor wagon driven by Henry Wells of Springfield, Massachusetts, collided with a bicycle operated by Evylyn Thomas. The bicyclist suffered a broken leg; the motorist, a night in jail. Three years later, in September 1899, the first automobile fatality was recorded, also in New York. The victim was a real estate broker named Henry H. Bliss, age sixty-eight, who had just gotten off a streetcar when he was struck and killed. The driver was arrested. Mishaps and fatalities abounded over the coming years. Before long, it was nothing short of "Slaughter on the Highways" (headline in *Outlook*, January 2, 1909).

The most direct way of dealing with the slaughter (then as now) was to regulate speed, the priority of which—as opposed to other forms of regulation—quickly became apparent. Speeding was a problem. Even an automobile with a top speed of 40 or so miles an hour could go four or five times as fast as the average horse-drawn vehicle. And it was the speed of the latter to which pedestrians were accustomed. Anything faster seemed dismayingly faster. As *Motor Age* summed it up at the turn of 1900:

> The people wanted it [the automobile]. But we doubt if they want it driven over them or over their rights in the public streets, and the warmth of their welcome is going to be a good deal cooled unless automobile owners exercise more care.

Although reckless or careless driving could also be destructive of personal rights, speeding was the easiest to define; and that is what early legislation focused on as a means of controlling the driver too susceptible to his motor car's potential for "scorching." By 1906 there were speed limits in effect in most states. A few left speed regulation to localities. Florida set a limit of 4 miles an hour, but only for curves, bridges, fill, and intersections. The most common state limit was 20 miles an hour; a few set it at 15, and some as much as 25.

Enforcement was not always an easy task for police. As reported in *Automobile* in 1904, a recourse of speeders was the use of "bogus license numbers . . . judiciously changed at frequent intervals, in order that no one number might become fixed in the minds of the police. . . . Goggles with face masks became quite popular, and all motorists with a love for fast driving came to look uniformly alike when the high gear was in mesh."

But law enforcement officials had their own devices. One was the "speed trap," a short stretch of road, usually a quarter-mile, manned at each end by a police officer with a stopwatch. If a car that was clocked speeding failed to stop at the officer's signal, a rope (sometimes a wire cable) was pulled across the road to force the car to a halt. Sometimes, as reported in *Horseless Age* in 1902, logs were thrown in the car's path for the same purpose.

WHAT IT COST TO OPERATE

1903 AUTOMOBILE

Estimated one year's upkeep and depreciation

Depreciation	$250.
Tires	75.
Gas (22¢/gallon @ 20 miles per gallon)	44.
Oil and other maintenance supplies	50.
Repairs	26.
TOTAL	$445.

The automobile for which this estimate was made was one that a "modest family" might own. It was figured to cost $1,000, be rated at five or six horsepower, have a cruising speed of 20 to 25 miles per hour, and be driven 4,000 miles a year (80 miles a week), which was considered "a reasonable average" for the time. Because of their open construction, most cars were little if ever used during the winter months. This car was considered to depreciate by half in two years, hence by $250 for the one year shown. The average cost of a car sold in 1903 was $1,160 wholesale. The least expensive was the "curved dash" Oldsmobile, the first mass-produced car, which sold at retail for $650.

Source of table: World's Work, "Can I Afford an Automobile," June 1903; average cost computed from "Motor-Vehicle Factory Sales and Registrations, 1900–1970," U.S. Census Bureau, Historical Statistics of the United States, 716.

As for insurance: Policies covering horse-drawn vehicles had been common; but when the horseless carriage arrived, it prompted reassessment on the part of insurance companies. Motor vehicles were obviously much more expensive to repair, and they were likely to cause greater injury and do far greater property damage. Automobile coverage meant venturing into an actuarial gray area, and many companies saw it as too full of difficulty to be profitable. Observed *Motor World* in 1902, "Nearly all insurance companies fight shy of such

A 1907 Buick. Although there were relatively few women drivers they wrote a disproportionate number of really good accounts of what early motoring was like, a few excerpts from which are quoted here. (Library of Congress)

risks, seemingly better pleased if the business does not come to them." In New York that year, only four companies were underwriting auto insurance, and they had gotten around the actuarial dilemma by arbitrarily jumping the standard $25 rate for a horse-drawn vehicle coverage to $100 for a motor vehicle. Companies in Cleveland, Ohio, took an even safer tack: They wrote policies insuring automobiles for damage "only when they are standing unused in the barn." For the immediate future, auto insurance remained expensive and hard to get.

There were other negatives to early automobiling. Safety and insurance aside, perhaps the greatest nemesis of the early cars was mud. Good roads were few. Really good roads (like modern superhighways) were nonexistent. What paving could be found in the early 1900s either was paving block or macadam, the original form, not the "blacktop" later incorrectly called macadam. The original form consisted of layers of stones of varying size (largest at the bottom, smallest at the top) topped with a layer of fine gravel mixed

with some sort of binder (water or bitumen) that formed a reasonably hard surface. Given adequate drainage, the result was a fairly good road surface reasonably resistant to bad weather. But most roads were unimproved, and rain, or even just spring thaws, meant mud that was often axle-deep (and axles were higher in those days). Mary Post, one of those daring women motorists of the early days who recorded their adventures, spent the summer of 1906 touring in her forty-horsepower Pope-Toledo and wrote a short book about it.

One day in June, on a trip through Bergen County, New Jersey, the Pope-Toledo's "forty horses" were no match for one real one. Mary Post's car got stuck on a "miserably small but muddy hill" near Englewood. The more the driver tried to get out, "backing, pounding, and spluttering," the deeper the car got stuck. She wrote:

> After an hour devoted to waiting, our one male guest started ahead along this lonely road on foot for succor. At the end of a three-mile tramp, meeting no one on the way, he found the first house, and then near it a ploughman working in the field with horses and a farm wagon near. Having secured the man's services, and put into the wagon a block and tackle, he came back to the waiting ones, waving his hat in triumph over his find, as the team and wagon bearing him and the driver descended from the top of our insurmountable hill. The tackle, rope and horses being applied to the car, they had us out in less time than it takes to read this story of that day's adventures. The poor auto had to bow her head in thankful deference to these rescuing beasts whom in happier times the auto (and probably its passengers as well) would have scorned. The horses looked upon us only with silent wonderment, although wild joy might well have shone from their eyes. Neither horse seemed anxious to say "I told you so."

Such predicaments helped fuel a phenomenon of early automobiling that had no real parallel with other emerging forms of technology: quirks and shortcomings that were magnified, fairly or not, into sometimes merciless joshings and ribbings. The overwhelming favorite butt of jokes was the Ford, largely because there were so many of them to make fun of; and it was often Ford owners themselves who did the joshing of their flivvers, tin lizzies, and henrys, as Ford cars were affectionately known. Ford jokes were so common they were collected and published. A notable anthology

Automobile humor, 1905. The caption reads, "Hey mister! You dropped your hat."
(*Auto Fun: Pictures and Comments from "Life,"* New York, 1905)

was *Ford Smiles: All the Best Current Jokes About a Rattling Good Car,* published in New York in 1917. In a brief preface, compiler Carleton B. Case took note of a common quality of Ford fun: At heart it was good-natured. "What perversity of human nature," asked Case rhetorically, "has developed the recent propensity to josh a wonderful machine, that has benefited the very people who laugh at their own 'tin lizzies' and 'henrys'? Perhaps . . . as being our faithful and constant chum, we feel free to make merry with it. Accepting this as the reason, there plainly is a compliment implied in the spontaneous outbreak of Ford witticisms." Henry Ford himself took no offense. "I hope they never end," he once said. "The jokes about my car sure helped to popularize it."

More serious were questions about the automobile's impact on quality of life. As a writer of a letter to *Outlook* complained in 1908: "It has been my lot to be passing the present summer in an old New England town, near the seashore, where the roadbeds are chiefly sand. It is a pretty town, where the houses are some distance apart and set from twenty to fifty or more feet back from the long street, and having porches where, under favorable circumstances, it is a delight to sit in the summer evenings. But since the advent of the automobile this pleasure is largely destroyed, especially in a dry season, when the air is filled with dust, which blows in clouds up to the doors and into the houses." In time this would pale against the far more serious impact on health of air pollution, although the early years actually produced a positive benefit—a reduction in horse pollution, the tons of manure left on the streets by all those horses tugging wagons, streetcars, buggies, and carriages.

A growing awareness of environmental impact was one thing. Cost was another matter. An early automobile was a major expenditure. The curved-dash Oldsmobile of 1903 sold for $650. That was roughly one-fourth of a doctor's annual income. And yet that defined the low end of the price scale. At the other extreme, midway through the first decade of the twentieth century, were such exotic machines as the Pierce Great Arrow at $5,000 or a Peerless limousine at $6,250. Even a more modest choice like a Maxwell at $1,400 or a Ford Model C at $950 was out of the question for a factory worker making $500 a year. And beyond what it cost to buy a car was what it cost to maintain.

Yet so great was the yearning that for many Americans it made no difference. As *Outlook* magazine reflected in 1910: "The price of the car, the cost of maintenance, the rapid depreciation, have no terrors for the uninformed. It is entirely natural that the family of moderate means, seeing their neighbors and friends in similar circumstances driving automobiles, should come to the conclusion that they can also afford to indulge in the same luxury. The fallacy concealed in this line of reasoning is that the average family can afford the expenditure of money involved in the ownership and operation of a motor car. This is the erroneous conclusion that has led to much loss and much deprivation. The chief difficulty in acquiring a sensible attitude toward the purchase of a motor car is that the prospective purchaser, in a large proportion of instances, refuses or neglects to inform himself as to the cost of maintenance."

While many a family would continue to get into a bind trying to keep up with the cost of maintenance, at least the purchase price was coming down relative to what the earliest automobiles cost; it declined substantially with mass production. In 1901, the year assembly-line production of automobiles began with the curved-dash Oldsmobile, there were altogether 7,000 passenger cars produced for a total wholesale value of $8,000,000, an average of $1,143 per car—a very expensive proposition for a family that was even moderately well-off. By 1929, with production at 4,455,100 and a total value of $2,790,000,000, the average wholesale cost had dropped to $626. The decrease is even more significant when considered against the wholesale price index*—55.3 for all commodities in 1901 and 95.3 in 1929—meaning the relative cost of a car in 1929 was only about a fourth of what it was in 1901.

The overall impact of the automobile on American life is far too broad to be considered here over and above restating some of the obvious: a general acceleration of the pace of life, creation of the suburbs (and suburban sprawl), traffic jams, gridlock, drive-in fast-food restaurants (beginning with Royce Hailey's Pig Stand in Dallas in 1921), and shopping malls (beginning with Country Club Plaza outside Kansas City, Missouri, in 1922).

But at least as profound as any of these was the automobile's significance as the collective mastering of a complex piece of machinery, with all that that portended for the vast technological change that lay ahead, most of all the computer revolution. In the case of the automobile—the nonautomatic kind, the mastery of which had to be accomplished in the process of its evolving into the relatively simple machinery it is today—this was a challenge to almost everyone. "I have taught a large number of persons to drive gasoline-cars," recalled Hiram Percy Maxim. "In my experience the beginner encounters his first difficulty in remembering to steer while he is operating the clutch pedal and selecting his new gear. It is rare that a beginner is found who can keep his mind on the steering, the clutch, and the gear change all at the same time. It is extremely rare to find a beginner who can add to these operations that of pressing down the foot throttle the right amount at the right moment."

With differing degrees of dexterity, albeit often also with a grinding of gears, people managed to learn. "It is a highly significant thing," observed Maxim in 1936, before even the automatic transmission and power steering had simplified things. "Today almost everyone drives a gasoline motor-car, just as almost everyone has learned to ride a bicycle. . . ."

---

*Bureau of Labor Statistics (U.S. Census Bureau, *Historical Statistics of the United States,* 200).

Is the gasoline motor-car the most complex machine the general public can handle? I do not think so. . . . We have washing machines, electric vacuum cleaners, electric stoves, oil-burning furnaces, radio receivers, motor-boats, motion-picture cameras and projectors, adding and computing machines, typewriters, and a host of other devices all of which call for no small amount of technical skill in their operation. . . . How much further can the public go in manipulating complicated mechanisms?

We are still finding out.

CHAPTER FOUR

LOOKING HEAVENWARD

AIR TRAVEL

[The news] created no little excitement about town [the Buffalo area], and hundreds were looking heavenward. . . . The majority of our people, however, looked upon the matter as a hoax, not believing it possible that such an unparalleled event could take place.

—*Albany Morning Express,* on the flight of the *Atlantic*

IT WAS ARGUABLY THE BEGINNING of air travel in America, this "unparalleled event." The overnight flight carried a party of four from St. Louis, Missouri, to central New York State, a distance of more than 800 air miles, at a speed of as much as 60 miles an hour and an altitude occasionally as great as 10,000 feet. It was a little slower but otherwise not unlike what a small, light, private aircraft might do today. The balloon *Atlantic* did it in July 1859.

What the *Atlantic* also did was to show an anticipation of air travel before its time had really come—a sense of expectation of what was possible while it yet seemed impossible. Thousands watched the *Atlantic* lift off in St. Louis promptly at 7:20 P.M. Friday, July 1, 1859, and disappear eastward into the evening sky. Here and there, others looking skyward observed its course: at dawn, passing just north of Fort Wayne, Indiana; at 7 A.M., over Sandusky, Ohio; east of Cleveland at 9:30; near Buffalo, New York, in early afternoon. After it had returned to earth, people in Adams, New York, near where it landed, gave the *Atlantic*'s crew a reception "exceeding in enthusiasm, the [local] celebration of the laying of the Atlantic Telegraph Cable." It was no small tribute; celebrations of the cable's completion, just the year before, were on a scale befitting its significance as one of the great events of the nineteenth century.

People had been hearing about balloons since the first ascension in America in 1793, and many had seen them at fairs and shows. But it was always for the spectacle of it: a balloon ascending majestically, sometimes levitating above, sometimes drifting just out of sight, but otherwise going nowhere. It had nothing to do with travel. Here, now, was a compelling demonstration that humankind could travel long-distance through the air, and at speeds faster than on the ground.

The *Atlantic* was chiefly the creation of balloonist John Wise (1808–1879), by then a veteran of some 230 ascensions. This was by far his most ambitious project. In the course of his trips aloft,

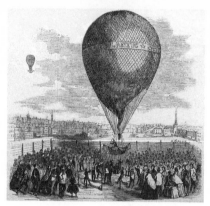

Liftoff. Departing from St. Louis the evening of July 1, 1859: the start of the record-setting flight of the balloon *Atlantic*. Besides the dignitaries and paying spectators in the fenced-off area here, thousands of others watched from streets and rooftops nearby. The small balloon at the left escorted the *Atlantic* for the first leg of its trip. (*Frank Leslie's Illustrated Newspaper*, July 16, 1859)

he had developed a theory as to a river of air flowing west to east. He wrote in the log of a flight in 1842 that "it is established now beyond a doubt in my mind that a current from west to east in the atmosphere is constantly in motion within the height of twelve thousand feet above the ocean." That being so, he asked himself, why could not a balloon soar clear across the Atlantic? Hence the name of his ship, whose purpose it was to do just that. The first leg—the shakedown cruise—would be the voyage from St. Louis to New York.

Wise engaged as his collaborator John La Mountain (1830–1870), another balloonist, who oversaw construction of the *Atlantic*. The financial backing, something like $30,000, came from O. A. Gager, of Bennington, Vermont, who was promised a spot on board for the historic trip. The fourth crew member was William Hyde, a reporter for the *St. Louis Republican*. As for the ship itself, it was probably the largest balloon in the world at that time, a giant sack of varnished silk 130 feet high and 60 feet in diameter, under which were attached an open wicker car and a lifeboat 16 feet long. The car carried scientific and navigational gear (charts, compass, barometer, thermometer), express mail (a 10-pound bag of letters and papers sent by the United States Express Company of New York), and provisions for the flight (sandwiches, cold chicken, potted meat, and assorted wines, much like an airliner of today). Like a modern airliner, there was a scheduled time of departure; unlike many a modern one, this one left on time.

The lift-off site in St. Louis's Washington Square was fenced off, since it was hoped many people would buy tickets at fifty cents each to watch the ascension close-up. A fence would have been necessary anyway because of the size of the crowd. Several hundred persons did pay admission, and the number might have been more had only twenty-five cents been charged, the *St. Louis Democrat* noted. As it was, said the newspaper: "The streets, and house-tops, and sheds and windows outside the inclosure, were completely crammed with a multitude of the curious"—as many as "fifty thousand," notwithstanding the intense heat of a cloudless day. Despite the fence, there were so many pressing around the launch site by the hour of departure that an appeal went out to all those not actually holding one of the balloon's ropes to retire a short distance away. As they did, the rope holders let go and the giant balloon lifted off—La Mountain piloting, Gager navigating with the compass and charts.

"At 8:30 P.M.," Wise wrote later, "the shades of the evening shut from our view the noble city of St. Louis and the Father of Waters, though it continued light until after nine. . . . At midnight . . . the whole dome of heaven was lit up with a mellow phosphorescent light, the stars shone with a crystalline brilliancy, and the Milky-Way looked like an illuminated stratum of cumulus clouds."

Navigation was rudimentary; yet, unconsciously, the crew made use of a sort of primitive radar system. As Wise recalled: "Whenever we halloed it was followed by a distinct echo, and even this served as a differential index to height. We always found a response in numerous bow-wows-wows, and these, too, were always indicative of the fullness and sparseness of the habitations below, as we could hear them for many miles around us."

At 3:00 A.M. Saturday, the crew took a fix on location, and "came to a general conclusion that we were somewhere over the State of Indiana or Ohio." At 4:00 A.M. they passed a city but could not make it out. By daylight a landmark of unmistakable proportions came into sight—an immense lake.

> Just as we merged upon the lake, a little steam screw [ship] that was propelling up a river or bay, headed for our track, and some one on board of her very quaintly cried aloud to us: "That is the Lake ahead of you." Mr. La Mountaine [*sic*] cried back, "Is it Lake Erie?" and the answer was, "Yes, it is, and you had better look out."

The first thought was to circle the lake along its southern shore, but La Mountain suggested heading directly across to Buffalo, sailing a few hundred feet above the surface of the water. That agreed upon, Wise opened the valve and the *Atlantic* gradually sank to within 500 feet of the water. There, said Wise, "we found a gentle gale of about a speed of a mile per minute, and we resolved to float on it until we should heave in sight of Buffalo, and then rise and sail over it."

According to Wise, that was the most interesting part of the voyage. "We overtook seven steamboats, passed mutual salutations, and would soon leave them flitting on the horizon in our rear. One of these lonely travellers remarked as we passed him: 'You are going it like thunder.'"

The "gentle gale" performed its service well, and the *Atlantic* traversed Lake Erie in record time. At about noon on Saturday, as reported by the *Buffalo Courier,* the balloon was spotted above Buffalo. At about a quarter after twelve, an observer saw it passing over Niagara Falls. Then it went rapidly out over Lake Ontario.

The part about "thunder" was flattery that would come back to haunt the *Atlantic*'s crew. According to Wise:

> Finding ourselves in the State of New York, but too far north to make the city of New York, it was agreed that we would make a landing near Rochester, detach the boat, leave out Mr. Gager and Mr. Hyde, and Mr. La Mountaine and myself pursue the voyage to a point at Boston or Portland. Accordingly we descended gradually, but before we got within a thousand feet of the earth, we found a terrific gale sweeping along below. The woods roared like a host of Niagaras, the surface of the earth was filled with clouds of dust, and I told my friends certain destruction awaited us if we should touch the earth in that tornado. The huge Atlantic was making a terrible sweep earthward; already we were near the tops of the trees of a tall forest, and I cried out somewhat excitedly, "For God's sake, heave overboard any thing you can lay your hands on." . . . Our carpet-bags, our instruments, the express-bag, our provisions, were all ready to go, and go they did, one after another, until we were reduced to the express-bag, that went overboard last.
>
> We now descried the shore, some forty miles ahead, peering between a sombre bank of clouds and the water horizon, but we were swooping at a fearful rate upon the turbulent water, and, in another moment, crash went the boat upon the water sideways,

staving in two of the planks, and giving our whole craft two fearful jerks by two succeeding waves. La Mountaine stuck to the boat like a hero, but lost his hat, and got a dash of the waves, but soon recovered and threw over the express-bag and the last remaining ballast, and cried out: "Be easy, gentlemen, I'll have her afloat once more." In another moment we were up a few hundred feet again. . . .

After dashing along this way for nearly a mile, crushing and breaking down trees, we were dashed most fearfully into the boughs of a tall elm, so that the basket swung under and up through the crotch of the limb, and while the boat had caught in some of the other branches; and this brought us to a little, but in another moment the Atlantic puffed up her huge proportions, and at one swoop away went the limb, basket, and boat into the air a hundred feet, [then] suddenly down upon the top of a very large tree and collapsed her. It was a fearful plunge, but it left us dangling between heaven and earth, in the most sorrowful-looking plight of machinery that can be imagined.

None of the crew was seriously injured. The *Atlantic* itself was all but destroyed, but its flight of more than 800 miles set a record that would last until 1910. Despite the flight's unhappy ending, aeronaut John Wise remained as optimistic as ever about the future of aviation. In 1850 he made the remarkable prediction that "the genius of our favorably gifted country . . . must inevitably place aerial transition [transportation] as far before railroad and steamboat transition, as the latter are before the old-fashioned sail and horse-power modes, and impact its advantages to the present rising generation"—exactly what came true in the next century. After the crash of the *Atlantic* he announced his intention to make repairs and fly it again—this time across the breadth of its namesake. He was confident, he said, that he could travel to Europe by balloon in one-fourth the time it took the steamers. Using another balloon built for the purpose with financial support from the New York *Daily Illustrated Graphic,* he attempted a transatlantic flight in 1873 but crashed in Connecticut. He was killed in 1879 when still another of his balloons, the *Pathfinder,* sank in Lake Michigan. Eventually transatlantic flight would become a reality, but only with a new generation of balloons known as dirigibles (from the French, *diriger,* to steer) as opposed to balloons subject wholly to the whim of the wind.

The crash of the *Atlantic* in western New York state, heavily damaging the balloon but sparing its crew of four serious injury. The flight nevertheless set a distance record for balloons that lasted until 1910. (*Frank Leslie's Illustrated Newspaper,* July 16, 1859)

RISING ABOVE TALL ELMS

Many, of course, doubted that humans would ever fly, and thought those foolish enough to try were destined only for tall elm trees. Certainly there was doubt about the practicality of the earliest balloons, those curious contraptions that first went aloft with the Montgolfiers and others in France in the mid-1780s.* One who didn't doubt was Benjamin Franklin. When asked what possible practical use balloons could have, Franklin replied (or words to this effect), "What good is a new-born baby?" Franklin probably saw the good of balloons chiefly for scientific experimentation, and meteorology in particular, rather than transportation or communications; nevertheless, he foresaw the crossing of the English Channel before it was first accomplished on January 7, 1785, by the Frenchman J.-P. Blanchard and American physician John Jeffries. In a curiously appropriate way Franklin was rewarded for his faith by being the recipient of the first airmail letter. Jeffries had with him, addressed to Franklin in Paris, a letter from London; and Franklin proudly hailed its significance as "the first thro' the Air."

This same Blanchard was also the first aeronaut to fly in

---

*The earliest balloons were hot-air, as when the Montgolfiers in September 1783 sent a sheep, a duck, and a rooster aloft in their famous demonstration for France's Louis XVI. Yet hydrogen even then was coming into use. It was easily generated in barrels by adding sulfuric acid to iron scraps, the resulting gas being conveyed to the balloon by leather piping. A hot-air balloon commonly used a straw-burning brazier suspended beneath the mouth of the balloon. Hydrogen balloons were by far the more common over the coming years.

America—at Philadelphia on January 9, 1793—although he had already made forty-four ascensions in Europe. As would be the case sixty-six years later in St. Louis, the sight of a human lofting into the air, well publicized in advance, attracted considerable public attention. A balloon launching, furthermore, was a good spectacle for a crowd, since the object of attention was so large as to be visible for a considerable distance. The crowd for Blanchard's liftoff was described by *Dunlap's American Daily Advertiser* as "an immense concourse of spectators"—among them, President George Washington. Its numbers notwithstanding, the crowd was notable for its awed silence at the moment of ascent. As *Dunlap's* explained: ". . . when it [the balloon] began to rise, the majestical sight was truly awful and interesting—the slow movement of the band, added solemnity to the scene. Indeed the attention of the multitude was so absorbed, that it was a considerable time e'er silence was broke by the acclamations which succeeded." Blanchard's flight took him east across the Delaware River into New Jersey. He landed in Woodbury, having covered a distance of roughly 15 miles in forty-six minutes, and then returned to Philadelphia by horse and carriage.

Between then and the 1850s, there were an estimated 3,000 balloon ascensions in America, with about 8,000 persons taking part. Few were the opportunities, so it is difficult to say how many would like to have flown if they could. Probably most people would have demurred, many flat out refusing. Just to watch a balloon rising majestically upward was exciting enough for spectators.

Or just imagining one. A balloon could really catch a kid's fancy, and children of the nineteenth century were hardly any less excited by balloons than children of a later age by planes and rockets. Children's books had accounts of balloons from the early 1800s on, but they presented sharply differing perspectives. The earliest known reference appeared in a book published in Philadelphia in 1807 appropriately titled *The Third Chapter of Accidents and Remarkable Events Containing Caution and Instruction for Children.* It had two accounts of balloon flight, both involving crashes, one in which the balloon burst into flames as it came down. Such tales warned that balloon flight had no practical value and only fools would risk their life.

Less gruesome but no less didactic was *First Lessons on Natural Philosophy* by Mary Swift, one of the most popular of children's authors of the mid–nineteenth century, which had this bit of catechism to remind children of the realities that went along with the romance of flight.

Do accidents ever happen to those who ascend in balloons?

Very often.

How?

When the balloon comes down, it sometimes falls into the sea, and the people in it are injured or drowned; and sometimes it strikes a tree suddenly, or is dragged violently along the ground, and the persons in it get hurt.

On the other hand, as *First Lessons* noted on the following page, fliers and their passengers were not wholly at the mercy of happenstance: "If a balloon bag bursts, or a car upsets, and the man in it has a parachute, he can hold upon the handle of it, and keep himself from falling quickly to the ground or sea." Given the nature of children's literature of the time, this was meant to convey a moral: that one's religion, if practiced dutifully enough, was one's parachute in life. As a practical matter parachutes had come into use in the late eighteenth century, a perfect case of inventiveness matching the instinct for survival against the impulse for adventure. Mary Swift described one as looking "like a large umbrella open," a primitive version of its counterpart in modern times.

The sentiment wasn't all negative. Edward Hazen's *The Symbolic Primer,* published in Hartford, Connecticut, in 1830, dispassionately presented a definition of balloon flight that was scientifically objective and as detailed as a primer format allowed: "The Balloon is a large hollow ball of silk filled with gas, which causes it to rise into the air." *The Talisman: A Tale for Boys* (Boston, 1829) showed balloon flight as positively thrilling: An illustration portrayed a number of children, all obviously excited, watching a balloon ascend.

The course of balloon flight in the years immediately ahead

was of a utilitarian nature hardly intended to thrill spectators. T. S. C. Lowe, at about the same time Wise was hurtling over eastern America, had unveiled plans for a balloon with which to cross the Atlantic. It was a grand plan that never came to be, but Lowe went on to distinction manning balloons for Union forces in the Civil War.

Balloons had two primary shortcomings that precluded their practical use for transportation. There was naught but the fickleness of the wind on which to depend for motion and direction; and a single gas bag could accomplish only just so much in terms of lift. A new generation of rigid and semirigid airships—generally speaking, the dirigibles—solved both shortcomings. A number of gas bags, or cells, could be accommodated, allowing for an enormous increase in lift; and means could be had for mounting a motor, or multiple motors, casting away dependence on the wind. Eventually these technological developments made possible the *Graf Zeppelin* and *Hindenburg* and other giant airships of the 1920s and 1930s. In other respects the earliest dirigibles were little different from John Wise's balloon. Certainly they remained crowd-pleasers in a way that the earliest airplanes could not yet do.

CELEBRATING THE AERIAL AGE

To get some sense of what Americans thought of aviation in the early twentieth century we can look at the first air show ever held in America, and probably in the world. It was called an "Aero Carnival" and took place near New York City in 1909, little more than five years after the Wright brothers' historic flight at Kitty Hawk. Here on a broad upland plain hard by New Jersey's vast open meadowlands—an open site favoring flight not far from the growing skyscrapers of Manhattan 10 miles away—was an opportunity for all those who had been hearing so much about aviation to see close-up what airships, airplanes, and air people were all about. Arguably the first of its kind, the air show provided a unique opportunity for gauging just how much public interest there was in aviation. Did many people really care about what was going on? Was flying yet relevant to most people?

The Aero Carnival was a huge success, but perhaps as much for the carnival part of it as the aero. Attendance the first day alone was as many as 50,000, pouring down upon the center of activity—North Arlington, New Jersey—a gathering of spectators more than a hundred times as great as the population (437) of the little town itself.

The weeklong carnival began the afternoon of Tuesday, May 25, 1909, with a grand parade featuring fourteen horse-drawn carriages for dignitaries, 125 vehicles and floats decked out with flags and bunting, a battalion of National Guard troops, various bands, and a procession of schoolchildren waving flags. Houses and businesses along the parade route, leading from the town hall in nearby Harrison, were decorated for the occasion.

At the opening ceremony, Governor J. Franklin Fort gave the main address, declaring with obvious pride that the air show was "the first of its kind ever held in the United States, if not in the world." This was now the "aerial age," proclaimed the governor; "I don't think it an extravagant statement to assert that within twenty-five years we shall be traveling the air with as much ease and security as we now make a journey to-day over steel rails in a comfortable [railroad] car."

But it was the show above, not rhetoric from a podium, that had brought the thousands there that sunny, but windy, day. The purpose of the extravaganza was to show off new flying contrivances and encourage aviation with a prize of $1,000 for the first aviator who could keep an airplane in the air for at least a mile (an achievement that puts the state of aviation development in perspective). Originally, there were supposed to be six entries, including one representing *Scientific American* magazine, but as of Wednesday only two craft were actually on hand, ready to fly. One was a biplane called the *Jersey Devil* that was described by the *New York Times* as "a strange contrivance constructed of tin, iron, and steel, with two enormous wings stretching out from the top." The other was a triplane built by inventor Morris Bokor of New York, which apparently was the only one that actually tried to get into the air. But the unpaved road used as a runway was too soft to allow Bokor his needed 35-mile-per-hour takeoff speed (he could only manage 12), and he gave up. No one won the prize of $1,000.

The real attraction of the show, however, was not a plane but a dirigible, the *California Arrow*, a duplicate of the U.S. Army's SC-1, the first United States military aircraft. Fifty-two feet long, it had a gas bag made of silk, coated with varnish, that held 9,000 cubic feet of hydrogen. For propulsion, there was a 7-horsepower Curtiss engine. The *Arrow* was a curious sight in a sky that had so rarely glittered with anything man-made, though it was tiny by comparison with the dirigibles that were to come along in a few years. For most of the thousands who were at the show, this was their first look at something carrying a human aloft. The ship's pilot, Army Captain Thomas S. Baldwin, had taken on the then-formidable challenge of flying from the air show grounds to Manhattan, circling the Pulitzer Building on Park Row, near the present City Hall, and returning.

Takeoff was scheduled for 5:30 P.M., and right on schedule Baldwin's crew moved the dirigible out into the open. But the captain needed additional time for adjusting and testing, particularly since a gusty wind made the flight all the more difficult. After half an hour he announced he was ready. As the *Newark Evening News* reported:

> Everything looked propitious for a dead beat against the wind to Manhattan when the balloonist inspired a few deep drawn gasps from the almost awestruck onlookers by suddenly ascending still higher. It was then that the machine became refractory. It see-sawed through the air like a chicken trying to dodge an automobile and then veered about in an apparently aimless manner. Although the pilot could be seen working at the levers in an effort to gain control of the craft, it soon began its downward flight and landed easily about 200 yards away from where the start was made. The crowd rushed in pursuit, and upon the shoulders of willing helpers the big balloon was carried back to its tent, where it was housed for the night.

On Wednesday Baldwin managed to fly for ten minutes, covering a little less than a quarter of a mile; and by Friday he had made four ascents, albeit short ones because of the wind. He never accomplished his feat of soaring to Manhattan and back. For the thousands of spectators the disappointment was mitigated by side shows and a circus, the popcorn and lemonade, the "gayety and holiday abandon . . . [the] Coney Island atmosphere" of the occasion (quoting the *New York Times*) mingled with the excitement of seeing a couple of flying machines up close and an airship that actually flew. In the opinion of the *New York World*, the world's first air show and the thousands it drew was "evidence of tremendous interest in aerial navigation."

Nevertheless, it was what had excited crowds for more than a century that caught the most attention; and that huge spectacle in the sky would continue for a time to represent the ultimate in air travel. The only difference is that the balloon would become an ever larger spectacle. The 52-foot length of Captain Baldwin's dirigible would soon be dwarfed by giant airships ten times as long and more. To travel by dirigible in the 1920s and 1930s was to achieve the ultimate in travel experience for the time. It was "Our most modern method of transportation," said a writer in *Living Age* in 1925, hugely impressed by a trip aboard the zeppelin ZR3. The 656-foot-long ZR3, completed in 1924, was produced by the zeppelin works in Germany as partial payment of reparations to the United States. After delivery in 1925, it was renamed the *Los Angeles* and became a Navy airship, making some 250 flights

The great age of dirigibles: the U.S.S. *Akron* over New York City about 1932. Unlike the *Los Angeles*, which was a German reparations zeppelin, the *Akron* was American-built. At roughly a seventh of a mile in length, the *Akron* was one of the largest airships ever constructed. A year after this photograph was taken, while making its fifty-ninth flight, it went down in the Atlantic in a storm. A smaller sister ship, the U.S.S. *Macon*, crashed in the Pacific two years later, effectively ending America's dirigible program. (National

Archives)

before being decommissioned in 1932. For the obvious public relations value, the ship occasionally took along civilians who recorded their observations for print. One such observer traveling aboard the *Los Angeles* in 1925 was delighted by such amenities as a phonograph and records. He found the main quarters resembling "more than anything else, an enlarged and glorified Pullman sleeper." When the *Los Angeles* went into service, it joined the *Shenandoah,* which was built in the United States in 1923 following zeppelin design. Two other giant American-built airships were added to the Navy dirigible fleet in the early 1930s, the *Akron* and the *Macon.* Both crashed, as did the *Shenandoah.* No other American dirigibles of rigid design were built.

American airships were military. For commercial travelers— those who could afford the cost—there were the German zeppelins. The first of these, the *Graf Zeppelin,* completed in 1928, inaugurated transatlantic dirigible service and flew more than a million miles, including 144 ocean crossings, before being decommissioned in 1937. The ultimate of dirigibles was the *Hindenburg,* 804 feet in length (nearly three football fields) and of sufficient power (four 1,100-horsepower diesel engines) for a maximum speed of 84 miles an hour. In comfort and amenity, it was as close to the level of luxury of a first-class steamship as could be put in the air. Each of its twenty-five cabins had two berths and running water. The lounge boasted a grand piano (albeit made of light-weight aluminum), and its dining room served such fare as brook trout and German wine. On each side of the ship was a 50-foot promenade with windows angled downward to facilitate observation. It made its maiden flight, from Germany to America, in May 1936. One of its fifty passengers was Louis P. Lochner, the journalist son of a Lutheran pastor in Milwaukee, Wisconsin, then serving as chief of the Berlin bureau of The Associated Press. Lochner flew round trip, from Berlin and back, and found the *Hindenburg* "Jules Verne come true!" One thing that struck Lochner about the trip was "the proximity of New York to Berlin, thanks to the zeppelin, brought home to us as the Tempelhof station master announces proudly, 'All aboard for Friedrichshafen–New York' "—like it was New York to Boston. Another profound recollection was of the infinite blue at cruising altitude, the transcending of what we know as weather;

it is a sensation that modern air passengers take for granted but was then known but to a few aviators. "What a difference between now and my ordinary ship crossings," Lochner wrote. "Then I could count with certainty upon foggy weather; now the clouds lay below us like a fluffy carpet, and we enjoyed the brightest sunshine above. . . . It is when I experience things of this kind that I am aware of the limitations of the human language."

It was May 6, 1936, that the Tempelhof stationmaster barked "all aboard" for the *Hindenburg*'s first flight. By remarkable happenstance—ten round trips and 1,002 passengers later—it was May 6, 1937, that marked its last trip. Limitations of human engineering—and especially the use of highly flammable hydrogen instead of safe but scarce helium, which only the United States possessed and which it refused to supply—put an end to the *Hindenburg* as it attempted a landing at the U.S. Navy's airdock in Lakehurst, New Jersey. The giant airship burst into an inferno that killed a third of those on board. Reported live on radio as a seemingly routine event that suddenly turned terribly tragic ("Oh, the humanity!"), it was a dramatic and irreversible ending to travel by balloon.

MACHINES WITH WINGS

There are many students of aerial locomotion who profess a contempt for the balloon, as a mere plaything, and consider that the only proper solution of the problem is by a flying-machine, which shall sustain itself in the air, like a bird, by mechanical means.

—Living Age, August 21, 1875

Long before the *Hindenburg*—long before anybody even dreamed of such a colossus actually flying through the sky—it was argued that the balloon was simply an anomaly: The key to humankind flying was in emulating the way the winged kind did it.

The trick was to make it work. Balloons worked because they were lighter than air, whereas a machine (say, of "tin, iron, and steel, with two enormous wings stretching out from the top," like the one at the 1909 Aero Carnival) was obviously heavier than air. Many were the attempts at heavier-than-air flight, even the use of steam for propulsion. It was not until 1903—with the gasoline engine brought up to a sufficient state of development and with a newfound understanding of aerodynamics—that there were really serious contenders, and the clear favorite was Samuel P. Langley, secretary of the Smithsonian Institution. But his boat-launched "aerodrome" failed one test in October of that year and another in early December, leading one journalist to remark that Langley's flying machine had all the aerodynamic properties of a handful of mortar.

It was December 17 of that year that humankind first flew in powered flight—Wilbur Wright sprinting down the sands of Kitty Hawk shepherding into the air, if ever so little, that massive crate-like contrivance he and his brother Orville had built. Orville was at the controls. A photograph recording the first instant of manned flight has perhaps been reproduced more than any photograph ever taken. The event itself was not only the most dramatic in the history of aviation but arguably the most pivotal of the twentieth century since it symbolically launched all the technological achievement of the century.

The Wrights arranged for the photograph of the first flight. There was no press photographer present, or even a single reporter. Modest and unassuming by nature, the Wrights were doubly anxious to protect the privacy of their experimental flights. They had a standing rule in the fall and early winter of 1903, as in the two prior years, that only close associates and necessary workers were allowed at the Kitty Hawk site. This first of all secured the design of their craft; it also avoided the negative publicity that would inevitably attend to failed launches. The brothers had a standing arrangement that news of the first successful flight would be announced in their hometown, Dayton, Ohio, by their father, Bishop Milton Wright, and through their "press agent" (as they referred to him), brother Lorin.

The press had been interested during various experiments at Kitty Hawk in the years immediately preceding the first flight. But the Wrights held the press at bay. Now on that cold, gray day of December 17, 1903, when powered flight became a reality, they were prepared to have the world know. Orville signed his name to a telegram sent to Dayton from the only telegraph key for miles about, the local office of the Weather Bureau, with whose observer, Joe Dosher, the Wrights had become friends. Dosher sent the message to the bureau headquarters in nearby Norfolk, Virginia, which passed it to a Western Union operator to send to Dayton. At half past five in the evening, Milton Wright read what he had hoped for:

> Success four flights thursday morning # all against twenty one mile wind started from Level with engine power alone # average speed through air thirty one miles longest 57 seconds inform Press home #### Christmas. Orevelle Wright.

As planned ahead of time, Lorin took the telegram to the office of the *Dayton Journal* and gave it to the local Associated Press representative for transmittal to newspapers throughout the country. But the AP man, Frank Tunison, who had visions of balloons traveling for hours and apparently knew nothing about winged flight, was unimpressed: "Fifty-seven seconds, hey? If it had been fifty-seven minutes then it might have been a news item."

The Associated Press took a pass. And that might have been the end of it, except that back in Norfolk the Weather Bureau operator, who was supposed to have kept the contents of the telegram to himself, tipped off a reporter friend at the *Norfolk Virginian-Pilot*. Next day the *Pilot* bannered its front page with:

FLYING MACHINE SOARS 3 MILES IN TEETH OF HIGH WIND OVER SAND
HILLS AND WAVES AT KITTY HAWK ON CAROLINA COAST

The headline, like the story accompanying it (which two *Pilot* reporters frantically pieced together by telephone just in time for the deadline), had almost as many errors as truths—flying 3 miles, for example. But the central fact—that manned, powered flight was a reality—was not only conveyed to readers of the *Pilot* but, through its quick recognition of what a news item really was, to readers all over America. The editor of the *Pilot* wired twenty-one other papers asking if they also wanted to use the story. Only two—the *New York American* and the Cincinnati *Enquirer*—did, using it in the next morning's editions; and then AP picked it up in abbreviated version and sent it out across the nation. The *New York Herald*, whose fondness for new technology was evident in its
championing of the telegraph, on December 19 used essentially

A boldly determined yet seemingly amazed Wilbur Wright running alongside as brother Orville ascends for the first time at Kitty Hawk on December 17, 1903. It is perhaps the most widely seen photograph ever taken. Yet it remains a singularly dramatic image of technology at the threshold. (National Archives)

the AP release augmented by 1901 photographs from *Scientific American* of the Wrights using a motorless version of their Flyer as a glider to give their coverage a sense of on-the-spot realism.

What in fact happened was that the Wrights made four powered flights the morning of December 17, 1903. Orville made the first, covering 120 feet in twelve seconds. Wilbur was the pilot on the best flight of the day, the fourth flight, soaring 856 feet in fifty-nine (not fifty-seven as reported) seconds.

Even before the brothers left Kitty Hawk to return to Dayton, they had telegrams from the *Woman's Home Companion* and the *New York World* bidding for exclusive rights to their story, then from *Scientific American* asking for photographs and *Century Magazine* wanting both photos and an exclusive story. On December 22 the Wright family home in Dayton was besieged by reporters. What the AP's man in Dayton didn't think was an item was chugging down the runway and taking off.

On the other hand, many people thought, as did an unidentified man quoted in a story titled "The Highway of the Air" in *Everybody's Magazine,* January 1909: "Those Wrights may be doing it, but seeing is believing." And seeing was not always convincing. The earliest planes were gangly and awkward looking; in flight, more like orange crates blowing about than devices meant to soar through the air. By comparison, balloons, though hardly speedy-looking, had a certain majesty to them. When Orville Wright demonstrated his Flyer at Fort Myer, Virginia, in August 1908, a disappointed spectator thought the celebrated Wright Flyer looked and sounded like nothing more than some overlarge piece of farm machinery:

> They warn you at Niagara that the only way to see the Falls the first time is to see them from below; that if you look at them from above you will have a quick, sinking sense of unfulfillment. My experience with the flyer was like that. There it was, barely skimming the tops of the grass and weeds of the parade ground, with only the edges of its broad wings visible, and its two propellers flapping awkwardly behind. I saw no sublimity in that; no realized ideal of vast, white pinions gleaming in the sky; none of the grace and ease I'd dreamed about. Instead there was what looked like a big, double-armed reaping machine trundling along, and the clack of its motor made but one sound in my ears—the noise of reaper knives hewing through the prairie wheat.

> And then . . .

> The ugly, pitching frame swooped upward, as if my fancied reaper had galloped to a prairie rise. Then it careened on that circling, skyward shoot, and, edging over as it soared, turned its surfaces toward us with a flash of snowy wings. A murmur broke from the crowd, a whisper of admiration. "Oh!" Out over the distant tree-tops and the shed's peaked roofs, above every background but the blue, rushed into view then the real picture—the one I'd dreamed about—the vast bird-thing, wheeling in a long, lazy sweep of gracefulness through the profundity of the sky . . . free of all restraint; and with all the power of a great sea bird drove away upon its course.

Wright's demonstration was made for the United States Army for the purpose of securing a contract to supply his great sea bird as a military plane. But the flight observed here turned out to be a prelude to disaster. On September 3, 1908, nine days after the trials began, Orville crashed, carrying with him to his death an Army observer, Lt. Thomas E. Selfridge, who was flying as a passenger. Orville was badly injured, but survived; Selfridge became the first powered aircraft fatality. A propeller had split, spinning the craft out of control. Giving Wright the benefit of the doubt that this was happenstance, rather than a fundamental flaw of air-craft design, the Army allowed Wright to return the following summer and resubmit to a new set of trials. Orville Wright, accompanied now by Wilbur, who was in France in the summer of 1908, returned to Fort Myer in late July 1909. In the all-important speed trial—the test that tripped up Orville the first time—the Wrights' plane not only passed but exceeded the minimum specifications set by the Army, averaging a speed of 42.583 miles per hour, 2.583 over the required 40. The Wrights got their contract.

Asked about the future of aviation in 1909, Alexander Graham Bell—who also had an interest in aviation—offered the opinion that, "The aerodrome [its original meaning was plane, not airport] has, at a stroke, rendered antiquated all present methods of warfare. . . . it is an era as critical as that of the Monitor and the Merrimac, the first two ironclads."

And so it turned out. World War I in fact brought the airplane to both a new prominence and a new practicality—and a new stage of development. At the outset of the war, planes were traveling 70 to 80 miles an hour at up to 7,000 feet; at war's end, 150 miles an hour at altitudes in the range of 20,000 feet. The airplane engine that Wright had wondered about had more than doubled in efficiency, producing twice as much horsepower per pound as before. What emerged in the 1920s was a far more modern craft. But still, what was it good for, now that bombing and strafing enemy lines was no longer its mission? Beyond stunts and air shows and crop dusting—and carrying a few passengers here and there—what could it do?

OVERCOMING SHYNESS

Americans, for the most part, remained skeptical. Distilling thought from such sources as the *New York Times, Popular Science Monthly,* and the *Magazine of Wall Street,* the *Review of Reviews* in 1927 declared it was a case of "Air-Shy America":

> The United States, except for its flyers, is air-shy. It quickly made an industry of the movies and the automobile; but of the airplane it made only a stunt performer, never considering it seriously as a vehicle for the civilian.

That was in August 1927, an article ironically followed on the next page with one titled "Lindbergh Jumps Head First." The latter was a reprint of an article that appeared earlier in the *U.S. Official Postal Guide, Monthly Supplement.* It was written by Charles A. Lindbergh, then a contract airmail pilot, about bailing out of his mail plane that past winter in a snowstorm just as his fuel ran out. He dove headfirst, pulled the rip cord, and wafted safely to the ground.

Symbolically, it was Lindbergh's history-making solo trip across the Atlantic in May 1927 that took a growing American awareness of aviation and propelled it into the air age. Newspaper headlines, magazine articles, and movie newsreels made it something nobody couldn't know about. Even before the year was out, Lindbergh's own story in book form (titled simply *We,* in respect for the plane that made it possible) was published in New York and London. Not everyone agreed as to the importance of what Lindbergh had done. To many, it seemed little more than a stunt. "What good will it do?" some asked.

What good it did, most of all, was convince people who had doubts about flying. Although Lindbergh's *Spirit of St. Louis* represented essentially no more in the way of technical development than other planes of the time, its dramatic demonstration of trustworthiness—it was all that separated Lindbergh from an open ocean—helped make people who cringed at the thought of flying think that maybe it was safe after all.

The notion that planes were fragile and dangerous contrivances best suited to daredevils had been slowly changing anyway. Airmail showed one very practical side of aviation, one that directly touched people who had never even seen a plane close-up and had their doubts about them. Airmail service began in 1918 and was greatly improved in 1924 by nighttime flights using beacons. The beacons themselves represented another degree of acceptance of aviation by the public. Each light was the responsibility of some private citizen who accepted the obligation under contract with the United States Lighthouse Service. A typical beacon was maintained by a farmer who, every evening at sunset, trekked out through his fields to the tower of a windmill, where he

unlocked a door and started a small gasoline engine that operated

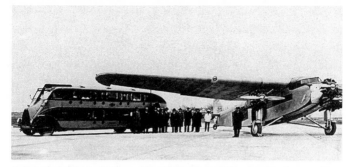

A trimotor plane and a Greyhound bus side by side. In 1929, when this photograph was taken, this was still thought to make an interesting comparison. In time passenger planes would dwarf the bus, and no one would think of setting up a picture like this again. (Library of Congress)

a generator. As the generator started, a lamp atop the tower burst into light. Next morning he turned the engine off. Such beacons were spaced about 10 miles apart from coast to coast; as of early 1927, they beamed some 3,000 miles of air routes.

Although commercial air carriers had briefly appeared as early as 1914, permanent, regularly scheduled airline service may be said to have started in 1926 with several lines that eventually became or merged into American, TWA, United, Northwest, Eastern, and Pan Am.

In 1929, Transcontinental Air Transport, a forerunner of TWA, was the first to offer coast-to-coast service, using planes for daylight travel and railroads overnight. This cut to two days a trip that took three by rail alone. Here also was another manifestation of Lindbergh's prestige in the wake of New York–to–Paris. Lindbergh, a technical adviser to the new line, pressed a button in Los Angeles that signaled the inauguration of the first transcontinental air-rail service and the start of that evening's first leg—a Pennsylvania Railroad "Airway Limited" that left New York's Pennsylvania Station at 7:05 P.M., Sunday, July 7, 1929. The flashing of a light occasioned by the press of the button highlighted a ceremony attended by railroad and local officials. A guest of honor, as well as passenger on the inaugural trip, was aviator Amelia Earhart.

Passengers using the transcontinental service alternated rail (Pennsylvania and Santa Fe Railroads) and plane travel (Transcontinental Air Transport). When they got to Winslow,

Arizona, the passengers found Lindbergh waiting to be their pilot for the final leg, the flight to Glendale, California, which arrived there at 5:40 P.M. on Tuesday, July 9.

Over and above the novelty of the experience, early air travelers tended to notice some of the same things as later travelers, though sometimes from different perspectives. Mrs. Frederick H. Colburn, who took a Western Air Express Fokker Trimotor to Los Angeles in 1928, said "the buzz and whirr of the motors reduced us all to sign language."* Later-day passengers who think jet whine loud on takeoff would perhaps think otherwise if subjected to the unrelenting clatter of piston engines resounding through the cabin of an early trimotor. Mrs. Colburn, who took the precaution of filling her ears with cotton, also found comfort in the fact she did not "feel any difference in pulse or heart action" while aloft; nor, "Was I seasick? Certainly not!" Like every later traveler, she would stare in awe at how "the ground underneath seems full of wrinkles, and that the trees are apparently not higher than a goblet." Unlike later passengers, she was presented with a gardenia corsage on boarding; like later ones, she "enjoyed a dainty box luncheon served aboard the airplane."

Louis Lochner, who had taken the first flight of the *Hindenburg*, was also an early airplane traveler. Of a flight into Newark, New Jersey, which then served as the principal airport for New York City, he wrote: "My first experience in an American plane! It was a 14-passenger Douglas . . . a very fast machine. . . . A pretty stewardess looks after the welfare of the passengers. They tell me that it is statistically proven that airplane stewardesses marry more readily than any other girls. They look quite trim and dapper in their uniforms." (Boeing Air Transport, a predecessor of United Airlines, inaugurated the use of stewardesses in 1930.)

---

*This was presumably one of three Fokker Trimotors that launched passenger service on Western Air Express, a forerunner of TWA, in 1928. By 1929 Western Air Express was the nation's largest domestic airline. The Fokker was a mainstay of early air travel until a crash in 1931 that killed Notre Dame football coach Knute Rockne. The plane's massive wings were of wood construction, and rot was blamed for the crash. The Fokker was superseded by a new generation of all-metal passenger planes, beginning with the Boeing 247 and the Douglas DC-2 and DC-3.

The fourteen-passenger Douglas must have been a DC-2, which appeared in 1934. There was only one DC-1 made, a prototype constructed in 1933. The DC series (for Douglas Commercial) along with the Boeing 247 represented a new generation of airliners—all-metal construction, stressed-skin fuselage, retractable landing gear, and such passenger amenities as reading lamps, stewardess call buttons, and upholstered seats (instead of the cane seats of earlier passenger planes).

The Boeing 247 appeared first, in 1933, and hence is remembered as the first of the modern airliners. An advertisement that year proclaimed it as "Club Car Comfort at 171 M. P. H." Actually its normal cruising speed was only 155 miles per hour, but that was the fastest of any airliner then in service. On its first coast-to-coast run, from San Francisco to New York, it set a record time of nineteen and a half hours, beating the old record by nearly eight. But the 247 was soon to be eclipsed by the larger and faster DC-2; and the DC-2 in turn by the legendary DC-3, with passenger capacity of twenty-one and a maximum speed of 230 miles per hour. The DC-3, which made its first passenger flight on the Fourth of July, 1936 (American Airlines, from Chicago to Glendale, California), so revolutionized air transportation that by 1939 it was carrying 90 percent of all airline passengers in the United States. The DC-3 remained the basic design of an airliner until the coming of jetliners in the 1960s. Except for pressurized cabins and tricycle landing gear, there would be no significant changes. Planes would get larger, and might have three or four engines, but all would carry on the basic concept of air travel as it came to public awareness with the Boeing 247 and the DC-3.

The post–World War II years saw air travel expand dramatically. Fares dropped in relation to the cost of living, and new routes opened up more and more of America to the convenience of flying. Even more significant: Whereas before the war air travel was for the well-to-do, it now came within the means of almost everyone; and going by air eclipsed the railroad as *the way* to go long distance.

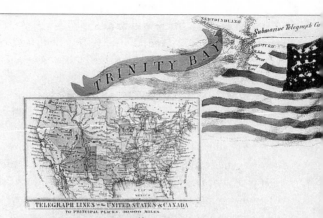

NEWFOUNDLAND

Submarine Telegraph Co

TRINITY BAY

TELEGRAPH LINES OF THE UNITED STATES & CANADA
TO PRINCIPAL PLACES, 30,000 MILES

The Queen's Message.

TO THE PRESIDENT OF THE UNITED STATES

Her Majesty desires to congratulate the President upon the successful completion of this great international work, in which the Queen has taken the deepest interest.

The Queen is convinced that the President will join with her in fervently hoping that the Electric Cable which now connects Great Britain with the United States will prove an additional link between the nations whose friendship is founded upon their common interest and reciprocal esteem.

The Queen has much pleasure in thus communicating with the President, and renewing to him her wishes for the prosperity of the United States.

NEW WORLD

PACIFIC OCEAN

ATLANTIC OCEAN

NIAGARA

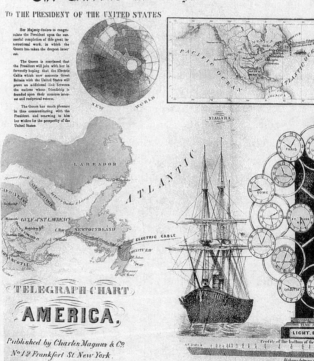

LABRADOR

ATLANTIC

GULF of ST LAWRENCE

NEWFOUNDLAND

ELECTRIC CABLE

NOVA SCOTIA

PARIS

ROME

CONSTANTINOPLE

CALCUTTA

LIGHT. ELE

TELEGRAPH CHART
AMERICA.

Published by Charles Magnus & Co.
No 12 Frankfort St. New York.

Profile of the bottom of the At

Entered according to act of Congress, in the year 1858, by Charles Magnus & Co. in

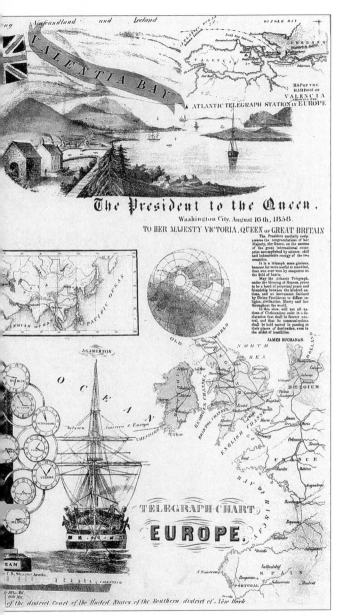

THE WONDROUS EVENT OF A WONDROUS AGE
"Celebration All Over the United States in Honor of Ocean Telegraphing, Sept. 1858"
(New York, 1858. Smithsonian Institution)

PART 2

COMMUNICATIONS

TO A CONTEMPORARY OBSERVER, they looked like "cobwebs in the air"—strands of wire looping from one pole to another to another. Those who watched as workmen in the mid-1840s began this transformation of a once unpoled, unwired landscape couldn't help but sense that something remarkable was happening.

The telegraph signaled a new era, one in which *speed* of communication—not merely availability or reliability—was a new factor in how business, government, and the everyday world would communicate. Even people who had no occasion to send or receive a telegram were beneficiaries if they read a daily newspaper, for the telegraph was the beginning of modern journalism and modern weather forecasting.

So profound was the telegraph's impact that when the telephone appeared, three decades later, it was first known as the Speaking Telegraph. And then the telephone eclipsed the telegraph to become the most taken-for-granted form of communications technology.

With the telephone came a continued transformation of the landscape—wires and poles in vast numbers added to or joined with those of the telegraph. And then more visual evidence of evolution in communications: aerials, antennas, and eventually satellite dishes.

But the most significant advance of all had no new outward sign. It was those same old telephone wires, hooked up to modems and thence to home computers in the late twentieth century, that made possible a communications revolution beyond anything ever dreamed of.

The story that unfolds here is thus largely one of how a cobweb became a Web.

CHAPTER FIVE

THE TRULY ASTONISHING CONTRIVANCE

THE TELEGRAPH

IT WAS NOT MERELY A "TRIUMPH OF SCIENCE" or even just the "Great Event of the Age." It was of biblical proportions, some thought. Pointing to the book of Revelation, the *New York Herald* declared on August 9, 1858, that there may have been "a prophetic vision" of the event: "That which we now see realized, the Evangelist may have seen eighteen hundred years ago on the island of Patmos, as in a glass dimly, and [his] prophetic words . . .

> He [the angel] set his right foot upon the sea and his left foot upon the earth . . . and swore there should be time no longer*

. . . may, without much straining, be applied to the great wonder of the age."

The great wonder was the spanning of land and sea by written word—the completion on August 5, 1858, of an Atlantic cable linking America and Europe by telegraph. As opposed to sending a letter by steamship "within the compass of nine days and a few hours," wrote a *New York Times* reporter on August 7, the "transmission of thought, the vital impulse of matter, by the completion of the submarine telegraphic line, has been brought within the limits of a few seconds; indeed, for all practical purposes, time, in transit, may be regarded as entirely eliminated."

The Philadelphia *Evening Journal* declared, "This is the greatest triumph of scientific and mechanical genius that has been achieved for centuries." A *New York Times* editorial paraphrased the astronomer, Johannes Kepler: "The Atlantic Telegraph is felt to be one of those great achievements 'beyond the reaches of the soul.' "

In Chicago, the Great Event was celebrated with the public firing of a hundred guns. In Portland, Maine, bells were rung. In

---

*"And I saw another mighty angel come down from heaven clothed with a cloud: and a rainbow was upon his head. . . . And he had in his hand a little book open: and he set his right foot upon the sea, and his left foot on the earth. And cried with a loud voice, as when a lion roareth. . . . And sware by him that liveth for ever and ever . . . that there should be time no longer." —*Revelation, 10:1–6*

Cincinnati, business was temporarily suspended on the mercantile exchange. In Albany, New York, it was reported that "the scene in the streets was as though each person had received some intelligence of strong personal interest." In Andover, Massachusetts, at the fiftieth anniversary dinner of the alumni of Andover Theological College, a dispatch announcing the event was read, whereupon the whole audience joined in singing "Praise God from Whom All Blessings Flow." In New York City on August 10, lawyer George Templeton Strong penned in his diary, "Everybody all agog about the Atlantic Cable. Telegraph offices in Wall Street decorated with the flags of all nations and sundry fancy pennons beside, suspended across the street. Newspapers full of the theme, and of the demonstrations the event has produced from New Orleans to Portland." All in all, there was an "irrepressible outburst of enthusiastic joy in all parts of the country" *(New York Times)*.

And the celebrating continued. Two weeks later, when the first historic message had traveled almost instantaneously the breadth of the Atlantic Ocean, sixteen-year-old Caroline Cowles Richards used her diary to save for later times a record of how the occasion was marked just in one little village in upstate New York: "August 17–There was a celebration in town to-day because the Queen's message was received on the Atlantic cable. Guns were fired and church bells rung and flags were waving everywhere. In the evening there was a torchlight procession and the town was all lighted up."

Yet by much the same reckoning, time should have been considered eliminated fourteen years earlier. It was at the Capitol in Washington on May 24, 1844, in the presence of members of Congress (whose appropriation of $30,000 made it possible) that Samuel F. B. Morse made his historic "What Hath God Wrought!" demonstration of the telegraph. But the response to that event was more of awe than euphoria, and mostly only close to home. It was an event witnessed first by those in attendance, those usually squabbling Whigs and Democrats who at last had something they could all agree upon–the success of what Morse had accomplished in the Supreme Court chamber. They watched, said one observer, with "mingled delight and wonder."

There had been little advance notice to the public, except for a

gradual march of workmen from Washington to Baltimore, driving poles into the ground and then stringing wires from one to the next. There was virtually nothing in the newspapers as to what was about to happen. But when it happened, there was quick recognition, in Washington and Baltimore at least, that it was something "truly astonishing." Reported the *Baltimore Patriot* next day:

THE ELECTRO MAGNETIC TELEGRAPH

Morse's Electro Magnetic Telegraph, now connects between the Capitol at Washington and the Railroad Depot in Pratt, between Charles and Light streets, Baltimore. The wires were brought in yesterday from the outer depot and attached to the telegraphic apparatus in a third story room in the depot warehouse building. The batteries were charged this morning and the Telegraph put in full operation, conveying intelligence to and from the Capitol. A large number of gentlemen were present to see the operations of this truly astonishing contrivance. Many admitted to the room had their names sent down, and in less than a second the apparatus in Baltimore was put in operation by the attendant in Washington, and before the lapse of a half minute the same names were returned plainly written. . . . The time of day was also enquired for, when the response was given from the Capitol–"forty-nine minutes past eleven." . . . This is indeed the annihilation of space.

The telegraph was a practical device, and its first really practical test came in its day-to-day use for reporting the Democratic national convention, which convened in Baltimore on May 27, 1844. There was actually an earlier test, even before the demonstration for Congress, but it was only over the 22 miles of wire completed northward from Washington to the junction of the Annapolis road with the Baltimore-Washington road. News of the Whig national convention, which opened in Baltimore May 2, reached that point by rail and was then relayed to Washington by telegraph.

Now, with the entire 40-mile line completed (and tried out) between Washington and Baltimore, there came a show of what the telegraph could do in real life. And the occasion was a fitting one in that the Democrats' convention was filled with suspense, going nine ballots to produce the first dark-horse candidate for president of the United States.

Manning the telegraph key at the railroad depot in Baltimore was Morse's associate, Alfred Vail, who sent back to Morse, now stationed in a tiny room below the Senate chamber in the Capitol, a running account of the nomination of a candidate for president. Bulletins were posted in the Capitol Rotunda as news arrived, and a crowd sometimes numbering several hundred congregated about "the Telegraph office" eager to hear what was going on.

Former President Martin Van Buren, who had lost reelection in 1840, was the early favorite, and indeed got a majority on the first ballot, but not the two-thirds required for nomination. As successive ballots were taken, the convention remained deadlocked between Van Buren and Lewis Cass. By the eighth ballot, there was a new candidate in the contest, a relatively little-known congressman from Tennessee named James K. Polk. The balloting continued for the ninth time. As members of Congress crowded around Morse's tiny office, the telegraph register began clicking out what everyone wanted to hear. The balloting was over. From the dots and dashes just received from Baltimore, Morse translated: "Polk is unanimously nom[inated]. 3 cheers were given in convention for restoring harmony."

The Democrat convention proved to even the most zealous skeptic the usefulness of the telegraph. As Morse himself recalled, "Even the most inveterate opposers have changed to admirers, and one of them, Hon. Cave Johnson [incoming postmaster general and formerly a congressman from Tennessee], who ridiculed my system last session by associating it with the tricks of animal magnetism, came to me and said: 'Sir, I give in. It is an astonishing invention.'" Reporting of the convention likewise made the first real impact on public perception of just what had been accomplished. The *New York Herald*'s Washington correspondent, writing on May 28, made clear that impact:

> Little else is done here but watch Professor Morse's Bulletin from Baltimore, to learn the progress of doings at Convention. Nothing will be done of any interest or importance, until after the adjournment of the Convention. Professor Morse's telegraph is not only an era in the transmission of intelligence, but it has originated in the mind an entirely new class of ideas, a new species of consciousness. Never before was any one conscious that he knew with certainty what events were at that moment passing in a distant city—40, 100,

or 500 miles off. For example, it is now precisely 11 o'clock. The telegraph announces as follows: "11 o'clock—Senator Walker is *now* replying to Mr. Butler upon the adoption of the two-third rule." It requires no small intellectual effort to realize that this is a fact that *now is,* and not one that *has been.*

What *now was* had immediate impact on the public. Newspaper accounts and word of mouth got the news around Baltimore quickly. By the hundreds, people flocked to the railroad depot, clamoring for a sense of presence at history in the making. As Vail wrote to Morse June 3:

> Every thing went well last week and such an excitement provided [there]by never occurred before in relation to any new thing brought before the public. Hundreds begged and pleaded to be allowed mearly [*sic*] to look at the instrument. They declared they would not say a word or stir and didn't care whether they understood or not, only they wanted to say they had seen it. . . . You cannot imagine the intense interest the Tel[egraph] excites.

Within the week, Vail had made arrangements for the public to have its firsthand look. On June 6, the *Patriot* advised: "We are requested to state, that the Telegraph office in Baltimore will be open for the admission of Ladies, from 5 to 7 P.M." And a few days later, in Vail's words, for "Tom, Dick, and Harry" also: "The Telegraph . . . will be in operation again this afternoon at half past 4 o'clock, when those curious to see its operation, are invited to attend." For those who wanted to know more than just what it looked like, the *Patriot* on June 15 printed a long and detailed account of exactly how the telegraph worked, along with an explanation of Morse code.

Yet the notion of elimination of time inevitably produced a good measure of perplexity as well. Just what did this mean, to be somewhere else *now?* Could one actually *go?* Early Morse biographer Samuel Prime, who tended to discount such stories as "undoubtedly fictitious," nevertheless put stock in an anecdote that, he said, Morse himself related. When Morse had his own telegraph station in operation in Washington in 1844, a lovesick young lady came in. How long would it take to send a message to Baltimore, she asked. "About one second," she was told. She then

THE TRULY ASTONISHING CONTRIVANCE

produced a neatly folded, gilt-edge note and instructed that it be sent by telegraph to her boyfriend in Baltimore. (They had quarreled; she had to reach him as soon as possible, and the mail was too slow.) But you can't send the actual letter by telegraph, Morse explained. "Then you will send *me*, won't you?" replied the girl. To which, responded a telegraph clerk, "Perhaps it would take your breath away to travel forty miles in one second!"

According to another contemporary anecdote, a curious fellow sat on the ground for nearly a whole day watching the telegraph wires above. Upon being asked what he was gazing at, he replied that he was waiting to see a letter go by.

The telegraph did not come into full-blown use immediately. Once the convention was over, there seemed to be so limited use for the line between Washington and Baltimore that it was used for occasional chess games between players in the two cities. When a line was in place between Philadelphia and New York, lottery agents and brokers were among the first to experiment with telegraphy. It was not until a wider network of lines was available that commercial use really began to come about: for example, by steamboat owners and shippers on the Ohio and Mississippi Rivers who could take advantage of the telegraph for information on changes in the condition of navigation. One of the most essential early uses of the telegraph was for railroad dispatching, which began with the Erie Railroad in 1851.

Nor did everyone in the early days of the telegraph send or receive telegrams. Most people did not. Telegrams were relatively expensive, and hence more generally used in business or among the well-to-do. Rates at first differed widely from company to company, but by the early 1850s they had settled to a typical charge of twenty-five cents for a message of up to ten words sent less than 100 miles and a dollar for one of twenty words going 500 miles compared with postage of three cents for a letter (of many more than twenty words) sent up to 300 miles.

PERCEPTIBLE PROGRESS

But for almost everyone—user and nonuser—the coming of the
telegraph was conspicuous in the poles and wires shooting up and

out around the country. Swedish author Fredrika Bremer, touring America in 1849, found it "remarkable that in all directions throughout this young country, along these rough roads, which are no roads at all, run these electric wires from tree to tree, from post to post, along the prairie land, and bring towns and villages into communication."

Those wires were something no one had ever seen before, and they prompted great wonderment as to how the telegraph worked—particularly among the young, who wonder about everything. By the early 1850s, even before Western Union was created, books for children were being revised to include the telegraph.

Forrester's Pictorial Miscellany for Boys and Girls, published in Boston in 1854, offered a detailed, technical description of the telegraph—including Morse code—that covered eight pages that was anything but "writing down" to children. As the opening of the article explained: "I propose to give my little readers some account of the Magnetic Telegraph, one of the most wonderful discoveries of modern times. I fear that I shall not be able to make some of my very young readers understand the operation of this curious contrivance fully, for it is one that requires deep thought, and some considerable knowledge of electricity and magnetism; yet I will endeavor to explain the various parts of the subject in a simple manner, and illustrate the most difficult portions with engravings, so that, if you study hard, you can master it."

The article covered such aspects of telegraphy as the galvanic battery and principles of electromagnetism as well as telegraph apparatus itself. Assuming that readers were most apt to be from the Boston area, Mark Forrester, the editor, noted that, "All the curious magnetic apparatus which I have mentioned, besides a great variety of other instruments, magnets, electrical machines, and the like, you can find at the store of Palmer and Hall, at number 526 Washington street, Boston. I have lately spent several hours in examining his various contrivances for testing the power of electricity, some of which I will hereafter explain to you and I can assure you that, old as I am, I gained a great deal of highly interesting and valuable information."

Among oldsters generally, the virtues of the telegraph quickly became apparent in various ways—reading a newspaper, for example.

From *Forrester's Pictorial Miscellany for Boys and Girls*, Boston, 1854. As originally published, this illustration was wrapped around a portion of text.

Interpreting the significance of the telegraph for children at mid–nineteenth century: an illustration showing Boston (left) connected to New York City by telegraph wires. The text accompanying this provided a detailed, technical description of the telegraph, including Morse code. Children were advised to study hard and persevere through the technical detail because this was "one of the most wonderful discoveries of modern times." (*Forrester's Pictorial Miscellany for Boys and Girls,* Boston, 1854)

Before the telegraph, out-of-town news got to a newspaper office the same way a letter got to a mailbox. Foreign news likewise traveled by international post and required a similar ten-day-plus interval coming from Europe. But increasingly intense competition drove newspaper publishers to cut the time of domestic transit by their own devices. The New York press was perhaps the most competitive. The *Courier and Enquirer* and *Journal of Commerce* by the 1820s each had boats that went out to sea to meet incoming transatlantic ships and race back to New York with foreign news dispatches. The *Herald* by 1837 had three boats capable of going out 150 miles to collect incoming news. What happened in Washington was the most important of domestic news. The *Herald* organized its own express service in 1840, using several connecting railroads, usually beating the regular mail by half a day. Early in 1845 the *Herald* had a daily express service running from New Orleans to report on the brewing Mexican War.

All this would change dramatically. Even as the telegraph was being demonstrated in 1844, *Herald* publisher James Gordon Bennett predicted that "once this extraordinary invention shall have been fully applied all over the country, the wonderful spectacle will be presented, of a vast continent, as consolidated and united, and possessed as much, nay, in greater degree, of the means of rapid communication as the city of New York." On May 24, 1844, the date of Morse's demonstration, the *New York Herald* had a column from Washington dated May 22 (what was happening in Congress two days earlier), a dispatch from Havanna dated May 12 (the worsening condition of sugar cane crops owing to lack of rain), and from Venezuela (news in general) dated April 26.

Late in 1845 Bennett suggested that the connecting of New York with Boston, Buffalo, and Washington by telegraph would make the post office obsolete. And while that never happened, the telegraph did more to change the newspaper in the nineteenth century than any other factor, technological or otherwise. What happened in Washington in the morning would now be news in that afternoon's editions, not the next day's, let alone the next week's, as had been the case before the mail went by railroad.

Even before completion of telegraph lines to Washington, Bennett arranged with the Magnetic Telegraph Company, organized by Morse and associates in 1845, to transmit reports during the 1846 session of Congress. But manual transmission of dots and dashes was slow—roughly fifteen words a minute in these early years compared with thirty words in 1900 and forty-five using automatic printers in the 1920s. The telegraph company, almost at the start, limited any one newspaper to fifteen minutes of wire time. The *Herald* by May 1846 joined with other New York papers to pool transmission time. This led to a formal partnership early in 1849 whereby the *Herald, Sun, Tribune, Courier and Enquirer, Journal of Commerce,* and *Express* (the *Times* was not founded until 1851) joined as the New York Associated Press to lease a telegraph line for their exclusive use. Each paper got the news at the same time and each shared equally in the cost of operation. The partnership grew nationwide into what has long since been known as The Associated Press.

Limitation of wire time changed the way news was reported. Heretofore news could be written essay-style—that is, subjectively, according to the writer's notion of the order in which facts should be presented. With time on the telegraph wire severely limited, it became necessary to adopt a wholly new style—what has since become known as the "inverted pyramid" presentation: the absolutely essential facts right at the top, followed by the next most important, followed by the next, and so on. No matter when wire time ran out, the fundamental story had been transmitted. Similarly, the editor making up the paper could cut the story at any point, knowing what was essential was there, even if only a paragraph or two got into print. News continues to be reported this way, and indeed radio and television reporting follow basically the same tradition.

The telegraph also had impact on the financial world. Financial reports from New York were available even in the Midwest on an immediate basis, as is evident in the following item in the *Milwaukee Sentinel,* April 15, 1848: "At nine o'clock yesterday morning we had, by telegraph, the news and markets from New York, distant some *fourteen hundred miles,* up to three o'clock of the *preceding* afternoon! This is, indeed, a startling fact, and may well make us pause and wonder at the agency which has brought it about."

Politics, ever the art of timing, continued to make good use of the telegraph. Philip Hone, one of the important diarists of the nineteenth century and also an influential politician, recalled its role in September 1846 in Utica, New York, at the Whig state convention, over which he presided. The contest for the nomination for governor was between Millard Fillmore of Buffalo and John Young of Livingston. The latter was the one nominated, and Hone's diary records how:

Saturday, Sept. 26 [1846]. *Magnetic Telegraph.* Strange and wonderful discovery, which has made the "swift-winged lightning" man's messenger, annihilated all space, and tied the two ends of the continent in a knot! The whole extent of this newly discovered phenomenon was never made so apparent to me as on the day of the meeting of the convention; during the hour of adjournment to dinner a message was sent by the telegraph to Mr. Fillmore, at Buffalo. The answer came immediately, that "Mr. Fillmore was not in his office, and could not be found." Soon after, another communication was received, authorizing the withdrawal of his name, and expressing his satisfaction at Mr. Young's nomination. This was handed to me on my taking the chair, and had traveled four hundred and seventy miles during our short recess of an hour.

While cross-country communication was flowering from tree to tree, as Fredrika Bremer found in 1849, and increasingly annihilating space around the country, communication with Europe, and indeed the rest of the world, remained as slow as always. Cross-Atlantic communication was still that nine or ten days; elsewhere in the world often considerably longer. The best the telegraph could do to help was in the way Bennett put it to work for the *Herald* in 1846: He arranged for shipborne news arriving in Boston to be relayed from there to New York by telegraph, thus shaving hours off a transmission time of days. News reaching New York by ship, of course, he had already in hand. It was one thing to string electric wires from tree to tree; quite another, from one shore of the Atlantic to the other.

Thus the sense of profound triumph—news that could "send an electric thrill throughout the world"—when it could be said that London now was "within a flash of New York." Hence, by 1858, with the telegraph so quickly being assimilated into American life (and landscape, with all those new poles), was there such an intense sense of fulfillment in conquering that seemingly unconquerable expanse of space, the Atlantic Ocean. Surely now both space and time were annihilated. Here was arguably the threshold of what we know as modern communications—global as well as instantaneous.

Alas, only for a few weeks. The cable that Cyrus Field completed in early August 1858 went into service August 16 with a brief message from Queen Victoria to President James Buchanan ("Her Majesty desires to congratulate the President upon the successful completion of this great international work, in which the Queen has taken the deepest interest"). That, said the *New York Herald,* "settles the important question whether or not the line would work." Soon after, though, somewhere between Trinity Bay, Newfoundland, and Valencia, Ireland, somewhere in 2,000 miles of insulated copper cable, something didn't work. In the coming weeks, the cable performed only sputteringly; and by October 20 it failed completely. In 1865 the laying of a new cable was begun; and with the help of the *Great Eastern,* the largest ship in the world, it was successfully completed in 1866. Additional cables were laid in coming years, including one promoted by the *Herald*'s James Gordon Bennett.

Santa Claus arriving by telegraph, 1874: a testimony to the assimilation of technology into everyday life. (*The Daily Graphic,* New York, December 24, 1874)

By this time, the telegraph was fast becoming an integral part of American life. It had proved its tactical importance on both sides in the Civil War and its strategic significance to the development of the railroad, thus spurring settlement of the West.

For most Americans, from the late nineteenth century through much of the twentieth, the telegraph was synonymous with the telegram, which in turn was synonymous with Western Union. The nation's foremost telegrapher began as the New York and Mississippi Valley Printing Telegraph Company in 1851 and became the Western Union Telegraph Company in 1856.

Western Union was able to offer transcontinental telegraph service within a few years. Its domination of the market in the coming decades made it, for a time, the nation's largest corporation. Through the time of the Second World War, and for some years afterward, it was a Western Union telegram by which some milestone of life was concisely first communicated, whether a birth or a death, a promotion or some other important news. Even after the telephone was nearly universal, the knock of a Western Union messenger at one's door signified something special to hear about. Rapidly changing communications technology in the later twentieth century changed all that, as will be seen.

But the telegraph was more than just the sending of telegrams. Over and above its significance in the development of railroads, it was an essential part of the growth of American business in the form of the stock ticker. A printing telegraph system with which to record stock transactions and make them available at multiple locations was established at the New York Stock Exchange in 1867 and subsequently improved by Thomas A. Edison. The system was computerized in 1965. And there was another spin-off.

THE TELEGRAPH AND WEATHER FORECASTING

There are probably few amenities of modern life so thoroughly taken for granted as getting a weather forecast. Predictions (usually very accurate) are available around the clock on radio, television, and Internet.

Yet not many generations ago, people had nothing more to depend on than simple observations about what was already impending (the sky clouding up) or hints from Mother Nature (an unusual bustling of bees or ants at their nests was thought to be a harbinger of rain while bats flitting long and late in the twilight signaled a fair day on the morrow) or folk wisdom:

> An evening red and morning gray,
>
> Will set the traveller on his way;
>
> But an evening gray and a morning red,
>
> Will pour down rain on a traveller's head.

Objective attempts to get some sense of weather patterns were tried in the early nineteenth century but fell far short of producing any significant results. The U.S. Army began a systematic recording of weather data in 1819, but reports from the field were sent to Washington only once a month.

It was the coming of the telegraph that brought with it not only unprecedented speed of communication generally but the means of making weather forecasting practical for the first time. As a contemporary story in the *New York Times* observed, monthly reports "only served to indicate the visitation of a storm long after it had passed. Still, it was evident [from this rudimentary system of reporting] that the progress of storms is governed by fixed laws, and that by the aid of the telegraph it is practicable to give warnings of their approach."

The use of telegraphy for weather forecasting—the first time anywhere—was undertaken by the Smithsonian Institution in 1847, one year after its founding, under its first secretary, Joseph Henry. By 1849 there were some 150 telegraph operators around the country who were transmitting daily weather updates to the Smithsonian in Washington. This resulted in 1850 in the first weather map—a large diagram of the entire United States, displayed for public access, showing weather conditions throughout the country. Anyone interested (ship captains, for example) could view the map in person. Weather conditions were apparently shown as handwritten inscriptions indicating "fair," "cloudy," and so on. In 1858 the map was improved by using colored disks—white signifying clear, gray cloudy, black rain, and so on—affixed to the map. Each disk also had a small arrow showing wind direction—a significant step since this provided a simple basis for predicting weather patterns. Meanwhile in 1857 the Smithsonian began supplying daily weather reports for publication in the Washington *Evening Star.*

In 1870 collection of weather data became the responsibility of the U.S. Army Signal Corps, whose War Department office in Washington for a time became popularly known as the Weather Bureau. Data was sent by telegraph from reporting stations throughout the country daily at 11:35 P.M. These reports were then analyzed at the War Department, and forecasts furnished to the press at 1:00 A.M.—in time for morning editions. The national weather picture was now plotted on a map at the War Department.

The following report for November 19, 1871, based solely on telegraph communication, was typical of the times:

THE WEATHER
Synopsis of Events and Probabilities

Washington, D.C. Nov. 19–7 P.M.—The area of highest pressure has moved since Saturday afternoon somewhat to the south-eastward, and now extends along the middle Atlantic coast. Light easterly winds with cloudy weather have prevailed during the day from Georgia to New York. The area of lowest pressure has advanced from the Missouri Valley north-westward over upper Michigan, with brisk south-east winds veering to south-west from Missouri to Michigan; and threatening weather and north-westerly winds, with clear weather, have prevailed from Mississippi to Texas. Telegraphic communication with Rocky Mountain and north-western stations remains interrupted.

Probabilities

The low barometer in Wisconsin will probably extend eastward, with brisk south-west winds from Lake Erie to Illinois and northward, preceded by cloudy weather, and possibly rain on the lower lakes. Northerly winds and clear weather will prevail on Monday in Mississippi and Texas; cloudy and clearing weather continue in the Southern States, excepting Florida; threatening weather, with falling barometer, in Florida and on the middle and east Atlantic coast.

Warning Signals Ordered

Cautionary signals continue at Chicago, Milwaukee, and Grand Haven.

From the perspective of the age of satellite communications, such a report may look relatively primitive. For its time, it was a remarkable—and remarkably useful—application of technology in everyday life.

CHAPTER SIX

THE FIRST COMMUNICATIONS HIGHWAY

THE TELEPHONE

It will be a "highway of communication" connecting "every home, every office, every factory, and every farm in the land."

–AT&T advertisement describing the Bell Telephone System, 1909

LONG BEFORE THE INTERNET and the "information super-highway" were ever dreamed of—long before superhighways, in fact—the telephone was laying a communications highway throughout the land, a highway that would eventually reach more or less everyone. In 1909, one-fourth of American households had telephones. By 1914, telephone ownership had increased more than eightfold since the turn of the century, raising the total number of telephones to 10 million.

It was a time of remarkable growth, reflecting a changing conception of what the telephone was meant to be. For roughly its first two decades, from 1876 through the end of the century, the telephone was for business and professional people and the rich. And to the extent it was used by the well-to-do in the household it was for the "business" side of domestic life—calling the butcher or the grocer—and not for calls of a sociable nature. At roughly the turn of the century, this began to change, although it was a transition that would not be fully realized until the 1920s. *McClure's Magazine* saw what was happening, reporting in 1914 that "Until [1900] the telephone was a luxury. About 1900, however, the Bell Company started a campaign, unparalleled in its energy, persistence and success, to democratize this instrument—to make it part of the daily life of every man, woman, and child." By the 1920s that democratization would make the telephone not just a device for calling the doctor or the grocer but for ringing up Mrs. Smith across town just to chat.

That it was not so in its earliest days owes partly to telephone company policy and partly to the fact that the telephone was perceived as an extension of the telegraph. As the *New York Times* editorialized in 1877: "It looks as if we're on the verge of a revolution in telegraphy; as if very soon it might be possible, by means of the electric wire, for friends to converse freely at the distance of many miles, and even to recognize the tones and peculiarities of each other's voices as distinctly as through a common speaking tube at the distance of a few feet. The instrument by which this is accomplished is known as the telephone."

The perception of the telephone as an extension of the telegraph was fairly universal. In England, it was called the "voice telegraph"; in France, "Le Télégraphe Parlant." While the concept of the telephone being a development of the telegraph has long since blurred in public consciousness, there was literally a connection at the outset: The first telephone messages traveled over rented telegraph wires. Beyond that simple practicality, people talked of the two as interrelated. When Alexander Graham Bell made use of telegraph lines between New York and Boston to demonstrate his telephone in July 1876, the *Boston Traveller* said he was "telegraphing voices." Reporting on a presentation in February 1877, in which a young lady performed a popular song of the day, a newspaper report said " 'Last Rose of Summer' sung by telegraph."

This perception of a speaking telegraph carried over into early use of the telephone. With the exception of its use in journalism, and for other special purposes, the telegraph was understood to be a medium for short, to-the-point, business-like messages. So too, it seemed, the telephone. Telephone company policy reinforced this in part out of practicality—to keep a still small network of wires and phones from being overloaded with lengthy conversations. Some early telephone officials also held a patronizing Victorian notion about protecting their new medium from frivolous, unsuitable, or indelicate talk (arranging a tryst, or any such horror as that). Furthermore, flat-rate billing—rather than billing by the message—became common in the early years, favoring larger users. It was a switch to message-rate in the early 1900s (in New York City the change came in 1896) that reduced the cost for the small user, spurring that democratization.

Cost and policy aside, the telephone of the late 1870s to 1890s was not yet ready to become a highway of communications because it was not universally trusted or accepted. Sometimes the reaction was confusion or disbelief. Many people were apprehensive confronting a telephone for the first time. The disembodied sound of a human voice coming out of a box was too eerie, too supernatural, for many to accept. Was it the work of the devil? Reactions of this kind were symbolized in a cartoon, "The Terrors of the Telephone," appearing in the New York *Daily Graphic* in 1877.

Some looked on the telephone as a mere toy compared to the

"The Terrors of the Telephone" was the title of this 1877 reaction to the telephone, barely a year old for all practical purposes. Was the telephone a device for good? Or was there some sinister side to being able to communicate at great distance? In reality the telephone so far could accommodate conversations of only a few miles. This vision of the future showed a speaker in New York being heard simultaneously as far away as San Francisco, London, Peking, and even the Fiji Islands—an extraordinarily imaginative conception then, but one injected with fear of the unknown, as depicted in the crazed face of the orator. (*The Daily Graphic*, New York, March 15, 1877)

telegraph, which was preeminent in the field of communications, shuttling more than 31 million messages a year over some 214,000 miles of wire at this time. In retrospect, one of the most short-sighted decisions in corporate history was surely that of William Orton, president of Western Union, when he had the opportunity to buy the patent rights to the telephone for $100,000 soon after it was introduced. The offer was made by Gardiner Hubbard,

Alexander Graham Bell's future father-in-law and partner in the business side of early telephone development. Orton is said to have responded, "What use could this company make of an electrical toy?"

Others saw a connection between the telephone and a coming wonder. Although "electric lines" at this time were only for telegraphy, experiments with electric light were hinting that electricity had usefulness beyond what had so far been demonstrated. That, at least, is what a correspondent for the *Boston Transcript* seemed to be saying in February 1877 in an article about the telephone: "Let us hope that the day is fast approaching when every man will be in a position to turn on the electricity in his house with the same facility with which he now turns on the water or the gas."*

In 1877, the age of electricity was still to come; the telephone was *now*. It had been drawing nigh through seemingly endless experiments when, on March 10, 1876, Bell and his assistant, Thomas A. Watson, at their tiny lab in Boston, finally assembled the right combination of coils and magnets, mouthpieces and diaphragms. It has been popularly thought, based on a later recollection of Watson, that Bell spilled battery acid on his clothes and blurted out, through their embryonic contrivance, for Watson to come to his aid. More recent scholarship discounts that and suggests that the critical moment was simply the culmination of systematic experimentation. Bell recorded that he shouted into a transmitting device in a room separate from Watson:

"Mr. Watson—Come here—I want to see you."

To my delight he came and declared that he had heard and understood what I said.

I asked him to repeat the words.—He answered "You said 'Mr. Watson—come here—I want to see you.' "

---

*Early telephones (as now) worked on low-voltage direct current supplied by the telephone company. Production of electricity for household use was a more complex process to devise, and there was debate over whether it should be AC (alternating current) or DC (direct current). Edison's historic Pearl Street generating station in New York went into operation in September 1882, supplying current to a small area of lower Manhattan, but electricity was available to relatively few households in the years immediately following. Practically speaking, the age of electricity came with the turn of the twentieth century.

Little is known otherwise about that historic day—except that a revolution in communications technology was under way.

But it was not automatically accepted that the spoken word could travel by wire, as could the written word by telegraph. Watson later wrote: "The common attitude toward anything new is apt to be pessimistic for the average man thinks that what hasn't been done, can't be done. It was so with the telephone. It seemed a toy to most persons. Some of Bell's friends, although they had heard the thing talk at the laboratory, were doubtful as to its practical value, and one of them of a scientific turn of mind had told me that he didn't see how the telephone could be accurate enough for practical use for every spoken word has many delicate vibrations to be converted into electric waves by the telephone and if some of them get lost the message cannot be intelligible."

And in fact, the telephone in its early days often made it easy to lose the message. Even by mid-1877, after actual commercial telephone service had begun, vibrations were not always delicate, although the instrument itself was not always to blame:

> The beginner needs a little practice to become perfect on the telephone. A number of confused noises issue from it, and conversing through it is like carrying on a conversation amid the whirr of machinery or the shouting of a mob. . . . A magnetic storm made sounds as if a battle were in progress.

As a professor at Boston University, Bell was used to speaking before an audience and thus was uniquely prepared for the next phase of the revolution—capturing public opinion. He had a knack for making the most of what attention was already being given by the press; and beyond this, for Bell, "speaking on the telephone" literally came to mean going out and speaking on its behalf.

Bell had already given a critically important demonstration of the telephone in June 1876, when he showed it to a panel of judges at the Philadelphia Centennial. The panel included the British physicist Sir William Thomson (Lord Kelvin), and Joseph Henry, the American physicist and director of the Smithsonian Institution.

SELLING THE PUBLIC

Through the latter part of 1876 and much of 1877, Bell frequently lectured and gave demonstrations of his invention. One time at least, in explaining the telephone, he employed another new device coming into use. As reported in the press: "Prof. Bell delivered the third and last of his series of lectures in Chickering Hall [New York City] last evening to a small audience. The apparatus used was the same as on the previous evening . . . [illustrations that were] shown to the audience on the screen by means of the stereopticon in the gallery."

Perhaps the best-known early portrayal of use of the telephone. From the front page of *Scientific American*, Alexander Graham Bell, during a lecture in Salem, Massachusetts, communicating by telephone with his assistant, Thomas Watson, in Boston, 10 miles away. The date was February 12, 1877. (*Scientific American,* March 31, 1877)

Perhaps Bell's most widely publicized lecture was that given at Lyceum Hall in Salem, Massachusetts, February 12, 1877. Newspapers around the country carried reports of the presentation, and illustrations of the event appeared in such well-read journals as *Scientific American,* giving Bell and his telephone nationwide attention. The lecture featured an actual demonstration of the telephone, using wires of the Atlantic and Pacific Telegraph Company linking Watson in Boston with the hall in Salem. The *Boston Daily Globe* took advantage by having Bell read, over the line to Watson, the report of the event written by the *Globe* reporter; and the next day a *Globe* headline proudly proclaimed: SENT BY TELEPHONE. THE FIRST NEWSPAPER DESPATCH SENT BY A HUMAN VOICE OVER THE WIRES. SPECIAL DESPATCH BY TELEPHONE TO THE BOSTON GLOBE. The report noted that about 500 people were present—a capacity crowd that included people standing in the aisles and doorways—and gave "frequent and long continued applause." The lecture began with Bell explaining the telephone—basically how it worked, and how he invented it. And then he turned the program over to the star of the show—a working telephone placed on a table at the front of the stage, its wires running up and over to a far wall, thence to a connection with the telegraph wires, and thence to Boston, 18 miles away. As the *Globe* told it,

> Professor Bell asked Mr. Watson for a song, and "Auld Lang Syne" came from the mouthpiece of the instrument almost before his words were ended. Mr. Watson was then asked to make a speech to the audience. He expressed himself as having more confidence eighteen miles away than if he were present. His speech was as follows: "Ladies and gentlemen—It gives me great pleasure to be able to address you this evening, although I am in Boston and you in Salem." This could be heard thirty-five feet distant—that is, all over the hall, and brought down the house with applause.

Accounts of the lecture appeared as far away as London (the *Athenaeum,* which published the story in March) and Paris (*La Nature,* which invoked that image of the new deriving from the old: "Le Télégraphe Parlant: Téléphone de M. A. Graham Bell"). Such stories as these, as often as he could collect them, Bell pasted into a bulging scrapbook.

With such stories, public curiosity also bulged; but it was still two months' time from the Salem lecture until the telephone was ready to become a part of the household. The first subscriber was Boston banker Roswell Downer, who lived in nearby Somerville, Massachusetts, and ordered a line and two telephones to connect his home and office. It went into service on April 4, 1877. Next day, reported the *Boston Globe:* "Professor A. Graham Bell, the inventor of the telephone, had the pleasure of assisting yesterday at the opening of the first regular telephonic line in the world.... The instruments worked admirably, and the enterprising gentleman is very much pleased with his private telephonic wire between town and home. The practical value of Professor Bell's invention is being newly proved every day."

But the real proof was in the talking. Just how fast did Professor Bell's invention catch on? By the end of June 1877 there were some 234 telephones in service, triple that number by August, and quadruple by November, though transmission was still generally limited to a few miles. Over the next two years the telephone was

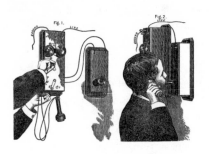

HOW TO MAKE A
TELEPHONE CALL (1878)

FIGURE 1 represents a person calling attention by pressing the knob at the end of Bell Box, and turning the crank, causing the Bell at the other station to ring. When the person at the other end hears the call, he will call back; then both will turn the switches to button marked T. The Telephone can then be used.

FIGURE 2 shows the same person talking with a distant [i.e., any other location] station, using a Box Telephone to talk into and keeping a Hand Telephone pressed against the ear. This is the arrangement that gives best satisfaction, but a very efficient arrangement is to use two Hand instruments at each station instead of a Box and Hand. If it is difficult to hear on account of outside noises listen with a Telephone at each ear.

When you have finished talking, BE SURE AND TURN THE SWITCH TO BUTTON MARKED B.

If a thunderstorm threatens, insert the plug that is supplied with the Bell, into the hole marked A, in Fig. 1. This cuts out all the instruments, therefore it must be removed in order to establish communication.

Quoted from a brochure of the New England Telephone Company, Boston, 1878.
(Warshaw Collection, Smithsonian Institution Archives Center)

gaining customers, not only in Boston but throughout the Northeast and then the country as a whole. Bell Telephone and New England Telephone merged into National Bell early in 1879, and by late that year there were some 70,000 phones in service. From this union in 1880 came American Bell Telephone Company, which by the following year had more than 130,000 customers, and by the end of 1882, some 245,000 customers and 700 exchanges.

Growth in telephone use (by 1890 American Bell had some 450,000 phones in use) came despite the fact that the early telephone was a fairly costly convenience. The first announcement of commercial telephone service by the Bell Patent Association, forerunner of Bell Telephone in Boston, set the charge for leasing two telephones at $20 a year for social purposes and $40 for business use, payable semiannually in advance. A few years later, in 1885, annual rates in major cities, as reported by the *Chicago Tribune,* included New York, $60 to $186; Philadelphia, $120; Chicago, $100 to $150; San Francisco, $60; New Orleans, $96 to $151; Washington, $48 to $100; and Minneapolis–St. Paul, $48 to $180. As a rough index, $50 then would represent about $1,000 now.

The two social telephones offered by the Bell Patent Association in Boston represented one line "connecting a dwelling house with any other building." If new lines had to be strung, there was an additional charge of $100 to $150 a mile. This was the earliest and simplest form of telephone service, one not yet involving a switchboard or central exchange. (Patrons were warned that "More than two [telephones] on the same line where privacy is required is not advised.") The coming of the central exchange allowed for interconnection of lines; but lack of privacy as manifested in the "party line"–more than one party to a line for a cheaper rate–remained a fact of life until after mid–twentieth century.

Roswell Downer's first telephone line and the few that followed were individual lines, whereas the basic nature of modern communications, telephone or otherwise, is interconnection. The means of interconnection in the early days of the telephone was the exchange, that place whereby Mrs. Smith's line was literally plugged into Mrs. Jones's. New Haven, Connecticut, was the first community with a commercial telephone exchange in operation, and therefore, for all practical purposes, the first to make tele-

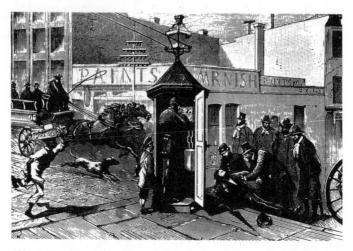

Chicago, 1878. One of the earliest uses of the telephone for emergency use: summoning aid for a man hurt in an accident. The booth was not a public telephone but one maintained by the police. (*La Nature,* 1878)

phone service a part of community life. New Haven's experience in the early years thus provides a glimpse of what the telephone was like when it first came into use.

The New Haven District Telephone Company was established with the granting of a charter by the Connecticut legislature in 1877 but did not go into business until February 21, 1878, with the opening of an exchange in a first-floor storefront at State and Chapel Streets. New Haven had an 1880 census count of 62,882, or roughly 14,000 households. Against this population base, telephone use was infinitesimally small. There were initially forty-seven subscribers—and not surprisingly, in light of rates, most were businesses. Only eleven of the forty-seven were private citizens. Subscribers included the police department, the post office, the *New Haven Register* newspaper, a law firm, a couple of social clubs, three physicians, two dentists and various factories, stores, and markets. None of these yet had a telephone number, that staple of modern life that was still off in the future. For now it was sufficient that "centrals," as the early operators at the exchange were sometimes called, could remember each subscriber by name and, more important, which plug went with which name.

A roster of forty-seven subscribers was not enough to make the telephone exchange profitable, and New Haven District Telephone sent out a thousand circulars in search of new customers. The thousand produced one new subscriber. Cost was certainly a factor, a prohibitive one for many. And among those who could afford a telephone there was that temptation, as Thomas Watson recognized right at the start, to see it as just a toy. It was one thing to exalt the transatlantic telegraph and another matter to install a telephone line into one's home. Was it safe? Did it really work? Would one really have to contend with the shouting of a mob or the sounds of battle while trying to hear one's neighbor down the street? For many, it was simply a matter of wait and see if it gets better.

TEAPOT-LID TECHNOLOGY

There was something of a case to be made for this. Early telephone service in New Haven was primitive. The first switchboard was improvised out of such assorted components as carriage

bolts, teapot lids, and wire. As recalled by a local historian a few years later, the switchboard at first was operated only between 6 A.M. and 2 A.M., and its crudeness was amply apparent: "Making a connection with a subscriber was not a rapid process, and when three connections had been made, that ended the extent of communication until somebody rang off. 'Wire's busy,' would have been an almost constant condition but for the fact that people had not

Philadelphia, 1890. A profusion of telephone and telegraph wires overhead meant no one could miss the coming of new technology. (*De Natuur,* 1890)

learned how to use the thing, and conversations . . . were brief and far between. Aside from this, connections were bad, the use of the instrument difficult and results often indistinct and unsatisfactory."

Notwithstanding a modest beginning and the bugs that had to be worked out, people in Connecticut took increasing interest. As one neighbor got a phone, another at least began to think about it. New Haven District Telephone expanded to include Hartford, Bridgeport, Middletown, Meriden, and New Britain, and in 1880 New Haven District became the Connecticut Telephone Company and then in 1882 the Southern New England Telephone Company (as it is still known today). By this time it had twenty-four exchanges and some 3,600 customers. By the second decade of the twentieth century, there was a network of sixty-nine exchanges; and those first 47 subscribers in New Haven had increased to 130,000 customers using 146,000 telephones to make as many as 700,000 calls a day.

One of Connecticut's early telephone users was Mark Twain, a soft touch for new technology (he also took up the typewriter), although as much as he expressed delight in new things he also professed consternation in getting them to work right. He later recounted his experience with the telephone while making his home in Hartford, Connecticut, in the 1880s.

When I lived up in Hartford I was the very first man, in that part of New England at least, to put in a telephone, but it was constantly getting me into trouble because of the things I said carelessly. And the family were also thoughtless. One day when I was in the garden, fifty feet from the house, somebody on the long distance wire who was publishing a story of mine, wanted to get the title. Well, the title was the first sentence, "Tell him to go to hell." Before my daughter got it through the wire and through him there was a perfect eruption of profanity in that region. All New England seemed to be listening in, and each time my daughter repeated it she did so with rising emphasis. It was awful. I broke into a cold perspiration, and while the neighborhood rang with it, rushed in and implored her to desist. But she would have the last word, and it was "hell" sure enough, every time. Soon after I moved to New York; perhaps that had something to do with my moving. When I got here and asked for a fire-proof telephone the company sent up a man to me. I opened up all my troubles to him, but he laughed and said it was all right in New York.

There was a clause in their contract, he said, allowing every subscriber to talk in his native tongue, and of course they would not make an exception against me. That clause has been a godsend in my case.

Twain was one of the first writers to incorporate the telephone into literature.* His *Connecticut Yankee in King Arthur's Court*, published in 1889, made the telephone one of those modern devices juxtaposed into old Arthur's England: *"Hello, Central! Is this you, Camelot?"* his telephone sequence began, followed with the observation:

Now what a radical reversal of things this was; what a jumbling together of extravagant incongruities; what a fantastic conjunction of opposites and irreconcilables—the home of the bogus miracle become the home of a real one, the den of a medieval hermit turned into a telephone office!

Elsewhere he observed that, "The humblest hello-girl [operator] could teach the highest duchess."

"Hello, Central" . . . the "telephone office" . . . "hello-girls": these few words, while serving immediate dialogue, also confirmed the progress of the telephone by 1889. *Hello*—that most casual of words—actually came into the language, for all practical purposes, with the telephone. It had a progenitor as far back as Chaucer in *hallow*, a common form of greeting; and in Shakespeare's day, a later ancestor as *halloo*. By the nineteenth century it was the *hullo* by which Americans often greeted each other. In person, that is. But what should one say on answering the telephone? What indeed? Never before did one have to enter into a conversation without first knowing who one was going to be talking to. You were always in person when conversing, seeing who was there in front of you before the first words came out. Now when that bell started ringing (a wholly new sound that had come into daily life), and you picked up the receiver, what did you say?

Bell himself answered by saying *ahoy* (or probably more often

---

*There was a toy telephone on the market at least by 1883. Probably the first, listed in that year's catalog of Ebbets & Co., was a "Bliss Telephone Set" selling for $1.25. It had a bell that could be rung by means of a crank. Later toy telephones had a spring mechanism by which the bell would ring when the receiver was taken off the hook. By the early twentieth century, children's telephone sets were sometimes electrified, using batteries.

just *hoy*) and thought everyone else should. It was a form of exclamation going back at least as far as hallow, and he continued to use it even after *hello* (said to be Edison's choice) became the popular favorite. *Hello, Central* was also the title of a popular song at the turn of the twentieth century, further evidence of *hello's* currency (as well as the telephone).

Now as to the *central* part of *Hello, Central.* The exchange, or central switchboard, of the early days of the telephone was at first manned by young men, whose agility and robustness were thought to make for a speedy switching of lines. But boys could sometimes be too robust, sometimes too prone to impatience and flippancy. The hiring of sisters Emma and Stella Nutt as telephone operators in Boston in 1878 began to turn the tide. Eventually it was taken for granted that the position of telephone operator was a woman's profession. Women were found to be just as fast and adept at the basic skills but also a lot more polite and dignified. With telephone companies quickly adopting high standards of etiquette and elocution, women were found to measure up far better; and by the mid-1880s they had replaced young men at most of the switchboards then in existence. The position of telephone operator in fact became a major career opportunity for women.

Operators—whether women or young men—originally had only proper names to go by in making connections; the first directories had no numbers, and a good memory for names was key to effective service. A measles epidemic in Lowell, Massachusetts, in 1880 helped to change that. A local physician, a Dr. Parker, fearing a virtual shutdown of the telephone office if its four operators were taken ill, recommended that each subscriber be assigned a number. This would make it far easier for substitute operators to take over. In short order, telephone operators everywhere were responding to customers with "Number, please."

It was in 1880 also that the first pay phone was installed in the lobby of the Connecticut Telephone Company in New Haven. Unlike a coin-operated pay phone of later years, the charges were paid to an attendant. Other companies followed. The 1884 directory of the Metropolitan Telephone and Telegraph Company in New York City listed thirty-two locations with a telephone for public use. All listings in the book had what became the standard form

LOVE BY TELEPHONE

In the late 1870s and early 1880s, just after it came into use, the telephone prompted differing reactions. Some people were shocked that the disembodied sound of the human voice could be heard coming out of a box and thought it the work of the devil. Others saw nothing sinister and delighted in it. Among the latter were songwriters who correctly sensed the wave of the future; within the first few years, there were at least fifteen pieces of music published in celebration of the telephone, including *The Wondrous Telephone*, the *Telephone Waltz*, the *Telephone Polka*, and the *Telephone Quickstep*. In *Love by Telephone*, written in 1880, three years after the first private telephone went into use, composer and lyricist C. R. Hodge rhapsodized about the age-old ritual of courting being transformed by modern technology: A sample verse:

I signaled. It was answer'd by Ella's charming voice.
"Are you alone?" I stammered out: my heart made such a noise
That I scarce could hear her answer. It came, "Yes quite alone":
"And so am I," I answered: then I kissed the telephone.

Refrain

I'll never cease to bless the thought that won her for my own.
Oh such rapture who'd have ever dreamed, could come thro' the
    telephone.

C. R. Hodge, "Love by Telephone," Chicago, 1880. Music Division, Library of Congress. Photograph, c. 1900. Smithsonian Institution.

of a telephone number through the mid–twentieth century and the coming of all digits—an exchange name (normally a geographic reference) plus a number. Thus New Yorkers of 1884 would ask for Nassau (for Nassau Street) 304 to reach the main post office, Nassau 133 for the *New York Herald,* and Spring 40 for the New York Gas Light Company.

Meanwhile telephone service that had begun as local-only—that line from Roswell Downer's Boston office to his home in nearby Somerville—was going long-distance: Boston to Providence in 1882, Boston to New York in 1884, Boston to Washington in 1888. By 1893, half the continent was connected. Just in time for the World's Columbian Exposition in Chicago was long-distance service established between there and New York. Mayor Grant of New York opened the new link in October 1892 by saying "hello" (what else?) to Chicago's Mayor Washburne. The connection was reported to be "perfect," except that Washburne tended to have his mouth too far from the transmitter at times, occasionally making it difficult to hear him. Otherwise the viability of long-distance conversation (nearly a thousand miles) was clearly proved. The engineering feat that accomplished it was thought worthy to be documented by *Scientific American:* The line was comprised of 826,500 pounds of copper cable strung across 42,750 poles, each 35 feet high, through New Jersey, Pennsylvania, Ohio, Indiana, and Illinois. "It is a remarkable achievement," said *Scientific American,* "indicative of marvelous possibilities in the future, in an art still in its infancy."

During its early years the telephone remained a rather expensive device best suited to the business world or the wealthy. As the twentieth century opened, it became more and more something for everyone. Pay phones made service available to those who could not afford a telephone of their own, and by 1902 there were some 81,000 of them. Usually they were phone company–owned and –operated. Some banks and drugstores offered free telephone service to patrons. And there was the occasional entrepreneur—be he ever so modest—who saw a business advantage in having phones available to his customers. One such was the Paterson, New Jersey, barber who in 1905 had a telephone installed next to each chair.

But was this necessarily good? Or was it an intrusion of technology on "chance intervals of relaxation and repose"? So thought one commentator of the day who argued against it: "The up-to-date barber's chair supplies to the customer a couch of ease for a quarter of an hour or so, giving him the rest of which, in a busy hard-working generation like this, he is likely to stand in so much need. . . . From of old, conversation there [the barber's chair] has been intended to go in at one ear and out at the other and not to wander off into the intricacies of an electrical system. Let the barber in New Jersey as elsewhere stick to his strops and lather pots." What would he have said about cell phones?

Barber shops or not, use of the telephone became so much a part of modern life in coming years—and Alexander Graham Bell so revered for his invention—that Bell's death in 1922 was marked by an extraordinary tribute: For the man who made conversation convenient, conversation stopped. At the behest of AT&T, telephone service throughout the country was suspended for one minute at 6:25 P.M. August 4, 1922, to observe Bell's funeral.

A few years later in 1926, taking note of the first fifty years of life with the telephone, an editorial writer at the *New York Times* observed the obvious: "How could we get along without it? . . . Now a suspension of the telephone service for a day would make about as much trouble as would the cutting off of our water supply."

And as for the telephone that was once only the instrument of businessmen and the wealthy: "[Now] the washerwoman or the odd-job man is almost as likely to have a telephone in the house as the banker or the manufacturer to have one—or a hundred—in his offices."

The telephone, of course, would continue to go through a process of improvement and development. A noticeable change was the coming into use in the 1920s of dial phones, which did away with the operator for routine calling. *Popular Science* took note in 1921 with the headline, NEARLY EVERY AMERICAN HOME IS GOING TO BE ITS OWN EXCHANGE.

The convenience of dialing directly, and not having to wait for an operator, was a welcome improvement for most people. But not everyone. When dial service reached the U.S. Capitol in 1930, many members of Congress interpreted it as meaning they would now have to "perform the duties of telephone operators in order to enjoy the benefits of telephone service." So read a resolution introduced in the U.S. Senate by Senator Carter Glass of Virginia. The resolution declared that "dial telephones are more difficult to operate than manual telephones" and directed the sergeant-at-arms to have the Chesapeake & Potomac Telephone Company get rid of the dialers and bring back the old manuals. The resolution passed; but progress, in the form of direct dialing, in due course won out even in the fusty old offices of the Capitol.

CALLING WHO KNOWS NOT WHERE

. . . if a person wanted to call to a friend he knew not where, he would call in a very loud electromagnetic voice, heard by him who had the electromagnetic ear, silent to him who had it not. "Where are you?" he would say. A small reply would come, "I am at the bottom of a coal mine, or crossing the Andes, or in the middle of the Atlantic." . . . Think of what this would mean. . . . It would be almost like dreamland.

—*Engineering Magazine,* July 1901

With it, you'll be reachable anyplace, even by callers who have no idea where in the world you are.

—*Fortune,* August 24, 1992

It took almost a century for dreamland to become a reality, but once it did there were electromagnetic ears and voices everywhere, calling everywhere. We call them cell phones (the subject of the *Fortune* article).

It was a remarkable imaginative idea in 1901, when it was broached by *Engineering Magazine* in an article about Guglielmo Marconi and the wireless. Dialing a number for yourself on the telephone was still off in the future, and even telephone *numbers*— as opposed to asking the operator for a party by name—were still relatively new. It was enough to have a telephone and be able to connect, by wire, with precisely whom you wanted.

A few years later, in 1910, an experimental mobile two-way radio was demonstrated in New York City. But the sheer bulk of **128** the sending set—two storage cells, a 10-inch spark coil, two Leyden jars, high and low voltage batteries, and a 7-foot aerial—made it wildly impractical; furthermore, it could transmit only a maximum of 3 miles.

Two-way radios generally came into use in the post–World War II period, especially in police cars and taxicabs; subsequently, conventional mobile phones, operating through the local telephone company, became available for private automobiles in small numbers. These mobile phones were generally limited to a radius of 20 miles. And since each metropolitan area was assigned only twelve channels, only twelve customers at a time could use the system. In New York City, by the early 1980s, fewer than 2,000 individuals had mobile telephones, and they had to wait sometimes as much as thirty minutes for a dial tone.

The breakthrough was cellular telephone service, approved by the Federal Communications System in 1982. Instead of one powerful local transmitter for an entire city or region, there was now a checkerboard (cells) of low-power transmitters and receivers by which local calls were relayed from one "cell" to the next; and a signal strong enough now for the local telephone company to relay anywhere—say the Andes, or the mid-Atlantic. In Chicago, for example, this meant that up to 50,000 calls an hour could be handled, as opposed to 1,400 with the old system.

The long road to practicality led a writer for *Forbes* magazine in 1984 to lament, "If he knew how long it has taken to develop a car telephone that could do what the desk phone can, Alexander Graham Bell would roll over in his grave." Yet this was not yet the ubiquitous cell phone of today. The cellular telephone of the mid-1980s was still an expensive device, often about $3,000 installed, and involved service charges sometimes running into the hundreds of dollars a month. Here was history repeating itself. As with the early conventional telephone, the early cellular was chiefly marketed to businesses and the very well-to-do.

Nor was it compact. Each cellular phone of the period was roughly three times the size of a later cell phone and clearly intended for use inside the car—as opposed to walking down the street or riding in a bus or in any of the vast number of ways a later cell phone is used. It was actually four separate pieces of hardware: a power source (a 5-pound box mounted in the trunk), an antenna, a cable, and the phone itself, which rested in a console on the floor. Even so, in 1984 a major brokerage research department predicted between 1 million and 1.5 million subscribers by 1990.

By the early 1990s, however, the same process of miniaturization set in as it had with other forms of technology—even more dramatically, perhaps—and with it a miniaturization of cost. What was priced at $3,000 in the mid-1980s had shrunk by 2000 to as little as $39.99 with monthly access charges of $29.99.

Besides being vastly less expensive, the cell phone of the turn of the twenty-first century was small enough to fit in a purse or a pocket. That made it so handy (and trendy) that cell phone ownership soared to some 85 million Americans by 2000.

Yet not without a certain degree of argument. The cell phone's cutesy chirping ring has sent stares and shushes to cell phone users in restaurants, concerts, libraries, and the like. In many such places, cellulars now are restricted. More controversial—and of more general concern—is use of cell phones while driving. By one estimate, 85 percent of the 85 million Americans owning cell phones admit to using them at the wheel. A late-1990s report of the *New England Journal of Medicine* concluded that drivers who use cell phones while driving are four times more likely to get into an accident; that is, the odds of a cell phone user smashing up are roughly the same as a borderline drunk. Americans, whose love for the automobile is exceeded only by their affection for wondrous contrivances, have been singularly resistant to any restriction on gabbing at the wheel, although a number of countries, including England, Germany, Australia, Israel, Italy, and Japan have enacted restrictions on car phone use.

Paradoxically, safety was a key reason for getting a car phone at the beginning of the cellular era. Many of those buying early mobile phones said it was comforting to know that a phone would be only an arm's length away in case of a breakdown or an accident. Yet more and more the phone became the cause of the accident. *Newsweek* in 1984 warned that "dialing while driving may be hazardous to your health." Its article was headlined HELLO? HELLO? CRUUUUNCH!

CHAPTER SEVEN

A NEW NECESSITY
OF CIVILIZATION

THE TYPEWRITER

The typewriter has become a necessity of modern civilization.

–*Education* magazine, June 1892

LARGELY SNUBBED in the years immediately following its introduction in the mid-1870s, the typewriter pounded to popularity in the 1890s. Some educators suggested that it was incumbent on schools to teach its use, and that perhaps no student should graduate without a practical knowledge of it. The typewriter transformed the business world of the 1890s. "If time is money," said one business writer, "it is easy to calculate what kind of a bargain one makes in purchasing one of these labor-saving machines." Said another observer in 1892:

> The machine itself has had a marvelously rapid development. If we turn back only ten years and read the descriptions of typewriting and typewriters in the then current periodicals it is like making a visit to the Smithsonian Institute to examine the first locomotive engine ever used in America.

Two decades earlier there was only a lukewarm response to this strange-looking device that was arguably the most challenging form of new technology yet confronted directly by the consumer. It meant putting words on paper in a way no one had ever done before, defying the tradition that one's penmanship was an extension of one's refinement and manners. Writing of the traditional and socially accepted kind—in neat and orderly motions of wrist and pen, as humankind had been doing for ages—was being shunted aside in favor of using one's fingers to bang little levers marked with letters of the alphabet—an alphabet beginning with the letter Q!

The first practical typewriter to be manufactured was the Remington Model No. 1, which went on the market early in 1874. Few people knew anything about it until two years later, when it was introduced to the public at the Philadelphia Centennial of 1876. So new in concept was it that *Scientific American* in January 1876 thought it appropriate to give a brief description: "The machine in appearance somewhat resembles an ordinary sewing

machine [itself little more than twenty years old], being mounted

The first Remington typewriter. Its keyboard was essentially the same as the keyboard of either a typewriter or personal computer of the present time. The ornate decoration, the sort one would expect to find on a sewing machine of the period, is no coincidence: The Remington division given the job of producing typewriters was the one that formerly made sewing machines. (Library of Congress)

on a stand of the size and appearance of a sewing machine stand. In front there is a keyboard with the letters of the alphabet, numerals, etc., upon it; and on pressing one of the keys, a small lever bearing the corresponding letter is caused to strike against a ribbon saturated with a prepared ink, over which the paper is held on a roller."

Just how innovative this was may be appreciated even more from a quaint account in *Nature*, May 1876: "The method of inking is excellent and unexpected. A strip of fine fabric, saturated with the ink is carried between two rollers so arranged that it intervenes *between* the paper to be printed on and the centre of the lever-circle. The type-carrying hammers do not, therefore, strike the paper itself at all, but only the ink-saturated band, which, as a result of the percussion, comes in contact with the recording paper, *but only in the parts where contact is made,* which are nothing more nor less than those corresponding to the configuration of the letter or figure employed."

The debut of the Remington Model No. 1 at the Philadelphia Centennial gave no hint of the meteoric rise ahead. The typewriter exhibit generated curiosity but made few converts. People looked but were neither dazzled nor convinced. A few people ridiculed the new device; a few others expressed serious interest. But very few machines were sold. The typewriter exhibit apparently made more money selling souvenirs—customized samples actually typed out on the spot for twenty-five cents apiece.

A huge hurdle for the typewriter was cost. At $125, compared with a few cents for a plain old pen, it was an expensive luxury that only a few people might even consider buying. And then there was the matter of needing to learn a whole new writing technique that no one had ever used before. Mark Twain, in one of the first letters he typed, observed what was hardly unique to his particular Remington No. 1:

> Susie has struck the keys once or twice, & no doubt has printed some letters which do not belong where she put them.

It was not just a matter of learning a completely new way of printing letters on paper, however. Even a seasoned typist of today would be perplexed with the Remington No. 1. There was no way to see what you were typing as you typed it. Though the keys and platen were in their customary locations, the keys struck underneath the platen, rather than in front. This meant you couldn't see what you were doing until you had stopped typing and rolled the paper upward. Furthermore, the No. 1 had only capital letters, and the carriage return was treadle-operated, like a sewing machine. (The typewriter, in fact, came mounted on a sewing machine stand and was decorated with a flowery design typical of a sewing machine—no happenstance, since it was Remington's old sewing machine department, with its thirty employees, that was given the job of producing the typewriter.)

Remington's Model No. 2, unveiled in 1878, essentially solved these problems. Though high and awkward by later standards, it had a carriage return lever on the machine itself and a shift mechanism to allow for printing both upper and lower-case letters.

The typewriter as we know it might have looked quite different. Devices with other configurations were tried—rotating wheels with letters around the circumference, for example. Or what looked like a miniature piano keyboard. Machines such as this were attempted but never manufactured. The design that prevailed—including the long-standard keyboard beginning with the letter Q—owes chiefly to Christopher Sholes, the principal inventor of the typewriter.

Remington, the only manufacturer of typewriters in 1874 and the principal producer for the rest of the century, had its model No. 1 on the market early in 1874. In five years, sales had totaled a disappointing 1,000 or so. By 1882, the total was up to 2,300; and by 1885, 5,000 a year. In 1890, sales reached some 20,000; and by 1892, with production running at a hundred typewriters a day, or more than 25,000 a year, Remington found itself unable

to keep up with demand. (In 1895 the federal government alone had 1,990 typewriters in use, more than 80 percent of them Remingtons.)

By now there were other manufacturers. One of them, the Hammond Typewriter Corporation of New York, in the late 1880s produced a pamphlet, *What Folks Say of the Hammond Typewriter,* that offered page after page of comments—all favorable, of course, since only those who liked the Hammond were included. Comments chosen for their usefulness to Hammond included: "I found it easy to acquire the rapid use of the typewriter" (the Rev. Frank S. Dobbins of Allentown, Pennsylvania) and "The fatigue of a day spent at the machine is not as great as that caused by continuous writing with pen or pencil" (city court stenographer John E. Norcross of Brooklyn, New York). These assorted comments show how widespread the use of the typewriter had become. As evidenced by the addresses given, the typewriter by the late 1880s could be heard clicking away in such seemingly remote places as Chemung Valley, Pennsylvania; Muscatine, Iowa; Wadley, Georgia; and Morrillton, Arkansas.

Mark Twain's joshing aside, it is hard to assess how difficult most people found it to learn to use the typewriter. Surely some were befuddled. After all, the typewriter's method of putting words on paper—by taps of the fingers rather than swirls of the hand—was without precedent. It was a wholly new process. As with other forms of emerging technology, especially in years to come, the motivation to master it superseded whatever difficulty it presented.

Perhaps the most troublesome thing was the very feature that has *never* changed—the layout of the keyboard. The Remington Model No. 1 had basically the same layout that is universal today—computer keyboards as well as typewriters—the so-called QWERTY (for its first six letters).

Why not a keyboard in alphabetical order? After all, the numbers on the standard keyboard, then as now, are in numerical order. And why a layout beginning with Q? Before getting Remington No. 1 on the market, Christopher Sholes in fact tried an ABC arrangement. At slow speed, it worked well enough; but as soon as a typist was going fast enough to give the typewriter an advantage over handwriting, the keys of the most used letters of the alphabet tended to strike at the same time, jamming together as they hit the platen. This might have been solved by redesigning the entire mechanism. Instead Sholes hit on the idea of rearranging the layout of the keys to lessen the likelihood of any two letters striking at the same time. He turned to his brother-in-law, a teacher and mathematician, for advice; after much calculating and experimenting, the result was an arrangement by which letters most likely to be successively hit would tend to come from opposite sides of the keyboard. As it happened, the first letters of this arrangement (top row, left to right) were Q, W, E, R, T, and Y.

Whether this is mathematically the best arrangement has been disputed ever since. That the new layout did largely solve the problem of jamming is evident: The Remington went on to become a commercial success, and virtually every typewriter (and computer keyboard) since then has been a QWERTY. Subsequent technical refinement has made the matter of layout moot, but the QWERTY tradition has proven insuperable to every challenge ever mounted. Sholes, however, sold the QWERTY layout to the public not for the practical reason he adopted it—to preclude jamming without resorting to a major redesign—but on grounds that it was a scientifically determined arrangement that would improve the speed and efficiency of the typist. This, according to typewriter historian Wilfred A. Beeching, "was probably one of the biggest confidence tricks of all time. . . . the idea that the so-called 'scientific arrangement' of the keys was designed to give the minimum movement of the hands was, in fact, completely false. To write almost any word in the English language, a maximum distance has to be covered by the fingers."

HOW DID YOU TYPE ON THE THING?

The QWERTY arrangement, nevertheless, worked; and it had the effect of making the typewriter practical without the need for further technical development that might have delayed its coming on the market for years. But something else needed to be resolved: How did you type on the thing? With one finger? One finger on each hand? Two on each hand? All five? Perhaps the first advice that sounded authoritative was offered by *Cosmopolitan Shorthander,* which said the proper way was to use only the first two fingers on each hand. It said that this was the way the best operators typed and it doubted whether any higher speed could be obtained with three fingers on each hand, let alone all five.

Not so, declared Frank E. McGurrin, the five-fingered stenographer for the Federal Court in Salt Lake City, Utah, and self-proclaimed fastest typist in the world. McGurrin often gave demonstrations of his prowess, sometimes typing blindfolded. He challenged anyone, with any typing method, to finger-to-finger combat. A certain Louis Taub, a two-finger specialist, took him up. They met in Cincinnati, with a prize of $500 at stake. McGurrin won easily. Five fingers eventually became the standard for a professional typist, and the touch method the generally accepted way of getting the most speed and accuracy. But many an early typist did quite well with a couple of fingers; and indeed the two-fingered Taubs of this world may be in the majority today, hunting and pecking with sometimes uncanny precision not at typewriters but at computer keyboards.

The first school of typing, of which there is a positive record, was opened in 1878 at 737 Broadway, New York, by D. L. Scott-Browne. Within a few years there were typing schools in most major cities. By the end of the century, typing was becoming a common part of the public school curriculum.

Sholes, who died in 1890, just before use of the typewriter became widespread, saw his own legacy as a broader one. He took pride in predicting that the typewriter would serve a purpose beyond simply speeding up the process of communication. At a time when women usually had to settle for menial labor, Sholes saw a social significance:

> I feel that I have done something for the women who have always had to work so hard. This will enable them more easily to earn a living.

And indeed, the typewriter revolutionized the role of women in the workplace. Before its invention, unless a woman had the means to an education by which to become a teacher or a nurse, a woman's work was in the factory or shop or in domestic service. The typewriter arrived gender-neutral. Was it inherently a man's machine? A woman's? Certainly, as opposed to other types of machinery, there was nothing about it that precluded a woman from operating it just as well as a man. And perhaps better. One of the first institutions to see in the typewriter a new career potential for women was the Young Women's Christian Association, which in 1881 began offering training for typists. The first class had eight girls enrolled. The idea spread. Within five years, it is estimated, there were some 60,000 young women with office typing jobs throughout the country. Every one of these jobs was a career opportunity that had not existed before the coming of the typewriter.

Meanwhile, the typewriter, like its keys that bounce back and forth, had had to do its share of bouncing before becoming widely accepted. A long forgotten aspect of the process is that it was not only the typist who had to get adjusted. Just as using one of the first typewriters was sometimes befuddling, so was getting a letter written with one. S. P. Johns, a Texas banker and insurance executive, bought a typewriter in the late 1870s and took pride in sending out typed instead of handwritten correspondence. But many people took offense at the strangely "printed" letters they received. Etiquette dictated proper forms of letter writing, and social convention prized penmanship for its expressiveness. A letter that looked like a printed handbill most assuredly did not meet any of those dictums of decorum. One of Johns's agents fired back (in handwriting): "I do not think it was necessary then, nor will be in the future, to have your letters set up like a hand bill. I will be able to read your writing and am deeply chagrined to think you thought such a course necessary." Apocryphal or not, there is the story of a Kentucky mountaineer who returned the first typed letter he ever received, explaining tersely: "You don't need to print no letters for me. I kin read writin."

Where it was not indignation, the reaction was often insatiable curiosity. So revealed Mark Twain when he was asked to write a testimonial to the virtues of the typewriter. Instead, in typical Twain fashion, he told Remington: "Please do not use my name in any way. Please do not even divulge the fact that I own a machine. I have entirely stopped using the Type Writer, for the reason that I never could write a letter with it to anybody without receiving a
request by return mail that I would not only describe the machine

A much-improved Remington of the 1890s. According to an 1892 advertisement in which this illustration appeared, Remington was producing 200 typewriters every two days—about what it averaged in a year its first five years on the market—and it was still not keeping up with demand. As the ad said, "The public were slow to realize the value of the invention." Not in the 1890s. (*Illustrated Phonographic World*, New York, November 1893)

but state what progress I had made in the use of it, etc. etc. I don't like to write letters, and so I don't want people to know that I own this curiosity breeding little joker."

It was curiosity, nonetheless, that helped fuel the take-off. Curiosity—followed by a realization that the typewriter was not a contraption but a serious tool for streamlining the process of modern communication.

Early marketing of the typewriter curiously overlooked business, by and large, and targeted such supposed typewriter users as lawyers, authors, clergymen, court reporters, and editors. A recession that began in 1873 automatically put a brake on acceptance by the business community. But ultimately logic and the business boom of the later nineteenth century won out. As writer Frank H. Palmer observed in 1892: "With one of these machines a business man can dictate with ease, and his clerk can neatly print, sixty business letters in a day. It has been demonstrated by many tests, that the typewriter as compared with the pen, saves forty minutes an hour, or five hours and twenty minutes in a business day. If 'time is money' it is easy to calculate what kind of a bargain one makes in purchasing one of these labor-saving machines."

A spin-off of the typewriter, especially in the workplace, was the popularization of carbon paper, by which multiple copies could be typed at once. With the decline of the typewriter in favor of computerized word processing—along with printers and copying machines—in the late twentieth century, carbon paper largely returned to obscurity.

If the typewriter was that kind of serious tool, and useful in everyday life as well as the business place, it was increasingly something that perhaps *everyone* should know how to use. And so fur-

"Young People's Typewriter," 1887. More than just a toy, it could actually type, although its mechanism was different and much slower in operation than a regular typewriter. (McLoughlin Brothers, *Catalog,* New York, 1887)

ther analogy with the personal computer. Just as in the later twentieth century the computer became an integral part of the classroom in America, so too in the later nineteenth century the infusion of the typewriter into the public school curriculum. And for the same reasons: It was both an efficient accessory to learning and a coming necessity for success in the workplace. In its adaptability to the classroom, the typewriter in fact prophesied computerized learning right down to a virtual description of it. Wrote Boston school board member Dr. William A. Mowry in 1891:

> The Typewriter makes it possible to place in every school room a little instrument, in compact and convenient form . . . where the pupil . . . manipulates the keys, so easily learned, and writes his answers to questions, his written exercises, his composition, or whatever he is required to express.

Acquiring a highly practical skill was (is) an even bigger plus. As one observer remarked in 1891: "The ability to use the typewriter is coming to be looked upon as a necessary part of a practical education, and in thousands of cases this knowledge is the means of earning a living." Even for those whose work would not require direct use of a typewriter, a knowledge of typing—as is oft said of Latin's contribution to a liberal education—would enhance one's overall acumen. Explained a report of the Bennington, Vermont, Public Schools in 1890: "There is no doubt that these machines will be used in the near future for their educational value alone in all high schools and grammar grades in the country. It is the testimony of educators who have tried it, that no other device in the hands of the pupil contributes so much towards a knowledge of correct business English." A writer in *North American Review* in July 1890 said it another way: "Not that it is probable that every one who learns would take up typewriting as a business, but spelling, punctuation, capitalizing, paragraphing, and greater still, prose composition, could be a dozen times better taught with the machine than without it." R. W. Burton, principal of the public schools in Polo, Illinois, summed it up: "Were it possible, I would have every pupil take a course in typewriting before graduating from the school."

In eerie echoes, every one of these arguments would reappear a century later in support of the personal computer as an essential part of every school's curriculum. Uncanny also was a certain precognition of the computer when the question was raised as to what the typewriter might be like in the late twentieth century. An artist for *Illustrated Phonographic World* in 1894 was given that challenge and came up with a curiously perceptive view of what was in store. The "1994" typewriter, as he conceived it in 1894, was voice-actuated, having dispensed with the keyboard altogether; and it was "programmed" (in a sense) to correct for spelling, punctuation, and grammar. It could be equipped to fold the letter, print and stuff the envelope, and add postage. A remarkable conception. And nothing there that turn-of-the-twenty-first-century technology couldn't handle.

The Animal Keyboard

The Animal Keyboard, Smith Corona, c. 1935: an imaginative approach to learning the typewriter. The idea was to teach children to type by having the keys labeled for different animals. Hence, on the left hand, as the instruction book explained, "Little finger is birdie finger, third finger is doggie finger, second finger is bunnie finger," and so on for each hand. As an added help, there was a matching animal ring for each finger. Despite its innovative charm, the animal keyboard seems to have had a short run and is virtually forgotten today except for one in the Smithsonian Institution. (Smithsonian Institution)

From *Illustrated Phonographic World*,* New York, June 1894: An eerie forecast of the computer. The artist's challenge in 1894 was to envision the typewriter in 1994. What he came up with was a voice-activated device that could correct for errors of spelling and grammar, print out the letters, and address (and even stuff) the envelopes. Pretty close to the mark.

---

*A journal devoted to typing and shorthand. *Phonographic,* in the contemporary sense, signified shorthand: hearing (from the Greek *phōnē* sound) and writing *(graphein).*

CHAPTER EIGHT

"YOU SHOULD GET ONE"

THE COPYING MACHINE

The finest invention of the present age . . .

–Thomas Jefferson, c. 1805, extolling the virtues of his copying machine

INSTANT IMAGES: By the millions, copying machines in offices and copy shops, libraries and supermarkets, feed the American appetite for making copies of everything on paper. The "xerox," as many people call it generically, is one of those seemingly indispensable things in modern life.

Yet while the technology for making instant photocopies is recent, the need for making copies—say, a letter just written—is hardly unique to modern times. Even in the eighteenth century there were those who wanted to—and could—make copies using a simpler form of technology.

Thomas Jefferson, for example. His "copying machine" was just as indispensable to him as the Xerox machine of modern times—not only "a most precious possession" but "the finest invention of the present age."

Jefferson was a prolific letter writer. The tradition of the time was for the writer, having completed an original in longhand with quill pen and ink, to duplicate it the same way in order to have a file copy—or perhaps, if needed, make two or more copies the same way. It was a tedious and time-expending process. Once he got his first copying machine in 1784, Jefferson used that device and an improved version for all of his correspondence the rest of his life. Prolific, indeed. Letters still existing that were written by Jefferson personally and so copied total some 18,000.

Jefferson was so delighted with his first copying machine that he began writing letters to friends (duly making copies thereof) suggesting that they also get copying machines. To James Madison he advised:

> Have you a copying press? If you have not you should get one. Mine (exclusive of the paper which costs a guinea a ream) has cost me about 14 guineas. I would give ten times that sum that I had it from the date of the stamp act.

Madison appears to have been less anxious to get one for himself. "[I] must postpone the conveniency to other wants which will absorb my little resources," he replied. But sensing its value for the institution that would eventually be the largest single user of modern copying machines, he went on to tell Jefferson: "I am led to think it would be a very oeconomical acquisition to all our public offices which are obliged to furnish copies of papers belonging to them." (It was under Jefferson indeed that the federal government got its first copiers, though neither for convenience nor economy. Jefferson had copying machines sent to consuls abroad so they could copy confidential correspondence without the need even for an aide to have a look.)

Although the kind of device Jefferson acquired was often referred to as a copying machine, it was more precisely known as a copying press. The one principally in use in the late eighteenth century was a device, or more accurately a process, patented in 1780 by James Watt. The machine part of it was a press, which might have either a screw-down mechanism or two wooden rollers to exert pressure on the page being copied. The secret to the process was a special ink based on gum arabic or sugar. A document written in this ink was placed in the bed of the press. Over this was laid a dampened sheet of tissue. The tissue and the original were then pressed together. Provided the copy was made within twenty-four hours, a legible copy was produced without damaging or changing the original. But the copy was a reverse image, and it had to be read from the back (the reason for using tissue). The Rev. Manassah Cutler, the Massachusetts clergyman and diarist, wrote in 1787 about seeing a copying press that Benjamin Franklin had brought back from England. Cutler described it as

a rolling press, for taking the copies of letters or any other writing. A sheet of paper is completely copied in less than two minutes, the copy as fair as the original, and without effacing it in the smallest degree.

George Washington also appreciated the virtues of copying presses, although he often found them breaking down. He was given one as a gift in 1782 and later bought a second. He complained in 1791 that the latter did "not work well; whether for want of more Springs I am unable to determine." A smaller one, he said, "used to be getting out of order frequently, but at present does tolerably well." Troubles or not, Washington made copies of official correspondence as well as business letters that he had bound into books; and some measure of his appreciation of copying technology may be gathered from the fact that he had paper bearing his personal watermark made just for his copying presses.

In a curious way, evolution to the next generation of copiers presaged experience of modern times. Copiers of the later twentieth century that produced copies that were obviously that—on thermal paper, for example—gave way to the plain-paper, "Xerox"-generation copier that could make reproductions virtually indistinguishable from the original. So too the second-generation copier at the turn of the nineteenth century. Instead of a thin tissue that was clearly a facsimile, the new polygraph made a copy (indeed up to five copies at a time) exactly duplicating the original, including the paper it was written on.

The polygraph was a refinement of the pantograph, a mechanical copying device going back to the seventeenth century. Probably the first successful one was designed by the French architect and engineer Marc Isambard Brunel, who in the mid-1790s fled France for the United States and then settled in England. He received an American patent for his "machine for writing with two pens" in 1799 and subsequently patented it in England as well. Soon after this an English-born inventor named John Isaac Hawkins, who had settled in Frankford, Pennsylvania, devised a similar machine that he called a polygraph. Under the patronage of Charles Willson Peale—whose fascination with natural history and technology was only barely secondary to his artistry—Hawkins developed his polygraph and through Peale had it sold from Peale's Museum, now occupying the upper floors and tower of the recently vacated State House, later known as Independence Hall. Peale announced the machine in such ads as this, which appeared in the Philadelphia *Aurora General Advertiser,* October 6, 1803:

> Neat Mahogany portable Polygraph Desks may now be had at the Museum. The price of those with two Pens, with convenient apparatus for letter writing, is 50 dollars, and those to write with three Pens 60 dollars. N.B. No machine will be suffered to go abroad before it has been proved and found to perform well.

Museum, Philadelphia Oct. 3

One of Peale's clearly satisfied customers was the White House. As Jefferson wrote to a friend in February 1805: "A Mr. Hawkins of Frankford, near Philadelphia, has invented a machine, which he calls a polygraph, and which carries two, three, or four pens. That of two pens, with which I am now writing, is best; and is so perfect that I have laid aside the copying-press, for a twelvemonth past, and write always with the polygraph."

The polygraph used wires and movable wooden arms holding duplicate pens to make from one to five copies of an original letter. As the writer's hand moved, inscribing the original, the arm or arms of the device (depending on the number of copies) duplicated the action of his pen on a second (and so on) sheet of paper, creating a virtual duplicate on the same kind of paper.

At $50 or $60, the polygraph was expensive—roughly half the price of a kitchen stove. A polygraph was for the few who had the means and who carried on such correspondence as would make it useful in the first place. Nevertheless, Peale, whose marketing skill was already evident in the huge success of his museum, promised for his copier more or less what would be promised in the age of the Xerox machine. Said Peale in announcing Hawkins's polygraph for sale:

> I have neither spared labour or expence to *simplify the machinery—* the having it *made durable—not easily deranged or put out of order,* and capable of being understood, and used, by any person on the first sight of it.

Peale said the device could be ordered so as to produce as many as five copies, but machines with two or three pens were likely to be most in use. Jefferson, as we know, liked the one with two pens.

Jefferson turned out to be probably the most enthusiastic user of the polygraph, ordering several more machines in the coming years. Otherwise sales were slow. It is estimated that Peale produced fewer than a hundred polygraphs, of which not all were sold. But this was handmade, rather than an assembly-line device; so total production was necessarily limited. On the other hand, it was sometimes difficult and clumsy to use, and popularity was limited to those who knew of or had need for such a device. It was also a delicate, fragile mechanism prone to needing repair or new parts. Peale actually lost money on the venture and seems to have stuck with it largely because of Jefferson's interest. Yet Peale's own fascination with new technology was also a factor; his museum, for example, was the first major public display of gaslight in America.

In coming years, copying technology echoed both the polygraph and the earlier copying press. A revival of the latter came in 1885 with Bushnell's Perfect Letter Copying Book, a flexible bound book of 150 pages of thin tissue. Much as with Jefferson's copying press of a century earlier, an original written with a special ink was placed facedown on the tissue, behind which was a dampened cloth and a blank manila page. The book was then closed and pressed tightly. In a few seconds, the copy was ready. Because of the use of better ink, it was no longer necessary to use an actual press. This made Bushnell's bound book easily portable. Samuel P. Langley, secretary of the Smithsonian Institution, used one on his European travels in the late nineteenth century. But because the image was reversed, the tissue had to be read from the back, as with Watt's original press.

An offshoot of this same process was the copygraph, which was also in use by the 1880s. This was perhaps the simplest form of copying of all. The copying medium was a tray of gelatin mixed with glycerin. An original was prepared using an aniline ink. When dry, it was placed facedown on the gelatin, which absorbed the image. To make a copy, a blank page was then laid down on the gelatin and gently pressed by hand or with a roller. A copy was produced almost immediately, and the image was right-reading since it was the gelatin image that had been reversed. The ink used was most commonly purple, so what was produced was likewise; and while hardly matching the results of a modern copier, reasonably good copies could be had, certainly so, given how simple and cheap a procedure this was. The gelatin process copier, eventually better known as the hectograph, was around until more or less the mid–twentieth century. A common use was for printing restaurant menus (lunch counter, not haute cuisine). Schools also used hectographs, for tests and

assignments.

Meanwhile it was also the 1880s that produced the first arguably modern copying machine, the mimeograph—another invention largely attributable (though hardly one of his best known) to Thomas A. Edison. It was his electric pen and autographic copying press combined that became the mimeograph.

Actually a by-product of development of Edison's automatic telegraph, the electric pen, patented in 1876, was a sharply pointed steel stylus topped by a tiny electric motor that caused a reciprocating motion of the stylus. At a rate of roughly 8,000 pulses per minute, it could make minute perforations in a stencil—perforations forming words or other images. A plain piece of paper was then placed under the stencil; thick ink was squeezed on the stencil and forced through the perforations with a roller, making a copy underneath.

By 1887 a much improved stencil with a waxlike coating did away with the need for the electric pen. Now a simple stylus accomplished the same results. More important, the stencil could be inserted in that newly invented contrivance, the typewriter, and an exact copy made of an entire letter. The "Edison Mimeograph," as this improved copying machine was known, was marketed by the A. B. Dick Company of Chicago. It could produce copies at a rate of up to 600 per hour—not only letters, but "Sketches of all kinds, Architectural Drawings, Music, etc." In making copies, the early mimeograph worked much the same as its nearly ubiquitous counterpart of the mid–twentieth century, except that each copy had to be made by hand rather than automatically by a revolving cylinder. The first rotary mimeograph was introduced by A. B. Dick in 1904.

As opposed to present-day photocopying machines, which are often used to make only a single copy of something, the mimeograph of the late nineteenth century and its counterpart, the "Autocopyist," were useful only for multicopying. Yet for their time these duplicating devices of the 1880s and 1890s were essentially analogous to the copying machine of the present.

But how were these devices received? Did people really use them, and if so, what did they think of them? Though copying

"YOU SHOULD GET ONE"

149

technology was still rather primitive from a modern perspective, many people, chiefly professionals, seem to have been impressed. That such machines were indeed in use, and probably appreciated as much as the Xerox of modern times, is suggested by what one Martin Mahoney wrote in the New York *Voice* in 1889. In "How to Reach the People" he praised new copying techniques for their value in shaping public opinion: "The mimeograph and the auto-copyist, which are not expensive, will give any number of copies of a letter, and such as would be taken by very many for actual handwriting. So that, given a carefully classified list of addresses, any number of persons may be easily and cheaply sent what will be as good as a private letter to each." Furthermore, the copying process was sufficiently assimilated that the noun had become a verb. Writing in the *Chicago Advance* in 1895, Mary Bamford observed that "the copies were mimeographed . . ."

As for "not expensive," A. B. Dick mimeographs of this period sold for between $12 and $29.50. The cheapest duplicated only an autographic (hand-stenciled) copy 6 by 8 inches. The most expensive made copies up to 11 by 16 inches, both autographic and typewritten. Stencils, of course, were extra. The cheapest option was a quire (twenty-four sheets) of autographic stencil paper for sixty cents. Typewriter stencils ranged up to $22 a ream.

While Mahoney's version of the modern computer letter was one use, the spectrum of potential uses was considerably broader. The Autocopyist Company, of New York, which in the mid-1890s was producing a variation of the mimeograph (handwritten copies only) at prices beginning at $11, claimed there were some 50,000 autocopyist machines in use by merchants, agents, bankers, brokers, manufacturers, architects, engineers, clergymen, scientists, school and music teachers, lawyers, accountants, designers, and hotel and restaurant owners.

A device that could actually make an exact copy of something already existing—as opposed to being generated on a stencil—was developed in France in 1906 but did not come into public use. Then there was the photostat camera—a special camera using photosensitized paper instead of film to produce what is known as a photostat. There were clear advantages, but the photostat camera

was not consumer technology.

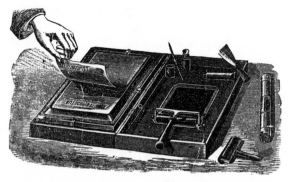

The Autocopyist, c. 1895: the "Xerox machine" of the nineteenth century.
(Warshaw Collection, Archives Center, National Museum of American History,
Smithsonian Institution)

The do-it-yourself mimeo machine, improved and electrified, remained the mainstay of multicopying for much of the twentieth century, turning out inestimable numbers of newsletters, legal briefs, school tests, publicity releases, church bulletins, restaurant menus, and cheap copying of all kinds, from a couple of pages to hundreds.

Yet the need remained for something stencil-less that could make copies from one of a kind to the hundreds. By the 1950s, copiers for office and personal use began to appear in significant numbers; and by the late 1960s, by one estimate, there were more than half a million copying machines in use producing more than 10 billion copies a year. The first wave of these were usually bothersome to operate and produced mediocre results by later standards. Special photosensitive paper usually was necessary. Some processes worked with fumes rather than liquid to avoid shrinking the paper; others, with infrared rays to produce heat by which an image was transferred to sensitized paper (thermography).

Still needed was what A. B. Dick had pledged back in 1889: "Absolutely no practice whatever is required to produce most Excellent Work." Indeed, what Charles Willson Peale had promised in announcing Hawkins's polygraph in 1803: "capable of being understood, and used, by any person on the first sight of it."

Simplicity. The new age began with a similar promise. Wrote a *New York Times* reporter in 1948: "Even an unskilled person can make good Xerographic prints easily."

"YOU SHOULD GET ONE"

Xerography (from the Greek, *xeros,* dry) was "a revolutionary process of inkless printing." And besides inkless, stencil-less. The key was a "dry iron powder" in place of ink and the use of static electricity to "sensitize" the paper so as to attract and bond the powder to form an image. The report explained that "a system has been discovered to make the static electricity appear only on parts of materials on which printed words or figures are desired . . . the dry iron powder that substitutes for ink actually jumps into place to form needed words or pictures . . . and makes a permanent mark when heated."

This was hardly yet the modern copier, and for the time being xerography was seen primarily as something for the printing and publishing industries. Nor was this yet instant-print. Nevertheless, it was still thought to be pretty impressive that, "During the demonstration, inkless printed copies of drawings and letters were made, and a portrait of a living subject was reproduced, while observers timed the work at exactly forty-five seconds."

The first commercial XeroX Copier (it was originally spelled with a capital X at the end) was introduced in 1949. A product of the Haloid Company (later Haloid Xerox, and then just Xerox), it was based on a 1938 invention of Chester Carlson. Praise of the day about its being "easy to operate" was clearly overstated. The first XeroX was in fact difficult and messy to use, requiring most of its processing to be done manually; and it often misprinted. But a vastly improved model—the Xerox 914, the first push-button, plain-paper copier—arrived in 1960, and with it the modern era of copying. It was the first marketable automatic, plain-paper copier; and while a bulky addition to the office (let alone the home) at 650 pounds, it caught on beyond anyone's expectations. Sales doubled in 1961 alone, and *Fortune* magazine called the 914 "the most successful product ever marketed in America."

Edison, who had guessed correctly about stock tickers, phonographs, motion pictures, and electric light, also had it right about America's need to make copies of things.

CHAPTER NINE

DROPPING ON TARGET

THE FAX MACHINE

"PHOTOGRAPHS BY TELEGRAPH: TELEVISION NEXT?" ran a newspaper headline in New York in 1907. The story was about pictures being "flashed by wire from one country to another," raising conjecture as to what else might lie ahead.

"Television," perhaps? The story represents one of the earliest known uses of the word, but it was not the visual medium as it is known today. The story was about sending photographs from the office of the London *Mirror* to the office of *L'Illustration* in Paris; and the reference to television was to a still inchoate idea that if still photographs could be transmitted over a distance, could not moving images likewise?

The emerging technology in this case was simpler yet sensational enough. The sending device in this 1907 demonstration was a rotating drum around which was wrapped a photograph in the form of a transparent film. Light passing through the film was reflected against a selenium cell and converted into electrical impulses. These traveled over a telegraph wire to Paris, where a receiving unit reproduced the image in the form of a negative that could then be printed as a photograph.

This is essentially what became the newspaper wire-photo machine. In the 1920s and 1930s it helped to revolutionize journalism by allowing the nearly instantaneous transmittal of pictures, just as the telegraph had done for words in the late 1840s and 1850s. More to the point, this (and similarly developing technology) is what eventually became the fax machine.

Sending pictures was a more demanding form of technology and yet it traced its origins back to the time of the early telegraph. In 1843, Scottish clock maker Alexander Bain got a British patent for a device that ostensibly could scan a flat surface with a stylus mounted on a pendulum; but the device was never demonstrated. A somewhat more sophisticated device for scanning and reproducing on cylinders was demonstrated at the 1851 World's Fair in London. But it was not until the early twentieth century that optical scanning made practical the sending of photographs—or for that matter, any form of image, handwritten, typed, or drawn. In the wake of the 1907 demonstration by Dr. Arthur Korn of the University of Munich—and experiments by others—newspapers were no longer limited to the use of photographs taken locally by their own photographers. Now photographs of national interest could be distributed to newspapers throughout the country. The first significant use of sending photographs by wire came with the Republican and Democratic national conventions of 1924, echoing pioneering use of the telegraph for the national conventions of 1844. Weather maps were another application.

Western Union in the late 1940s offered a relatively small desk-size facsimile machine for office use; but only some 50,000 were manufactured and the service was discontinued in the 1960s. By the late 1980s technological refinement had produced a facsimile machine—now coming to be known as a fax—roughly the size of a portable typewriter that was practical for the small office or home, and the boom began. Retail sales increased from $283 million in 1982 to more than $900 million in 1988. Fax machines seemed to be turning up almost everywhere in the business world. Law firms had them placed in partners' homes so important documents could be sent for review at night and on the weekend. Newspapers used them to send ad layouts to advertisers. Artists sent sketches to clients. Businesspeople took advantage of night rates to send letters after-hours instead of making telephone calls at costlier daytime rates. There were facsimile machines in such places as hotel lobbies. With the boom came a new verb, as the *New York Times* explained in May 1988: "Spreading along with the machines is the expression to fax, as in 'I faxed the letter this morning.'"

But a fax machine was still expensive, precluding widespread use in the average home. It was estimated in 1988 that fewer than 20,000 households had faxes. Machines of the type used in law offices and small business were selling on average at about $1,500. The least expensive fax available was still $800. In the early 1990s, however, the price dropped sharply, and by the turn of the twenty-first century a fax machine could be had for $100 or less.

While providing a new dimension to communications, the fax brought with it ancillary effects, both good and bad. On the good side, according to one newspaper report, the use of faxes in New

York City was cutting down on the number of bicycle messengers darting helter-skelter around the canyons of Manhattan, lessening fright for pedestrians and motorists alike. On the negative side for the average fax owner: the realization by direct-mail advertisers that faxes offered a huge new shooting gallery of sitting ducks for junk mail. The usual time for sending was overnight, when phones rates were lowest; and many were the fax machines found in the morning overflowing with unwanted, unneeded missives of all description. Federal legislation signed in December 1991 gave the Federal Communications Commission power to regulate "junk faxes."

And then there were those who argued that the fax was just one more intrusion. Complained *New York Times* columnist Russell Baker with typical wry humor: "The fax is just the latest in a series of machines that constantly escalate the message wars. . . . For centuries whenever people had felt an urge to send a message, they sat down and wrote a letter [and] the act of thinking about it usually showed it wasn't worth the price of a stamp. Thus were perhaps billions of superfluous messages happily aborted between the impulse and transmission. . . . With a fax machine whenever you felt a message coming on you could drop it immediately on the target. Bingo! Bombo! Message delivered."

CHAPTER TEN

DOING WHAT CAME NATURALLY

THE HOME COMPUTER

IN THAT MEMORABLE YEAR OF 1976, when America observed the bicentennial of its independence, it also marked the centennial of two major milestones in the history of technology. One was the invention in 1876 of the telephone, which in the coming century would become perhaps the most taken-for-granted application of technology in everyday life.

In 1976, writing about a new technology that almost everyone had heard of but few really knew much about, *Popular Mechanics* magazine avoided making a comparison with the telephone and instead predicted that sometime soon "you'll buy a computer for your home about as naturally as you now buy a dishwasher." To have said as naturally as a telephone seemed too implausible. The analogy was kept, well . . . dishwasher-safe.

And far short of the mark. By 2000, personal computers easily outnumbered dishwashers and were challenging even the telephone as the most-used way of communicating.

By a remarkable happenstance, 1976, for all practical purposes, was also the centennial of the typewriter. As we have seen, the typewriter presaged the personal computer in mode of interaction between user and task as well as the keyboard shared in common. Beyond that, there is a parallel in how the typewriter and the computer were assimilated into everyday life a century apart, almost year for year.

We thus have a watershed in the year 1976, from which to look backward and forward at the progress of what is undoubtedly at the top of almost every list of wondrous contrivances.

But what exactly was the computer like in 1976?

"Everybody knows what a computer is," said *Popular Mechanics* in September of that year: "a roomful of multimillion-dollar boxes looking like refrigerators with a dazzle of flickering lights, all working swiftly and efficiently to screw up your charge-account bills."

In a few words, that was probably what many people thought:
158 an office-sized device that prompted awe and fascination mixed

with a certain amount of suspicion. Most people as yet had no direct, firsthand experience with a computer.

The "roomful" notion was the essential concept of the modern computer that emerged right after World War II. It was something entirely new to almost everyone. The closest thing to it, as far as most people knew, was the calculating machine that had been around, in one form or another, since the early nineteenth century—and the calculating machine didn't even come close.

The computer was in a new galaxy. As reported by the *New York Times* on February 15, 1946:

> One of the war's top secrets, an amazing machine which applies electronic speeds for the first time to mathematical tasks hitherto too difficult and cumbersome for solution, was announced here tonight [February 14] by the War Department. . . . Its inventors say it computes a mathematical problem 1,000 times faster than it has ever been done before.

Built at the University of Pennsylvania, the giant device was technically an Electronic Numerical Integrator and Computer, or ENIAC for short, and at the time of the announcement was being used on a problem in nuclear physics. In sheer size, it was awesome: It nearly filled a 30-foot by 60-foot room with 9-foot-high cabinets, some forty in all, full of plugs and plug boards (like a telephone switchboard), clumps of wires, dials, knobs, and blinking pink neon lights. Its circuitry used 18,000 vacuum tubes (compared with a home radio with 6 or 8 tubes), half a million soldered joints, and several miles of wiring. And what it could do was awesome. As a demonstration for reporters, ENIAC was asked to multiply 97,367 by itself 5,000 times over, which it did, according to one who was there, "in less than the wink of an eye."

As revolutionary as ENIAC was, it shared something critical in common with calculating and tabulating devices going back to the nineteenth century—the punch card. In the case of ENIAC, it was for the input of data by way of "a series of cards in which holes are punched . . . dropped into a slot in a 'reader.' The man who wants the answers may then sit down and await results. He seldom has to wait long."

In principle, the punch card actually existed in the late eighteenth century in the case of musical instruments that could be "programmed" to perform mechanically with rolls of punched paper. A more significant use was for the Jacquard loom invented in France about 1800 by Joseph-Marie Jacquard. A series of interchangeable cards automatically controlled the weaving of intricate patterns, a task heretofore requiring the attention of two or more skilled workers that now could be done by one. The Jacquard loom, which quickly went into use in the United States as well as Europe, was the first significant use of automation in industry. Punch cards then appeared in British mathematician Charles Babbage's Analytical Engine, plans for which were developed in the 1830s. Although his machine was only experimental, it presaged the modern digital computer in its capacity for accepting information and instructions from punch cards remarkably similar to those of later times—for processing data (in what Babbage called a "mill"), for storing data (literally in a "store"), and even for determining what calculations to do next on the basis of calculations already performed. A slightly earlier, slightly simpler calculating device designed by Babbage was his Difference Engine—almost certainly the first computer with a printer. As Charles Tomlinson's *Cyclopaedia of Useful Arts* explained in 1868, "A most valuable feature intended to be introduced into this machine is the power of printing the tables as fast as it calculates them ... accomplished [with] a plate of copper ... shifted from place to place, until it is punched all over with figures arranged in tabular form." Copies could then be made from the copper plate "without the slightest chance of an erratum [notice] being required."

HOLLERITH AND THE 1890 CENSUS

The first really successful data processing machine mixed the abstruse and theoretical of Babbage with the down-to-earth practicality of a railroad conductor punching a kind of ticket largely forgotten today. As Herman Hollerith recalled of the initial inspiration for the electronic tabulating devices he designed for the 1890

Census:

> I was travelling in the West and I had a ticket with what I think was
> called a punch photograph . . . the conductor . . . punched out a
> description of the individual, as light hair, dark eyes, large nose, etc.

From this evolved a punch card that recorded twenty-six personal characteristics (age, sex, race, health, country of birth, literacy, employment, and so on) as well as state, county, and city of residence of the 62 million Americans counted in the Census of 1890.

Use of automation came at a critical time. When preparations were begun for the 1890 Census, manual tabulation of returns from 1880 still had not been completed. The census process was overwhelmed by a burgeoning population coupled with an increasingly broader range of characteristics to measure—a need to know more about "us." Facing a potentially staggering crisis, the U.S. Census Office declared a competition for a mechanical tabulation system to replace the manual counting that had been used since 1790. Herman Hollerith, an engineer who had worked for the Census Office after graduating from Columbia University, was the easy winner with his punch-card electric tabulating machine— "an interesting alliance of the abstract and concrete" (*Scientific American*, 1890).

Tabulation of the census with Hollerith's equipment essentially involved two functions: converting handwritten census reports from the field onto punch cards, then recording data from the cards using a tabulator. The first was a relatively simple punch procedure. The second was more sophisticated, making use of electricity from storage batteries in the basement. The tabulator looked like a rolltop desk minus the roll, its upright section in back faced with clocklike dials. There were four rows of dials, of ten each. On the desktop was a device into which the punch card was inserted. A handle mechanism with spring-loaded pins was then pressed down on the card. Wherever there was a hole punched in the card, the pin penetrated to make an electrical contact with a tiny cup of mercury in the base of the press. Each cup was wired to a corresponding dial, making electrical contact and causing a hand on the dial to register one unit each time the handle was pressed. Since each dial registered up to 9,999 units, cards could be tabulated in quick succession up to that number, at which time totals for all cards in that group were written down by hand—so much for the

Various views of Herman Hollerith's tabulating machinery for the 1890 federal census took up the entire front page of one issue of *Scientific American* that year. In the upper right is one of the punch cards Hollerith designed for the system. It was the immediate forerunner of the data processing punch card of the twentieth century. Other views show how cards were punched with incoming census data and then tabulated automatically. (*Scientific American,* August 30, 1890)

automation part of it—and the counters reset to zero and the process started over again with a new batch of cards. By later-day standards, it was a primitive system. But what was accomplished was figuratively as well as literally electric. Said *Electrical Engineer* magazine in 1891: "This apparatus works [as] unerringly as the mills of the gods, but beats them hollow as to speed."

This first-ever use of automatic electrical tabulation in the workplace created a need for a new kind of skilled employee. So far none existed; but there were many interested, once word got around. There was a certain fascination in doing something no one had done before. And there was also the allure of "electrical tabulation": It looked like an easy way to make a living. Many of those who had clamored for jobs found out, however, that electric tabulating involved a lot of constant repetition. It was nowhere nearly as exciting as thought. Boredom set in. One woman curtly told the superintendent of the census, "Mr. Porter, I'm going home. It is no fun here." Supervisors found that workers were spending considerably more time than usual reading in the rest room. The draconian solution was to have toilet seats wired to a dynamo, and

when someone was suspected of sitting there too long—zap!

The hiring of workers for census tabulation coincided more or less with Christopher Sholes's reflection, shortly before his death, that the typewriter he invented would enable women more easily to earn a living. So too the electric tabulator—more easily than men, as it turned out. It was found that male clerks could tabulate about 32,000 cards a day while women, on average, could do 47,000. The record of 80,000 in one day was set by a female clerk.

The Hollerith tabulator caught the attention of the public. Newspaper and magazine stories heralded its accomplishments. It was generally known that tabulation of the Census of 1880 was far behind schedule, and that the 1890 was being done in record time, and the reason was obvious. The "Hollerith System," further refined, was used again for the 1900 Census, affirming that a new age had indeed arrived—an age anticipating the revolution of "the personal equation" that would eventually come with computerization. As *Scientific American* summed it up in 1902:

> The machine has been adapted to this [census] work and made to take the place of the erring eye, the faulty memory, or the careless hand to such an extent that to-day the Census Office presents the appearance and busy hum of a vast machine shop rather than that of a great counting-house. Electricity has lent its expedition and subtle force to supplement human service, and the clerical work, largely emancipated from the errors of the personal equation, is brought under the control of physical laws.*

No other milestone of such magnitude would come to public attention until ENIAC almost half a century later. Yet ENIAC and others in its wake—notably UNIVAC (Universal Automatic Computer), which took over census tabulating in 1951, as well as the IBM 1401 of 1959, the first mass-production computer, and subsequent computers for business and institutional use—were mostly "out of public view . . . tucked away in corporate offices," as *U.S. News & World Report* observed in 1976. But not for long,

---

*Among the first major customers for Hollerith's tabulating machines were railroads. Other nations also bought them for census use, beginning with Canada and Austria in 1891 and later Czarist Russia. In 1896 Hollerith formed the Tabulating Machine Company, which, after several mergers, became IBM.

as *U.S. News* went on to point out: "Every corner of society is going to feel the computer's impact. Hardly a facet of American life will be left untouched in the age of the computer now taking shape."

FROM ENIAC TO BRAINIAC

Little by little, in various ways, awareness of computers had been growing. For millions of Americans, their first glimpse of a computer (and only glimpse, for the time being) was of one actually in operation on television, election night 1952. While rival networks settled for lower-tech (at NBC, a compact computer known as Monrobot) or no-tech (at ABC, just an old-fashioned blackboard), CBS unveiled one of the first Remington Rand UNIVACs in order to forecast election results as the polls closed.

For millions of Americans, it was also their first experience with computer glitch. Or so it seemed. Shortly after 9:00 P.M., CBS reporter Charles Collingwood was to announce UNIVAC's prediction. Would it be Dwight D. Eisenhower or Adlai Stevenson? Recent polls forecast a close vote—Eisenhower leading, but nothing like a landslide. Just before going on the air, UNIVAC divulged to CBS and Remington Rand that its on-air prediction was going to be a landslide for Eisenhower. Wary in light of the polls, company officials told UNIVAC to go back to work and recalculate. The result was that UNIVAC, once on the air, got stage fright, then suddenly stopped working. A puzzled Collingwood told viewers, "I don't know. I think that UNIVAC is probably an honest machine—a good deal more honest than a lot of commentators who are working and he doesn't think he's got enough to tell us anything yet." When it turned out UNIVAC had been right in the first place—Eisenhower indeed won by a landslide—CBS explained that to have erred was human, and it wasn't the computer's fault.

On the motion picture screen, five years later, ENIAC became EMMARAC, or Emmy for short, a computer-like electronic brain in the romantic comedy *Desk Set* (1957), starring Spencer Tracy and Katharine Hepburn. In 1961, there was *The Honeymoon Machine,* a comedy in which a computer aboard a Navy ship was used in a
164 clandestine attempt to break the bank at a gambling casino. Then

there was Hal, the humanlike, paranoid talking computer in the motion picture *2001: A Space Odyssey* (1968). Movies such as these took advantage of the public's hazy perception of computers for comic and dramatic effect, but they also built awareness of what was just around the corner.

Meanwhile, the computer as an educational toy was making its appearance long before the home computer was even dreamed of, further emphasizing how computers largely entered the mainstream of American life through the young rather than their elders. There were two of them, in fact, in the 1962 catalog of toymaker-par-excellence F. A. O. Schwarz in New York:

> ANALOG COMPUTER. (12 yrs. up)—Teaches electronics and mathematics . . . memory panels and audio indicator with 3-transistor amplifier solve puzzles and mathematical problems quickly and with ease. $29.95

> BRAINIAC LABORATORY (12 yrs. up)—A miniaturized "electric brain" with real problem solving abilities can be built with this fascinating construction kit. 64-page illustrated manual and materials provided to build 50 different reasoning machines and even a digital computer. Machines, completely safe, are easily assembled with nuts and bolts—no soldering required. $18.95

Other science kits in the same catalog included an Advance Electronics Lab ("over fifty fascinating experiments"), a Transistor Radio Kit, a Transistor Transmitter Kit ("broadcasts can be received on any closeby standard home radio"), a Solar Power Electricity Lab (thirty experiments using solar power), and an Astroscope (for launching a miniature satellite above a miniature globe).

In reality, the impact of the computer on daily life was already there by 1976 but often not recognized for what it was. Computers in the form of microprocessors were often lurking about unknown to those using them—for example in the new Singer sewing machine, which used a minicomputer to provide better control and a greater variety of stitching. Amana's Touch-Matic kitchen range had one too, unbeknownst to the average housewife. Other everyday uses of computerization at that time included: controlling traffic lights; helping police to identify fingerprints; and devising video replays at Boston's Fenway Park. Libraries—especially at the college and university level—were beginning to explore the use of computers to replace bulging card catalogs, following the lead of the nation's largest, the Library of Congress, which in 1976 was processing new books using bar codes that could be read electronically.

Bar codes generally were just coming into use in 1976. The Universal Product Code, or UPC, at the checkout counter, represents perhaps the most widespread of all interactions between the individual and the computer. Some consumers at first objected because the price usually no longer appeared on the item; but the UPC has since become so much a part of modern life that it isn't even thought of as an example of computer technology.

But the real revolution was a computer not for the grocery store or the corporate headquarters or the Census Bureau but, as a 1977 headline in the *New York Times* put it: COMPUTERS FIND A HOME (YOURS). What made the revolution practical was reducing the computer both in size and price. As the use of vacuum tubes, the mainstay of ENIAC, gave way to transistors in the late 1950s, size decreased dramatically. Far more dramatic was the development of integrated circuits (the various electronic components, once including vacuum tubes and later transistors, implanted on a chip of a semiconductor, typically silicon). *U.S. News & World Report* explained it in 1976 by saying that a microprocessor "the size of a half stick of gum . . . can provide as much calculating power as the giant room-size computer of a decade ago."

Soon barely the size of a fingernail, the microprocessor was first encountered by many people, perhaps most, as the pocket calculator—in retrospect, a simple, easy-to-grasp introduction to something of what the computer was all about. Pocket calculators at first sold for hundreds of dollars but the price dropped, eventually to as little as a couple of dollars. Sales of handheld electronic calculators went from a few hundred thousand in 1971 to an estimated 20 million in 1976.

THE FIRST PC

The real impact of the microprocessor, however, was to make practical the personal computer. Generally acknowledged as the first popular one was the Altair 8800, which appeared in 1975 and was cheap enough to be accessible to anyone with the inclination to assemble it (it came in kit form and the primary tool was a soldering iron). But those two essential means of interacting with the computer so taken for granted today—the keyboard and monitor—weren't part of it. The Altair worked by flipping switches. Its limitations notwithstanding, here was the computer that had once been "tucked away in corporate offices" made into something for the home. So was its price. Honeywell had tried a home computer that went on the market in 1969 for $10,600. Although the price included a two-week course in programming, few Honeywells were bought. The Altair sold for $387.

By 1976, other small personal computers were beginning to appear, and there were now estimated to be as many as 15,000 in use in America. The Apple II, the most successful of the first wave of PCs, arrived in 1977, selling for $1,195. Less expensive, at Radio Shack, was a setup including keyboard, microprocessor, monitor, and cassette recorder for $599. Monitors and keyboard were becoming standard. Whatever the equipment and whatever the use, the computer revolution was on. A sure sign of it: You could buy a computer at Macy's or from the Montgomery Ward catalog.

Of course, the computer was still a mystery to most people. The writer of a *New York Times* article on home computers in 1977 thought it necessary to explain software: "What's software? With a phonograph you need a record. With a home computer, you need software. To play Beethoven's Ninth, you put on the record of Beethoven's Ninth. To get your computer to figure out your income tax, you give it the income tax program. The problem is, there aren't many ready-made programs on software around yet." That would change, and software programs would abound. Meanwhile, computer manufacturers sought to allay fears. Timex Sinclair, which claimed to have the world's largest-selling personal computer in the early 1980s, reassured new owners in its 1982 user's manual: "You shouldn't be afraid of the computer. You are smarter than it is. So is your parakeet, for that matter. You will make mistakes as you learn. The computer will not laugh at you." Some dealers explained that there was an ultimate fail-safe: If everything went wrong, you could always pull the plug.

The personal computer, 1977. As shown here, it had six separate parts, including a monitor and keyboard and user-supplied cassette recorder for storing data. A printer was not yet a common accessory. The small placard over the monitor reads, "To err is human, to really foul things up requires a computer"–a sentiment undoubtedly shared by many an early (and later) computer user. (Library of Congress, Prints & Photographs Division, *U.S. News & World Report* Magazine Collection)

The personal computer, 1982. Digital Equipment Corp. In five years, a perceptible trend toward compactness. (New York Public Library Picture Collection)

Once people and their computers got plugged in to each other, what did people do with them? Many bought them for video games. What has come to be known as the video (or electronic) game—like the pocket calculator—was a use of a microprocessor application as an introduction to the personal computer. Video games began to appear as coin-operated amusements in video arcades in the early 1970s and quickly became popular, especially with young people. The first video game for use at home was *Odyssey,* which was announced by the Magnavox Company in the spring of 1972 and went on sale in September of that year. Once its computerized master control was plugged in, the family television set became an electronic Ping-Pong table, football field, tennis court, or hockey rink, or even a game of "Simon Says" for toddlers. It was hardly inexpensive at $99.95, but it sold briskly; in the first month, some 9,000 sets were bought in southern California alone. One father in San Bernardino explained that, "It keeps the kids quiet, so I couldn't afford not to buy it." An arcade game called *Pong* (Atari, Inc.) that followed became an immediate sensation in cocktail lounges, bars, pizza parlors, hotel lobbies, and train stations, showing broad social acceptance. A version for the home went on the market in 1974. In coming years there were such sensations as *Space Invaders* (1978) and *Pac-Man* (1980). Popularity of the former was struck home by the *New England Journal of Medicine* in 1981 when it reported a new malady, "Space Invaders Wrist." By 1983, video games were the principal use of a home computer and the major incentive for buying one. Either as software used in a home computer or as a console attached to a television set, video games are a huge business today. Many people would rather play electronic games than watch television or go to the movies: In 1999, video game software/hardware sales in the United States totaled $8.9 billion compared with $7.3 billion for movie box-office receipts. Games simulate space travel, war action, adventure, sports, auto racing, mystery plots, and countless other kinds of situations and challenge motor skills as well as mental coordination by the use of a joystick or other form of control.

Meanwhile, there were other uses—more practical ones, some people thought—for the home computer as it evolved in the late 1970s and early 1980s. A Personal Electronic Transactor marketed

HOW TO SET UP A HOME COMPUTER (1982)

The PC revolution began with the $387 Altair 8800, followed by a Sinclair PC in kit form for just under $100. In 1982, the Timex Sinclair T/S 1000 was said to be the world's best selling computer. Yet home computers were still so unusual the user manual went to great pains to make the new owner feel comfortable.

GETTING STARTED

Welcome to the world of computing. . . .

We want to assure you that:

1. You will enjoy computing.

2. You will find it easy as well as enjoyable.

3. You shouldn't be afraid of the computer. You are smarter than it is. So is your parakeet, for that matter.

4. You will make mistakes as you learn. The computer will not laugh at you. Your mistakes will not do any harm to the computer. You can't break it by pushing the "wrong" button.

5. You are about to take a giant step into the future. Everyone will soon be using computers in every part of their daily lives, and you will have a head start.

The T/S 1000 was basic. There was no monitor; the manual explained how to hook it up to a television set. Another essential was a tape cassette recorder, since the T/S 1000 had no means of storing, let alone directly accessing, data. The manual suggested a recorder with a counter to "help you find programs on your cassettes." Potential uses included "answering your telephone . . . watering your lawn."

User Manual, Timex Sinclair 1000. Timex Computer Corporation, Waterbury, Conn., 1982. (Smithsonian Institution) by Radio Shack could teach languages and mathematics as well as answer, make, and log telephone calls—and play games. Many people used computers for personal and household business.

Word processing today is one of the principal uses of a home computer, for everything from a short report for school to the manuscript for this book. It was coming into use in the mid-1970s but was still primarily something for the workplace. Some idea of the speed of assimilation of the computer since then is evident in looking at a definition of word processing as it was understood in 1978: "Word processing is the big buzzword right now. . . . What, in fact, is word processing? Essentially, it is a means of speeding up an organization's communications process through the integration of technology, people, and procedures. Dictation, by one of several means, is funneled into the word processing center. There, a typing specialist makes a rough transcript on an automatic typewriter, which simultaneously records the material on a magnetic tape, a magnetic card, or a paper punch tape." It is a curiously archaic definition for so relatively recent a date. Paper punch tape seems as antiquated as Herman Hollerith's census tabulator. Yet that very juxtaposition of definition compared with what is understood to be word processing today reaches to the core of the phenomenon that is the computer revolution. The "5,000 to 15,000" home computers estimated to have been in use in 1976 have multiplied by galactic proportions. In 2000, by one estimate there were 161 million computers in the United States (out of 557 million worldwide).*

THE SIMPLIFYING OF COMPLEXITY

Paradoxically this most wondrous of contrivances is arguably the most complex to use. No form of consumer technology has ever been as challenging to learn. And yet, people do learn it. The computer has been so assimilated into society that using one is doing what comes naturally. The "connect the dots" approach to most of what one does on screen—this step dictating that step—goes a long

---

*The estimate of 161 million computers (not exclusively PCs) is from *Time Almanac*, 2000, p. 554.

way in explaining it. So does assimilation of earlier technology. If the computer had inexplicably arrived on the scene, say, in 1876, it would have been so baffling as to have had no chance of acceptance other than among mathematicians and engineers. The absorption of other simpler technology clearly paved the way: the typewriter with its "computer-like" keyboard and indeed the very mode by which we interact with it . . . the telegraph and telephone, by which we got accustomed to speaking and writing from afar . . . television, by which we got used to having a brightly lighted screen communicate with us . . . simpler contrivances like pocket calculators, which, as the price plummeted, found their way into almost every pocket. These and other similar advances of technology helped hugely to make it possible for so complex, so inherently baffling a device as the home computer to have more than 80 million Americans who claim to be able to use it.

Even so, it wasn't actually all that easy. The computer first had to be accepted as a part of everyday life and then had to be learned. In 1976, there was still that perception of the computer as Big Brother. *U.S. News & World Report* in July 1976 found that there were "a lot of obstacles that stand in the way of any unbridled love affair with the computer. People continue to resent the feeling of depersonalization that hits the individual when he is classified as a number, and they fear threats to privacy that go with the growth of large computer banks."

Even in 1984, as MIT sociologist and psychologist Sherry Turkle observed in *The Second Self: Computers and the Human Spirit:* "Computers call up strong feelings, even for those who are not in direct contact with them. People sense the presence of something new and exciting. But they fear the machine as powerful and threatening. They read newspapers that speak of 'computer widows' and warn of 'computer addiction.' "

Meanwhile there was that intimidating challenge of having to contend with this brainy device by actually going head-to-head with it. It was a process that tried the patience of otherwise normal and perspicacious people. In 1982, senior writer Elizabeth Peer of *Newsweek,* a computer novice, told of trying out an upscale Apple III ($8,000) to see how someone would fare without special

instruction. Although she eventually got the hang of it, the ordeal of self-doubt had to be endured first. She began having words with the machine. "Aw, com'on," she would plead; then, "Dammit, I did exactly what you said." "Finally," she wrote "unable to contain my outrage, I shouted a command that Apple III is anatomically unable to obey and then, remembering that computers have no ears, took to the keyboard. '— you,' I typed furiously, slamming the return button to provoke a reply. What I got is what I probably deserved. '?SYNTAX ERROR,' replied Apple III, haughtily."

On-the-job training in the office, workshops, courses of study, help from a friend: these were the key for many. And most important of all: learning the computer in school. We have seen a remarkable parallel between the assimilation of the typewriter in the late nineteenth century and the computer in the late twentieth. "The typewriter has become a necessity of modern civilization," said *Education* magazine, June 1892. "Were it possible, I would have every pupil take a course in typewriting before graduating from school," said the principal of the public schools in Polo, Illinois, about the same time. The analogy, however, breaks down in another respect. No kid of the time, so far as is known, ever asked for an 1890s typewriter for Christmas. No kid in 1900 likely rushed home from school to play with the family typewriter. The typewriter was of enormous significance, but not of enormous allure—not of the sort that has made kids and computers such natural friends. Yet new things do fascinate children. It could be seen in the "electric toys" (probably magnetic gadgets of some sort) that came out only a few years after the invention of the telegraph and toy telephones that appeared on the market by 1883, before very many older people had real ones. It could be seen in the early days of radio when everything later said about kids and computers could be heard about the wonders of wireless:

The young man or boy who takes it up as a hobby becomes more and more interested [and] acquires a valuable education. . . . One man wrote us saying: "I don't know the first thing about wireless; I am just ordering these few things for my boys. . . . My boys talk Radio all day—and dream it all night, I guess. . . . They certainly get a lot of amusement and good, sound and useful knowledge out of their work. Their radio outfit is the best investment I ever made." (*The Wireless in the Home*, 1922)

Change wireless to computer in the above and it works equally as well. Probably the greatest groundswell in computer use came from young adults and older children, who naturally have a high receptivity to new things, and quickly gained the advantage, over their elders, of having had computer instruction in school, often as early as kindergarten.

"The computer is a machine that brings out the kid in all of us," wrote Ted Nelson in *Science Digest* in 1978: ". . . kids get turned on to computers by the excitement of being a part of what's happening . . . by the sense of mastery, the same excitement of control that comes with learning to drive a car or swim . . . [and because kids] love to make things happen." In 1979 children in the San Francisco area could lease time on small computers for $2.25 an hour. Some kids played host at birthday parties at the Marin Computer Center, Marin County, California, treating guests to free computer time. A nineteen-year-old named Evan Katz explained to *Science Digest* in 1982 that "Kids have no fear of computers at all—it hasn't been ingrained in them. People who've grown up with the computer have a totally different attitude toward it."

Children as young as four were taking to the computer as easily as toy ducks to bath water. "They feel so comfortable with the machines that they offer to teach baffled adults how to use them," observed *Newsweek* in 1981. The magazine looked in on a five-year-old drawing trucks and airplanes on the screen of her computer at the Lamplighter School in Dallas, and quoted her as crowing, "See how easy? You can really make it do a lot."

"A kid's whole life is set up for experimenting," explained Sandra Hanna, educational programs director at a family theme park in Pennsylvania, as reported in *Science Digest* in 1982. The park had sixty Apple II computers for kids to use in the company of their parents. Parents tended to hang back and let the kids go at it, she said; "Then, after the kids have taken the risks of making mistakes and the parents have learned by watching, parents move the kids aside and take over." Children aren't put off by programming symbols that seem illogical to adults. "Kids aren't mad when asked

to do something for no apparent reason, they're used to it," commented Mary-Alice White, director of the electronic learning laboratory at Columbia University Teachers College, in *Science Digest;* "In much of life they're asked to do things that don't seem to make sense."

Kids had a big head start over most of their elders. Some school systems were using computers for instructional purposes in the 1960s. One of the first was the Philadelphia public school system, which began computer-assisted instruction for several hundred students at five schools in 1966. By 1976, computer instruction was an integral part of the curriculum for some 70,000 students at thirty-two schools. Today kids from age three up have their own software to use in the family computer (or their own PC, in many cases) that combines fun with learning.

In 1971, the National Association of Secondary School Principals embarked on a nationwide survey of how many and in what way schools were using computers, then sharing the data with the many that were not. Use of computers in education increased substantially during the 1970s. By 1979, a third of the nation's 30,000 high schools had computer education; and it was predicted that virtually all would within five years.

At the college level, computers caught on quickly, both as an aid to instruction and as preparation for a career. Dartmouth College president John G. Kemeny explained that the computer, as an instructor, "has the infinite patience that the teacher doesn't have to continue a drill." At Dartmouth in 1979, more than 90 percent of all students graduating had a fundamental knowledge of computers, and more than half the faculty was incorporating computer work into regular course assignments. Kemeny, before assuming the presidency, was chairman of the mathematics department and took the position that all students, not just those in math, computer science, engineering, or physics, should have a working knowledge of computers.

It was during the 1980s that classroom use of computers really accelerated. A "frenzy," said *Newsweek* in 1982. Pressure came especially from parents. As *Newsweek* observed, "Even parents who know nothing about computers tend to fear that their children will be unemployable if they haven't mastered computer technology."

In 1981, computers were being used in an estimated 18.2 percent of America's public schools. By 1991, the total was 98.4 percent.* By the mid-1990s, the educational process had spawned a whole generation that was both computer-savvy and computer-crazy. A vast part of the population, primed for even broader and more sophisticated use of their IBMs and Macintoshes, Dells and Packard Bells, was ready to wave in the next phase of the computer revolution, the Internet.

THE INTERNET

The Internet is a phenomenon of modern times. Nothing like it existed before. And yet, as an imaginative reaction to the wonders of earlier technology, especially the telephone, it can be seen germinating long before its flowering. Just as we can find in acceptance of earlier technology, especially the typewriter, an unsuspected preparation for the computer era, so can we look back, even as far as the 1870s, and find both conceptions and primitive applications presaging the Web of today.

The wonders of the telephone triggered the imagination. One of those caught up in the wondering was the noted French caricaturist, Albert Robida, in whose mind and pen resided one of the most extraordinary imaginations of the later nineteenth century. Robida's contemplations of *La guerre au XXe siècle* (1883), for example, included remarkably accurate predictions of twentieth-century submarine and air warfare. But his imaginary *téléphonoscope*, foretelling both television and the Internet, is what interests us here. Robida unveiled it in *Le Vingtième Siècle* (c. 1883) and *La vie électrique*, a separately titled work that was published as Part Four of *Le Vingtième Siècle*. Robida's drawings showed his *téléphonoscope* functioning remarkably like a home computer using the Internet. For example, it could be used to receive the news of the day, to shop for clothes at home, and even to take a course of instruction in mathematics at home (see illustrations). In other cases, the *téléphonoscope* worked like a television. One drawing shows madame in her boudoir watching late at night. All this, in the mid-

---

Statistical Abstract of the United States, 1993, 165.

Intuiting the Internet: As conceived by Albert Robida, c. 1883: Shopping for clothes (A) and taking a course in mathematics at home (B) via *téléphonoscope,* and getting the latest news via *journal téléphonique* (C). (Robida, *Le Vingtième Siècle,* Paris, [1883]). (D) Newark, New Jersey, 1912: "A quiet evening at home with The Telephone Herald." Subscribers received a fixed schedule of news, weather, music, stock quotes, sports, theater, and fashion news, and information on sales at local stores. Unlike the Internet, it wasn't interactive—though as an early user noted, a way of "expressing disapproval of bad news is to hang up the receivers, tho if circumstances warranted he might slam them against the wall." (*Literary Digest,* March 16, 1912).

1880s—but only on Robida's drawing board. Robida, almost totally forgotten today, was best known in his own time not for his prognostications of the future but as an antiquarian and author of charmingly illustrated works about French history and culture. He died in 1926.

The phonograph, meanwhile, inspired a concept curiously like a modern CD-ROM. Wrote Philip G. Hubert Jr. in 1889 in *Atlantic Monthly:* "I really see no reason why the newspaper of the future should not come to the subscriber in the shape of a phonogram [a cylindrical wax recording]. It would have to begin, however, with a table of contents, in order that one might not have to listen to a two hours' speech upon the tariff questions in order to get at ten lines of a musical notice. But think what a music critic might be able to do for his public! He might give them **177** whole arias from an opera or movement from a symphony, by way of proof or illustration." Hubert was music critic of the *New York Evening Post*.

About this same time there was an actual application of the telephone line for a use comparable to the Internet. This was the *Telefon-Hirmondo* (literally, telephonic news-teller), which opened in Budapest in 1893. As reported first by the *New York Sun* and reprinted in *Scientific American* in 1895:

THE TELEPHONE NEWSPAPER

The telephone newspaper . . . has 6,000 subscribers, who receive the news as they would telephone messages. . . . Within the houses long, flexible wires make it possible to carry the receiver to the bed or any other part of the room. The news is not delivered as it happens to come in, but is carefully edited and arranged according to a printed schedule, so that the subscriber at any time knows what part of the paper he is going to hear. It begins with the night telegrams from all parts of Europe. Then comes the calendar of events for the day, with the city news and the lists of strangers at the hotels. After that follow articles on music, art, and literature. . . . To fill up the time when no news is coming in, the subscribers are entertained with vocal and instrumental concerts.

The Telefon-Hirmondo was the inspiration of Theodore Puskas, a Hungarian-born entrepreneur who came to the United States about 1877 looking for telephone equipment and became associated with Thomas Edison. Recognizing the value of Puskas's contacts in Europe as well as his interest in electricity, Edison made Puskas his European agent for the phonograph and the Edison version of the telephone. Sometime after this Puskas returned to Hungary and established his Telefon-Hirmondo. It grew to include 15,000 subscribers, including Emperor Franz Josef. Subscribers were connected by telephone wire with a central exchange. In the home was a pair of receivers, typical of a telephone of the time, that one held to one's ear. News was provided at regular intervals, or by breaking into other programs with bulletins. Besides general news one could receive stock market reports, sports news, music, theatrical reviews, children's concerts, instruction in foreign lan-

guages, and even occasional live transmissions from theaters. In a further respect did the Telefon-Hirmondo nearly presage the Internet. Although it apparently never came about, there was at one point a proposal to attach a phonograph to the telephone receiver "in such a way that the first sound over the wire would start the phonograph, which would then record the news, and make it available for the subscriber at his convenience."

Getting news "while it was actually happening" was what most impressed many observers about the Telefon-Hirmondo. This was before radio had come into use, and keeping up with the news meant waiting for the daily newspaper to arrive after whatever it was *had already happened*. Now in Budapest, you could get the news at home almost as it was happening. As *Living Age* recounted it in 1903: "Probably there are few who would be so rash as to aver that the capital of Hungary ranks as one of the most progressive and up to date cities in the world; yet this city is setting an important example, inasmuch as one of its intelligencers publishes information of an event while it is actually happening—not as quickly as possible after it has occurred."

While visiting in Hungary, Manly M. Gillam, an American advertising executive and former newspaper editor, discovered the Telefon-Hirmondo and sensed that it had at least as much potential in the United States. On his return home, he obtained American rights and organized the United States Telephone Herald Company, which, by early fall 1911, had secured rights to operate in New Jersey. With assistance from an engineer recruited from Budapest, it set up operation in Newark. By the middle of November there were more than a thousand customers signed up, including a department store and a restaurant. The charge for service was five cents a day. Programming began at 8:00 A.M. and continued until 10:30 P.M. and included news, weather, stock market reports, news of sales at local stores, fashion notes, sports, stories for children, and music and vaudeville.

Although the Telephone Herald had 2,500 subscribers by early 1912, only half could actually be supplied with service because of the limitations of equipment. Financial woes piled up. The company's liabilities were placed at $12,000 against assets of $8,000. Eleven employees who went unpaid filed suit for back wages. By the beginning of March 1912, as announced in *Editor and Publisher* magazine, the Telephone Herald had suspended service. The Telefon-Hirmondo of Budapest was still in operation in 1918, but the future of any such enterprise was doomed by the ascendancy of radio. With the coming of broadcasting after the First World War, who wanted to pay for a service that could be had free of charge just by turning on a radio? Yet basically all that radio was in its earliest days—the daily schedule of news, music, and features—was there first in the pioneering programming of the Telefon-Hirmondo and the Telephone Herald.

Clearly only a few people ever used either the Telefon-Hirmondo or the Telephone Herald (or their British equivalent, the Electrophone Company, founded in 1894, which never had more than 600 subscribers). And not everyone thought they were necessarily such good ideas. A British journal, the *Electrician,* warned of "dangers" in 1892: "It seems to us that we are getting perilously near the ideal of the modern Utopian when life is to consist of sitting in armchairs and pressing a button. It is not a desirable prospect."

But the concept of the telephone newspaper represents only part of what the Internet is all about. What about the Internet in its broader sense, as the information superhighway? Let's look at a remarkable prediction by British author H. G. Wells, probably best known to Americans for his *War of the Worlds.* In 1937, he suggested that, "The time is close at hand when any student, in any part of the world, will be able to sit with his projector in his own study at his or her own convenience to examine *any* book, *any* document, in an exact replica." Wells's technology was microfilm, charted to a new level of refinement. Substitute *computer* for microfilm projector and we have the Internet essentially as we know it today. Wells, who died in 1946, missed seeing how it really could be done.

When it was done, there was a certain "war of the worlds" aspect to it that Wells would have found intriguing. What we know as the Internet originated in 1969 with the Advanced Research Projects Agency (ARPA) of the U.S. Department of Defense as a means of safeguarding communications among key agencies in government, research, and education in the case of catastrophic enemy attack. The first link, inaugurated in December 1969, connected computers at four major universities. As it widened in number of computer sites connected, it became known as ARPANET. During the 1970s it grew slowly but branched out internationally. By 1981, there were still only some 200 computers on-line. Growth remained slow, owing in large part to the complexity of accessing the system—something well beyond practicality for home computer users. In time other smaller computer networks were absorbed, and what was once ARPANET (and then NSFNET, under the auspices of the National Science Foundation) became the Internet. But it was not until 1991 and the development of the World Wide Web—in effect, access made easy for ordinary people—that the Internet began to zoom in popularity: from some 300,000 computers on-line in 1991 to nearly 10 million in just five years. By 1999, by one estimate, there were more than 92 million Internet users just in North America.

PROMISING THE WORLD

Clearly this was also the period when computer use zoomed. Not only were home computers far better, and less costly relative to what they could do, but there was potential usefulness of new magnitude. In 1982, Timex-Sinclair promised a computer "to dial and answer your telephone [and] water your lawn." Front lawn, indeed! The Internet promised the world.

Just as was the case with computers, kids and the Internet turned out to be made for each other. In 1983, exactly a century after Albert Robida and his *téléphonoscope*—while technology was catching up to expectations and the Internet was still barely known except to a relative few—some schoolchildren were asked what they would like computers to do for them. They had it all figured out:

> When I have a computer I hope it will be a computer that tells you how to do certain things and answers you. I hope for my computer to also give me reports on the news so I won't have to buy a paper. —*A sixth grader*

> I would tell it to tell me where to find the prettiest clothes and tell me where to get my hair done. Tell me where the most famous restaurant is in the world.—*A seventh grader.*

In 2000, teenagers were running ahead of the general population in use of the Internet in the United States, with predictions that, within a few years, 72 percent of teens would be on-line versus 56 percent of the general population. Beyond just having easier access, teens use the Internet more. One survey in 2000 found that 28 percent of participating high school students were on-line twenty or more hours a week compared with 16 percent of the adult participants. Teens, who like to feel connected anyway, were using e-mail and chat rooms most of all. But they had great expectations about everything on-line. "I think the Internet will be the basis for almost everything that needs to be done," said one sixteen-year-old at Boston Latin School. A West Coast student put it another way: "The Internet will replace phones, answering machines, television and libraries."

For some people, use of the Internet—like Robida's imaginary *téléphonoscope* browsing for clothes at home—has been replacing traditional methods of shopping, even for automobiles and insurance. E-business quickly became an Internet phenomenon, so much so that dot-coms—all too often overvalued and under-profitable—went through a severe shaking up in the spring of 2000. As a whole, Internet stocks plummeted 50 percent in value; some had catastrophic losses. *iVillage.com* ("The Women's Network") went from an initial price offering of $24 to a high of $130 and had plunged to $12.16 as of April 20, 2000. Another site, *drkoop.com*, launched by a former surgeon general of the United States, went from an IPO of $9 to a high of $45.75 and then collapsed to $2.50. Right and left, dot-coms became dot-gones. Some, like e-brokerages and travel businesses (airline tickets in particular) proved hardy. Others, like specialty sales outlets (pet food, for example), fell by the e-side.

The Internet now is most widely used for e-mail. In 1998, for the first time, e-mail surpassed hand-delivered mail in volume in the United States. Its soaring popularity literally took e-mail into— or more accurately from—space. When the space shuttle *Endeavor* went into orbit in December 1998, its six astronauts had a laptop that they passed around among themselves, taking turns sending e-mail back to family and NASA officials on Earth. In twelve days they logged 620 messages, an average of eight and a half a day for

each crew member.

As for soaring on Earth: E-mail messages totaled some 300 million a day in the United States in 1995; by 2002, they were predicted to reach 8 billion.

Perhaps especially significant was how e-mail was catching on among older people—the very ones who had been most hesitant about computers in the past. As *New Choices* magazine explained in 1999, "Many users [over fifty] find that e-mail is even handier than the phone for staying in touch with family members. . . . everything from calling family members to researching your genealogy is just a click away. Such convenience is among the many reasons for e-mail's fast-growing popularity." *New Choices,* which is marketed to an over-fifty audience, quoted a seventy-two-year-old retired bookstore owner on Cape Cod in Massachusetts as saying, "My entire family is online. Practically all of my old friends are on, and whenever possible I encourage those who are slow to join to get with it."

As for the overall population, *Business Week* in 1999 explained the snap-snap efficiency of e-mail this way: "Whether for work or for personal correspondence, the 3 billion-plus messages zipping back and forth each day have become the oxygen of the Internet Age. E-mail's convenience, ease, and efficiency are unparalleled. E-mail can let two people transact business like machines calibrating: 'Get it?' 'Got it.' 'Good.' "

As the twenty-first century opened, the Internet was easily the most dynamic new force in society. It had revolutionized communications, changed the way business works, altered everyday living patterns, and spurred an economic boom of unparalleled proportions. Was there a tarnished lining anywhere?

Amid the euphoria, there were those who lamented an erosion of intimacy that seemed linked to communicating by e-mail. U.S. Librarian of Congress James H. Billington was quoted as worrying that e-mail was sparking a decline in the use of language—that handwriting, and even typing, sharpens the message, better informs as to actual content, and imposes some logic and sincerity by its very physical form. "The letter is an artifact and emblem of civilization," said Billington.

Some people pointed to the increasing disparity between the have-computers and the have-nots, calling it the "digital divide."

For example, while computer literacy was a taken-for-granted part of the curriculum in most schools, there were accounts of schools that had no instructional computers at all. *Forbes* magazine in 2000 told of a blue-collar worker in such a school district; he sold his car to buy his son a computer, figuring the two-hour bus ride to work it would mean for him was a reasonable price to pay for his son's future. At home, computer use directly reflected household income. In 2000, in homes with income under $15,000, roughly 7 percent were on-line; where income was greater than $75,000, roughly 75 percent. How to adjust the disparity? Solutions ranged from computer recycling centers (turn in your old one to be refurbished for a poor family) to outright buying every single student his or her own computer (in Maine, just that was proposed for every junior and senior high school student by 2007).

A greater uncertainty—proportionately greater *for* the haves than the have-nots—was a decline in human contact that seems to go with the Internet—THE WEB'S CHILLING TREND, as *Business Week* headlined it in June 2000. It was about a nationwide survey on the social impact of the Internet by Stanford University's Institute for the Quantitative Study of Society. Its key finding: "The Internet promises to have profound effects on the way Americans live."

The survey found that well over half the adult population has access to the Internet at home or in the office. Some 60 percent say they have cut down on television, and about a third indicate they read newspapers less. Some 25 percent of regular users say they are spending less time at social events and talking on the phone, and a like percentage less time shopping in stores; 13 percent say they have less face-to-face social and family contact.

In the opinion of Norman Nie, director of the study, the Internet poses "a powerful isolating technology that undermines our community participation." E-mail, he conceded, gives people a way to stay in touch, but "it's not the same as listening to someone's voice or giving them a hug."

Then there is the question of whether society is getting too dependent on computers generally. In a poll conducted in 2000 by *Popular Science,* more than half of those responding (53 percent) said yes.

On the other hand, e-commerce—shopping and doing business by Internet—is seen as having a beneficial effect on the planet. The Center for Energy and Climate Solutions in 2000 figured that the Internet will save 1.5 billion square feet in retail floor space and 2 billion in office space, cut annual energy needs by 53 billion kilowatt-hours, and reduce by 35 million metric tons the amount of greenhouse gases released into the atmosphere.

THE MAGIC OF THE SCREEN: A MAGIC LANTERN SHOW, 1866
(*Godey's Lady's Book*, New York, January 1866)

PART 3
ENTERTAINMENT

THE MAGIC OF THE SCREEN. How curiously appropriate we first find it coming to light with a device known as the *magic lantern*.

The magic lantern is a real fossil of a thing now, yet in the obvious delight of those watching the show pictured on pages 186 and 187 there is a lure of projected reality no less exciting than for later generations. Then it was an image on muslin stretched over a wooden framework, or even just shown on a light-colored wall. Today there are motion picture screens, television screens, and computer screens to dazzle us.

The increasing dominance of the screen over American life (between the workplace and television, vast numbers of people spend most of their working hours in front of one) is something we will find emphasized in Part 3. Another recurring theme is something Thomas Edison put his finger on without intending to, when he was talking about improvements to the phonograph in 1912. Declared Edison: I will make it "the greatest musical instrument."

What is a musical instrument? A piano? A trumpet? A tin pan, even? Arguably, a musical instrument is a device with which to *create* music. Is turning the crank of a phonograph *creating* music? Edison thought so, proclaiming the phonograph not merely a musical instrument but the greatest instrument of all—"his favorite invention . . . the achievement of which he is proudest."

And there we have a pivotal moment. From then on, as we will see, the application of technology will act exponentially—radio, stereo, television, and so on—so that *production* of entertainment (making music for yourself) is largely superseded by *consumption* of entertainment (turning the crank). We will look briefly at what home entertainment was like before the age of technology. Essentially, you had to do it for yourself, however modest your talents—be it parlor magic, singing, playing the piano, or even banging on a tin pan. That began to change, largely after the Civil War, with such simple technology as the magic lantern, the stereoscope, and the stereopticon.

Since this section focuses on entertainment in and about the home, motion pictures will not be covered. Arbitrarily included here is photography, which might as plausibly be placed under communications; but for most people it is the entertainment value of taking pictures, rather than the communications aspect of photography, that is foremost. Hence its appearance here.

Paradoxically, photography is a form of entertainment that brings out the creativity in people.

CHAPTER ELEVEN

A SUCCESSION OF WONDERS

HOME ENTERTAINMENT

THE ZOETROPE is one of those long-forgotten things that seem so terribly quaint in the age of television and movies. Yet in the later nineteenth century it was sometimes called the "wonder cylinder" for what it could do: in effect, present moving pictures in one's own parlor.

Invented in the mid-1860s, it had a name coined from two Greek words (*zoe*, life, and *tropos*, turning). The zoetrope was a revolving drum through which to watch a succession of images rotating within. It symbolizes the application of technology to home entertainment in a way that began to evolve in the mid–nineteenth century, and as it continues to evolve today in ways unimaginable not long ago—a succession of wonders.

There has always been "home entertainment" of one sort or another, but in earlier times it was generally too simple to be called that. Throughout the colonial period and into the early nineteenth century, while America was still largely an agrarian society, farm and household obligations were so all-enveloping that there was precious little leisure time. Reading the Bible, or perhaps a book or newspaper, or just having a family conversation, generally sufficed for occasional times that could be called leisure. And during the winter months, when the days were short and even candlelight was something of a luxury, there was almost no time for which one needed to *find* something to do.

The advance from the simple to the sophisticated in home entertainment began with the Industrial Revolution and accelerated with an increase in leisure time that came about with shorter working hours, a process that continued well into the twentieth century.

Even in the 1830s, before either of these factors had had much impact, the idea of home enjoyment was taking on a new dimension that reflected a new emphasis on science. A book for young people published in Philadelphia in 1838 titled *Parlour Magic*, for example, included chapters with tricks and experiments based on "Light and Heat," "Gas and Steam," and "Transmutations." In a

The zoetrope, c. 1880: a wonder of the Victorian parlor. As the drum atop the pedestal was spun, looking through slits in the side produced the effect of a motion picture. Zoetropes essentially like this one continued to be produced into the 1940s. (New York Public Library Picture Collection)

sense, the book was serious frivolity. It was intended that the young reader should learn something constructive while entertaining friends. As the preface made clear, *Parlour Magic*'s purpose was "to furnish the ingenious youth with the means of relieving the tediousness of a long winter's or a wet summer's evening . . . to qualify the hero of his little circle to divert and astonish his friends, and, at the same time, to improve himself."

Among the book's 363 tricks and experiments were a considerable number reflecting basic scientific principles. One hinted at photography, which was just around the corner: "Pin-Hole Focus: Make a pin-hole in a card, which hold between a candle and a piece of white paper, in a dark room, when an exact representation of the flame, but inverted, will be depicted upon the paper, and be enlarged as the paper is drawn from the hole."

Seemingly at odds with the book's rather noble purposes was another experiment that, by modern reckoning, was downright dangerous. It was a detailed explanation of how to get, well . . . high—meaning "the very agreeable sensations excited by inhaling" laughing gas. The ingenious youth was instructed to put three or four drams of nitrate of ammonia in crystalline form in a small glass retort and hold it over an alcohol lamp. As the crystals melted, the resulting gas was to be collected in a bladder with a stopcock. Then came the fun.

> Have the person first exhale the atmospheric air from the lungs, and quickly placing the cock in his mouth, you turn it, and bid him inhale the gas. Immediately, a sense of extraordinary cheerfulness, fanciful flights of imagination, an uncontrollable propensity to

> laughter, and a consciousness of being capable of great muscular exertion, supervene.

Just the thing for relieving the tediousness of a long winter's night.

With photography came a new diversion with vast potential for entertainment, in the home and out. Until the Kodak roll-film camera of 1888, taking pictures was primarily for the professional, and then photography became an amateur sensation. Even before this, commercially produced photographs in stereoscopic form became a staple of parlors throughout the country. A parlor without a stereoscope was as rare in the later 1800s as a living room without a television set today. In its original form—using mirrors placed at angles—the stereoscope came into use in England in the late 1830s. But it was its later form, dating to the 1850s, in America as well as England, that made the stereoscope popular. This was the small handheld device with twin lenses for viewing a double-image photograph—or stereo view, one image from a slightly different point of view than the other. When the user held it up at eye level and peered through the twin lenses, the resulting image gave a sense of three dimensions. The first stereo views were produced in America by E. Anthony of New York by 1859. Particularly popular in coming years were Civil War scenes, many Mathew Brady photographs included.

GAMES AND PUZZLES

Meanwhile, mass-produced games and puzzles, utilizing new advances in printing and manufacturing techniques, were also coming into the American home. A notable figure here was a young printer named Milton Bradley, a onetime draftsman who settled in Springfield, Massachusetts, and opened a small lithography firm. Business was bad. One evening, whiling away the time playing a simple game, Bradley hit on an idea: invent a better game that used lithography in its manufacture. That would keep his largely idle press busy and perhaps open up a profitable sideline.

What Bradley created in 1860 he called *The Checkered Game of Life*. It was basically a checkerboard, with eighty-four red and white squares labeled with various periods and conditions of life, from "Success," "Fame" and "Wealth" to "Crime," "Prison," and

"Poverty." Four could play. At each corner of the board was a tee-totum, a device with a wheel on which was inscribed an arrow. The wheel was spun. When it stopped, the number to which the arrow pointed was the number of the square to which that player advanced a small disk. The winner was the first to land on Happy Old Age.

Bradley himself landed on Success, Wealth, and Fame all at the same time. After lithographing his first batch, he went off to New York City to offer the games to merchants. He sold out, went home and printed more, and sold all those, and as many more as he could print. By 1872 the Milton Bradley Company was preeminent in the field. Its catalog for that year still offered the *Game of Life* for one dollar and took pride in noting that it "had greater sale than any other similar game ever published." In its broad assortment of games, puzzles, gadgets, and devices, the 1872 catalog also shows the degree of diversity that was developing in home entertainment in the post–Civil War period, a time of greatly expanding manufacturing capacity in a wide range of consumer goods.

Among them was something new—that wonder cylinder, the zoetrope, the revolving drum through which to observe, in effect, motion pictures. It used a printed paper strip showing images in successive phases of motion (a horse running, boxers boxing). The strip was attached to the inside of the drum, which had vertical slits. As the drum was quickly rotated, the spectator, looking through the slits, could see the action inside as if watching a motion picture, albeit one that was only a matter of seconds in length. The 1872 Bradley catalog explained that the "simple figures printed on strips of paper become animated so that the movements of life are imitated in the most natural manner."

Zoetropes were by no means limited to Bradley; other manufacturers also produced them in considerable quantity. But they largely disappeared with the coming of real motion pictures. Even so, there were zoetropes manufactured at least until the mid-1940s. One produced by Mastercraft Toy Co. of New York in 1945 is on display in the Strong Museum, Rochester, New York.

A related home entertainment device of the later nineteenth century was the praxinoscope, a projecting form of zoetrope. According to a contemporary report, "To make these moving figures visible to a large number of people at one time, the wonder

A SUCCESSION OF WONDERS

cylinder can now be combined with the magic lantern [which] first throws its rays of light through the lens on to the screen, projecting, for example, some landscape or other; part of the light then passes through a prism which projects the light-rays on the moving figures. These reflect them back to the top lens, which throws them on the screen in magnified form, thus enabling the spectators to see the moving figures."

The magic lantern was a relatively simple device by means of which a magnified image was projected on a screen or wall. In England, a device of this kind was known by the end of the seventeenth century. As described in 1696, it was a "small Optical Macheen, that shews by a gloomy Light upon a white Wall, Spectres and Monsters so hideous, that he who knows not the Secret, believes it to be perform'd by Magick Art." This may have been a one-of-a-kind, and such other devices that came into use in England during the eighteenth century remained rare.

The magic lantern became popular in America in the post–Civil War period. Although it could be made to simulate hobgoblins and monsters, its principal use was the same as a modern slide projector—and indeed the magic lantern of the later nineteenth century looked more or less like a projector. A typical one of 1870 sold for $20 to $30 and had a small kerosene lamp as the light source. Slides were readily available. T. H. McAllister, of New York, a major supplier of optical equipment, offered a wide variety in its 1870 catalog. The largest single category was the Civil War. There was a seemingly limitless selection of images of battles, skirmishes, camp life, soldier life, and portraits of prominent officers. Other sets included "Views in the Holy Land," "The Ten Commandments," "The Drunkard's Career and End," "Scenes from Cooper Novels," and "Illustrations to Milton's *Paradise Lost.*" These sets were hardly inexpensive, ranging in price from $16.50 to $33 (the latter more than the price of the magic lantern). Individual slides offered by McAllister were typically priced at $2.75. But there were other suppliers, and prices varied. Slides could also be borrowed or traded.

Another, and often considerably more expensive, optical device of the time was the stereopticon—in effect, a projecting stereoscope. It could be used as something of a double magic lantern to produce a stereo image on a screen; or by manipulating left and right light sources separately, it could create such special effects as dissolving one image into another. The term stereopticon, however, appears also to have included simple large-scale projectors of the kind *Frank Leslie's Illustrated Newspaper* featured on its front page shortly after the presidential election of 1872. A full-page illustration showed a "stereopticon" projecting election results on a giant rooftop screen at Broadway and Twenty-Second Street in New York, with a huge crowd gathered in the streets to watch. In the century to come, an electrically operated signboard in Times Square would serve the same purpose.

Whether the show in one's parlor was produced by a simple magic lantern or a top-of-the-line stereopticon, the modern home of the later nineteenth century was doing away with using just a light-colored wall. Something new was appearing that has remained in one form or another to the present, and today is the usual focal point of a living room—a viewing screen. Today it is television; then it was muslin stretched over a wooden framework. In its directions for the stereopticon, McAllister instructed: "The first thing to be done is to put up the Screen. The Screens are made with a wide hem, and with loops placed two feet apart all around the four sides of the Screen. By these loops the Screen can be attached to a wooden frame." Screens of the same kind could be used with magic lanterns and sold for as little as $8 (a screen of 9 square feet).

Music-producing devices first appeared in the form of the clockwork music box early in the nineteenth century. The first ones were expensive, but by mid-century mass production was making music boxes widely available and highly popular. Selections included excerpts from favorite operas as well as sacred and popular music of the day. But the music box eventually fell victim to the phonograph, and production effectively ended early in the twentieth century.

HANDS (AND FEET) FOR MUSIC

While its manufacture employs a certain degree of technology, the piano would seem to fall outside of what is generally considered here as the application of technology to home entertainment. But let us take a closer look: First, there is relevance in that the piano's demise as a common part of the household was the direct result of technology in entertainment; and second, the piano itself underwent technological evolution to become the mechanical player piano (or piano player; they're different).

The piano as a form of home entertainment goes back to the eighteenth century, but its cost then put it out of reach of all but the most wealthy. Even in 1850 the cost was still formidable. A grand piano cost anywhere from $700 to $1,000; a square piano (forerunner of the upright) $250 to $500. A skilled craftsman's annual wages at this time ranged from roughly $500 to $1,500.

By 1867 production was increasing, and sales likewise. It was estimated that every working day in America some 112 new pianos were being bought. The numbers did not surprise a writer in *Atlantic Monthly:* "When we consider, that every hotel, steamboat, and public school above a certain very moderate grade, must have from one to four pianos, and that young ladies' seminaries jingle with them from basement to garret (one school in New York has thirty Chickerings), and that almost every couple that sets up housekeeping on a respectable scale considers a piano only less indispensable than a kitchen range, we are rather inclined to wonder at the smallness than at the largeness of the number."

Overall production of some 25,000 pianos a year in the United States in 1867 was second only to England, with an estimated 30,000. American pianos were selling at retail for anywhere from $450 to $1,500. But a good used piano could be had for less than half the original price.

Many of these expensive pianos may have been little played, and perhaps served more as decoration. With increasing proliferation and a market in used pianos there seemed to come something of a transformation. So said *Atlantic Monthly* as it reflected of the piano in 1867: "Cold, glittering, and dumb, it stands among the tasteless splendors with which the wealthy ignorant cumber their dreary abodes—a thing of ostentation merely. . . . But a fool and his nine-hundred-dollar piano are soon parted. The red flag of the auctioneer announces its transfer to a drawing-room frequented by persons capable of enjoying the refined pleasures. Bright and joyous is the scene, about half past nine in the evening, when, by turns, the ladies try over their newest pieces, or else listen with intelligent pleasure to the performance of a master. Pleasant are the informal family concerts in such a house."

By the 1890s, mass production and the coming of the upright model were making the piano generally affordable for middle-class families in America, so much so that by the turn of the twentieth century there were an estimated 1 million pianos in use. Smaller than a grand and suited to the use of more standardized parts, the upright was generally less expensive. And it had the virtue of taking up considerably less space, so that it fit literally, as well as dollar-wise, into middle-class domestic life.

Yet having a piano required not only the dollars to buy it but the dexterity to play it. Anyone could take piano lessons, but not everyone could actually learn to play well. Could technology make up the difference? Could someone devise a machine to do the playing?

A machine literally to sit down in front of the piano, having its own built-in bench, so to speak, and play flawlessly with felt-tipped wooden fingers was a development of the late nineteenth century. It was called a *piano player.* A cabinet somewhat larger in dimensions than the average piano bench, it was meant to be wheeled up to the piano keyboard and set in place so that "fingers" in the device meshed with the keys of the piano. It was pedal-operated, much the same as a parlor organ. As a perforated music roll unrolled, suction generated by the pedals drew air through ports exposed by the perforations. This activated pneumatic valves that forced the "fingers" to "play" their corresponding keys. Where there were multiple perforations, multiple keys would play chords. Levers in front of the cabinet controlled tempo and relative loudness of treble and bass.

"It is bringing into use thousands of pianos which have been silent for many years," explained a 1900 advertisement for the Aeolian Pianola; it is a "piano-player for those who do not play the piano and for those who do." Also for those who were relatively well-off. The Pianola sold for $250; a 1903 Oldsmobile cost $650.

The piano player had fairly brief popularity, although versions of it were made as late as 1931. Coming into use, meanwhile, was

Home entertainment was sometimes less than entertaining, as in this portrayal of a frazzled mother apparently hearing more than just an occasional wrong note. The coming of player pianos made it possible to eliminate wrong notes but also diminished the degree of creativity that the pretechnology era encouraged. (*Our Boys and Girls Monthly*, October 1871)

a *built-in* mechanism to do what the player had done. This is what came to be known as the *player piano*. The first ones were normally pedal-operated, although an electric model could be found as early as 1895. In time electric motors predominated, allowing the listener to sit back and listen without having to rock a foot back and forth. (And with the player piano's demise came the end to such humor of the times as a mother boasting of her child, "You can see she has a great foot for music.")

Player pianos had great popularity during the early twentieth century. Here was a unique application of a simple form of technology going back to the Jacquard loom that was also an inspiration for data processing.

The player piano (or piano player), as opposed to a phonograph, played one's *own* instrument right in one's *own* parlor–live. It was almost as if one were performing oneself. As an early advertisement noted, "With its aid any number of your household may play upon the piano even if he or she literally does not know one note from another." There was never anything like it–nor would there be afterward. On the other hand, there were drawbacks. A piano was

relatively expensive, and it took up space even if an upright model, which virtually all player pianos were (although a piano player worked with a grand as well as an upright). And, of course, a piano, mechanical or otherwise, played only piano music.

Player pianos peaked in popularity in the mid-1920s. More than 200,000 were produced in 1923, and in 1927 fewer than half that many were sold. Between 1927 and 1929 all piano sales dropped off by 40 percent–player pianos by more than 60 percent.

There were now other ways of indulging in one's love of music. The phonograph played music of all kinds and by the mid-1920s had evolved into essentially its modern configuration–disk records, loudspeaker, and electrical operation. Even a greater challenge to the parlor piano was the radio, which was soaring in popularity at just the same time the piano was falling out of favor. And while radio offered music of considerably more diversity–a pop singer, a symphony orchestra, an opera–it had one other huge plus: It was also free.

Early player pianos were usually pedal-operated. An exception was this "electric piano," dated 1895. It could be operated either by a storage battery or by household current, the latter then normally being used only for electric light. Player pianos, more and more commonly electrified, became highly popular in the early twentieth century and then lost favor to the phonograph and radio. (Byrn, *Progress of Invention,* 1900)

CHAPTER TWELVE

WHERE'S THE BAND?

THE PHONOGRAPH

A 1901 ADVERTISEMENT for an Edison phonograph shows a boy, baffled to the point of exasperation, trying to figure out how the music got inside. He is ready to use a hatchet to find out. The caption reads, "Looking for the Band."

It was a clever advertising concept, of course—one that reinforced a perception of realism that seemed remarkable in its day. As primitive as the early phonograph is by modern standards (and indeed as it yet was by its own standards of only a few decades later), it was an extraordinary instance of new technology. Which brings us to an often overlooked point: Until the coming of the phonograph, no one had ever heard a note of music except in the presence of the performer. The phonograph, perhaps more than any other form of consumer technology to date, generated that compliment of incredulity: "How do they do that?"

Disbelief greeted the phonograph at the very outset. Some prominent scientists derided it. There were accusations that Edison was secretly using ventriloquism. A Methodist bishop went to Menlo Park and put the phonograph to a unique test, one the bishop calculated would trip up even the best ventriloquist: He reeled off a list of obscure biblical names that hardly anyone would know how to pronounce. The machine reeled them back, each one correctly.

Once its legitimacy was accepted, the phonograph was greeted with nearly universal adulation. When Edison gave a demonstration for the National Academy of Sciences in Washington, doors had to be taken off their hinges to accommodate the crowds. Edison also played his machine for members of Congress in the Capitol and for President Hayes in the White House. Hayes showed his fascination by keeping the inventor there until three-thirty in the morning. A few years after this, a member of the Electric Club in New York, on hearing a demonstration, proclaimed the phonograph "the most ingenious thing that was ever worked out of the human brain."

It was the phonograph that was responsible for getting Edison the title "Wizard." "Aren't you a good deal of a wizard, Mr.

Edison
PHONOGRAPH
The Acme of Realism

LOOKING
FOR THE BAND

PERFECT REPRODUCTIONS OF SOUND
are obtained by using **Edison Records** and
Genuine Edison Phonographs
Nine Styles.   From $10.00 to $100.00.
Catalogues everywhere.   All dealers.

NONE GENUINE   THIS
WITHOUT   *Thomas A. Edison*   TRADE-MARK
NATIONAL PHONOGRAPH COMPANY,
135 Fifth Avenue, New York,   144 Wabash Avenue, Chicago.
Foreign Dept., 15 Cedar Street, New York,

While no one likely took a hatchet to an early phonograph to find out where the music was coming from, "Looking for the Band" as an advertising slogan reinforced a sense of realism that was in fact remarkable for the time. Until the coming of the phonograph, no one had ever heard a note of music except in the presence of the performer. Today, live music represents only a small portion of all the music that is heard. (*St. Nicholas Magazine,* May 1901. General Research Division, the New York Public Library, Astor, Lenox and Tilden Foundations.)

Edison?" asked a reporter for the New York *Daily Graphic* visiting the inventor in 1878, shortly after the invention became public. "Oh no!" chuckled Edison, "I don't believe much in that sort of thing." But the *Graphic* used wizard anyway, and it stuck. Edison became "The Wizard of Menlo Park" forevermore.

So wonderful was this new device that it set off a chain reaction of imagined wonders. "If words may be converted into electricity and back again into words," suggested *Popular Science Monthly* in March 1878, "what is to hinder their being converted into something more lasting than electricity—something that will endure, so that spoken words may be reproduced in the future exactly as spoken now; that persons, though dead, may yet speak? What is to hinder? Nothing! The thing is already done." *Scientific American* went a step further into the surreal: "We have already pointed out the startling possibility of the voices of the dead being reheard through this device. . . . It is already possible by ingenious optical contrivances to throw stereoscopic photographs of people on screens in full view of an audience. Add the talking phonograph to counterfeit their voices, and it would be difficult to carry the illusion of real presence much further."

Elsewhere there was talk of people using phonograph records to communicate, making written letters obsolete. Speeches could be recorded and sent out, allowing great orators of the day to deliver their silver-tongued rhetoric to audiences far and wide in the same breath. And the most fascinating prospect of all, thought some, was that great singers of the age could be captured on record cylinders and then perform for grateful music lovers who might otherwise never hear them. Edison himself, in *North American Review,* added such other uses as preserving the voices of famous people, having books read aloud, teaching elocution and music, and inserting voices into toys and clocks. Voices of the famous actually recorded included British Prime Minister William Gladstone, Robert Browning, Florence Nightingale, and Sir Arthur Sullivan. Theirs were voices Edison's agent managed to record for demonstration purposes when an improved Edison machine went on sale in England in 1888. Browning recited some of his verses. Sullivan, of Gilbert and Sullivan fame, offered for posterity: "For myself I can only say that I am astonished . . . at the wonderful power you have developed, and terrified at the thought that so much hideous and bad music may be put on record forever."

Terrified, in another way, among early hearers of phonographs were dogs. The somewhat high-pitched, disembodied sound coming from the horn of the player was enough to drive some of them wild. Occasionally, a dog would try to jump into the horn to get at the mysterious, unnatural voice in there. Here and there, people too had uneasy feelings, as if it were the devil making the sound.

But these were exceptions. For the most part, public response was positive. It was only in early November 1877 that information first leaked out in the New York press about a new Edison project—something on the order of what we would call a telephone answering machine—a device that could record a brief telephone conversation and then retransmit the message later by telephone. Hence the somewhat confusing etymology of "phonograph" (Edison coined it from the Greek *phōnē,* sound, and *graphein,* to write). The telephone also was brand-new, and Edison saw great potential in such a device.

Scientific American reported Edison's idea on November 17,

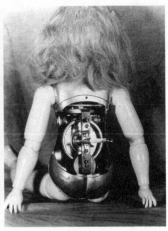

The Edison Talking Doll, c. 1889. The "talking" came from a hand-cranked miniature phonograph using a 3-inch wax cylinder. This one could talk "slow or fast," by how it was adjusted, and could recite the entire verse of "Jack and Jill went up the hill." The Edison Toy Manufacturing Company of Boston, a subsidiary of the Edison National Phonograph Company, began manufacture of talking dolls in 1880 and ceased production in 1890, apparently in the face of increasing competition from European manufacturers. (Smithsonian Institution)

1877. But it was not until the end of the month that Edison had refined it into an actual sketch from which a working model could be constructed. As Edison later described it, ". . . I designed a little machine using a cylinder provided with grooves around the surface. Over this was to be placed tinfoil, which easily received and recorded the movements of the diaphragm." He turned the sketch over to one of his artisans, who promptly told Edison it was absurd. Edison himself had doubts it would work, and some of his staff bet cigars against it. When a brass-and-iron working model was completed and ready for a trial run, Edison hoped at best to hear a couple of words but he gave it twenty-two as a test: the entire four-line first stanza of "Mary Had a Little Lamb," which he personally shouted into a little diaphragm on the device. When he turned the crank to replay it, with some of his staff assembled, the machine astounded them all, not the least Edison, who later wrote that "I was never so taken aback in all my life. Everybody was astonished."

Satisfied that his talking machine really could talk, Edison personally took it to *Scientific American*'s office in New York to demonstrate it. By this time the machine had graduated from the recitation of a nursery rhyme to simulating a brief conversation. As reported in *Scientific American* December 22, 1877:

> Mr. Thomas A. Edison recently came into this office, placed a little machine on our desk, turned a crank, and the machine inquired as to our health, asked how we liked the phonograph, informed us that *it* was very well, and bid us a cordial good night. These remarks were not only perfectly audible to ourselves, but to a dozen or more persons gathered around, and they were produced by the aid of no other mechanism than the simple little contrivance.

Simplicity was a secondary factor that contributed to awe of the phonograph. The device was not merely the "acoustical marvel of the century," observed *Popular Science*, but "as simple as a grindstone . . . as simple as a coffee-mill. . . . By the simple turning of the crank, the machine talks, sings, shouts, laughs, whistles, and coughs, so naturally and distinctly, that the listener can hardly believe his senses, or escape from the suspicion that there is some ventriloquist hocus-pocus about it, or a little fellow concealed somewhere about the arrangement."

Paradoxically, this miniature of sound reproduction came at a time when public performances were going through a "monster"

One of the earliest illustrations of the phonograph. (*Scientific American,* December 22, 1877)

phase—one music festival trying to outdo another for sheer massiveness of sound. The World's Peace Jubilee and International Musical Festival, held in Boston in 1872, promised a chorus of 20,000 trained voices and a grand orchestra of 1,000 skilled musicians, as well as a military band 1,000-strong. All in all, it would be "the Grandest Series of Concerts ever given in the world." A few years earlier a Handel Festival at London's Crystal Palace employed a chorus that numbered 735 each of sopranos and altos and 665 each of tenors and basses. "Monster entertainment" was the phrase for this sort of thing, and it was used unselfconsciously. The percussion section of an orchestra, for example, might have a "monster drum."

At the start there had been delight in imagining the phonograph's possibilities. "Imagine an opera or an oratorio, sung by the greatest living vocalists, thus recorded, and capable of being repeated as we desire," reflected *Scientific American* before the phonograph had even been patented. But trying to squeeze an opera aria, let alone a monster chorus, on a cylinder covered with tinfoil was infinitely beyond what the machine could do.

The simplicity of the first production phonograph, otherwise a virtue, limited what it could do over and above tell about Mary's Lamb or inquire as to the listener's health. It was still as Edison had first envisioned it: a sheet of tinfoil tightly wrapped around a grooved cylinder. As the cylinder rotated, a stylus—reacting to vibrations in a thin diaphragm—recorded the vibration in "hill and dale" fashion (ups and downs) in the foil. The process was then reversed for playback: As the cylinder turned, a stylus turned the ups and downs into vibrations that a diaphragm reproduced as sound.

"SOUNDS OF ALL KINDS"

In 1878, with the help of a group of venture capitalists (the principal stockholders included Alexander Graham Bell's father-in-law), Edison formed the Edison Speaking Phonograph Company and set out to manufacture and market the phonograph. It was still a crude device. Words were hard to distinguish. The tinfoil "record" gave only a minute and a half of performance and could be used only a few times. Nonetheless the public was enthralled. Five hundred machines were used for demonstration around the country at fairs, amusement centers, and exhibition halls. People had to hear for themselves and gladly paid the small admission fee charged. They turned out in such numbers that in one week at one

site in Boston, Edison's royalties on admissions amounted to

$1,500. The Speaking Phonograph Company put the device on sale for $10, announcing in an early advertisement that it was

> a machine that not only talks, but will record sounds of all kinds, and REPRODUCE THEM INSTANTLY, with FIDELITY AND DISTINCTNESS. The adaptation of this wonderful invention to the practical uses of commerce not having, as yet, been completed, in all its mechanical details, this company is now prepared to offer to the public only that design or form of apparatus which has been found best adapted to its exhibition as a novelty. The "PARLOR SPEAKING PHONOGRAPH" is intended for use in the parlor or drawing room, and will hold 150 to 200 words. The cylinder is so arranged that the foil can be taken off and replaced at any future time, thereby reproducing the same sounds that have been imprinted on it. It speaks loud enough to be heard in any ordinary room. We have a limited number now ready which we will sell for $10 cash, packed for shipment, with all needed appliances ready for use.

Yet its use "as a novelty," to quote the advertisement itself, best describes what the phonograph was still all about, although Edison himself had originally wanted it developed only for business purposes, not "sold for amusement." Once people heard it and the originality was gone, they lost much of their interest. Wonder gave way to disenchantment. One listener complained that the machine gave only a "burlesque or parody of the human voice." In any event, Edison, while he realized there were shortcomings, did little to improve the phonograph for the time being, and the phonograph remained largely a curiosity for its first decade, although by 1889 a German toy manufacturer had produced a small model that played toy disks 5 inches in diameter.

By 1888, Edison had an improved version ready, one that seemed to satisfy even the toughest of listeners, a music critic. *New York Evening Post* critic Philip G. Hubert Jr., writing in *Atlantic Monthly* in 1889, gave his opinion that "when it comes to music, the present achievements are wonderful. The phonograph will reproduce any kind of music—singing, the piano, violin, cornet, oboe, etc.—with a beauty of tone and accuracy which will astonish the musician." This was still a windup phonograph. In 1896, Edison introduced a spring-wound model for the first time. He preferred a battery-operated machine, but considerable **209** experimentation failed to produce a workable one. The spring-wound price was $40. Phonograph sales tripled in one year.

Meanwhile, other inventors were taking a spin, so to speak. Notable among those also working on development of an improved phonograph was Emile Berliner, who in 1887 developed the first successful flat disk. The flat disk, as opposed to Edison's cylinder, in due time became the established form of recording, remaining so even today in the CD player. Berliner's disk machine became known as the gramophone in England and was the origin of the Victor Talking Machine in the United States.

A worn-out Thomas Edison, photographed at the end of a seventy-two-hour marathon of work perfecting the phonograph in 1888. This image became one of the best known of the inventor because it was reproduced as a painting and widely distributed by the Edison Phonograph Company as an advertising poster. (Smithsonian Institution)

Edison, however, remained committed to the cylinder, which he believed (and he was probably right) gave better quality of sound with existing phonograph technology. By the turn of the century the cylinder had undergone considerable improvement. The tinfoil was long-since gone in favor of a hard wax cylinder. Then in 1908 Edison brought out a longer-playing, scratch-resistant cylinder called Blue Amberol, which played for four minutes instead of two and a half. Victor had its disks, which by the early twentieth century were made of solid shellac mixed with lampblack—essentially what was used for 78 rpm records into the 1950s. A disk, using both sides, could play for five minutes. Disks were also easier to store, taking up considerably less space than cylinders.

The phonograph craze was on. Edison had his factories working two shifts a day; and at that, the company had to apologize to **210** dealers in 1906 for being a million records behind schedule.

Edison cylinders sold for thirty-five cents each and generally featured popular music of the day: "Pretty Peggy" waltzes, heart songs, and "darky" (African American) melodies.

Victor took the tack of promoting more serious music, opera in particular. It sought to appeal to a potentially large audience of people who professed to like opera and symphonic music but could not afford, or were otherwise unable, to attend in person. What it offered was "opera at home," suggesting in its advertising that this was just as good as actually being there—better, in fact, in the sense of a phonograph in the parlor being more convenient and allowing a greater choice of repertoire to listen to. Opera was at a particularly high level of prominence, and Victor sought to take advantage by having the public identify it with a high level of culture. Preeminent among those whose talents Victor enlisted was Enrico Caruso (who also made the first opera broadcast in 1910). Along with the level of culture, however, also went the price: top-of-the-line Victor Red Seal records sold for as high as $2.

With Caruso, and such other opera stars as Nellie Melba and Adelina Patti, Victor began the "star system" that soon took over the record field, and somewhat later motion pictures. Hereafter, it was not only the musical selection one took into account in buying a record but who was performing as well. Edison for a time continued with his more folksy fare but soon also went to recruiting major talent in serious music as well.

An early Victor phonograph (Model "B"). As opposed to early Edisons, which used wax cylinders, Victors played shellac disks. (Smithsonian Institution)

By 1919, with radio broadcasting still just around the corner, the phonograph was *the* entertainment in the home. Said *Popular Science,* "Years ago . . . the parlor organ was the principal source of music in the home. . . . Today, however, the phonograph holds sway." In the years immediately ahead, electric power would replace the hand-operated windup crank, and the loudspeaker would

HOW TO PLAY A PHONOGRAPH
(C. 1908)

Directions attached to a windup Victor Talking Machine of a type produced from c. 1908 to the early 1920s.

Carefully unpack all the parts and—

1st. Screw the horn bracket to the motor case.
2d. Insert horn in elbow until pin goes into angular slot and turn elbow to right until firm on horn.
3d. Loosen screw "A" about three turns until plate "B" is quite loose and insert elbow of horn underneath plate, then tighten screw "A."
4th. Unscrew the needle-clamp screw, in soundbox, insert the blunt end of the needle as far as it will go into the socket and tighten screw firmly, then raise the soundbox so that it will rest on the tapering arm.
5th. Place a record on the turntable.
6th. Wind up the machine with the winding crank.
7th. Release the brake which will allow the turntable to revolve. The speed of the turntable can be controlled by adjusting the speed regulator. A speed of about 76 revolutions per minute will be found to give the best results for most selections.
8th. While the machine is running, place the soundbox so that the needle will enter the sound wave on the extreme outer edge of the record on the winding handle side of the machine.

A NEW NEEDLE should be used EVERY TIME a record is played.

Instruction card. Victor Talking Machine Company, Philadelphia, c. 1908. (Smithsonian Institution. Division of the History of Technology) antiquate the horn that had acoustically amplified the sound since the earliest days. This also marked the end of acoustical recording (a strictly mechanical process) in favor of an electrical recording process.

Although the coming of radio broadcasting in the mid-1920s sent sales of phonographs and recordings into a temporary nosedive, the phonograph had a permanent place in the parlor—or living room or den. The 1950s saw the passing of the 78 rpm record in favor of the LP; and in the 1980s cassettes and CDs began to supplant traditional phonograph records. And the coming of the Walkman and other micro-portables eventually made listening inside the parlor as ancient as the parlor itself.

CHAPTER THIRTEEN

THE CRAZE THAT STAYED

PHOTOGRAPHY

The craze is spreading fearfully. Chicago has had many fads whose careers have been brilliant but brief. But when amateur photography came, it came to stay.

—*Chicago Tribune*, 1891

WITH THE SHARP, SUDDEN, BRILLIANT burst of a flash picture, amateur photography became a part of American life.

It was an event that can be pinpointed: the introduction of the Kodak roll-film camera in 1888. That is not to say that photography was new. People had been taking pictures, and in far greater numbers posing for them, for nearly half a century. But those taking the pictures had made a career of it. Only the most diligent, patient, and persevering amateur would attempt the highly involved procedures required for taking and processing prints, and frequently with less than happy results.

As a profession, photography dated back to the days of Louis J. M. Daguerre, who in France in 1839 patented the first commercial photographic process. It was immediately hailed as "one of the wonders of modern times." A collection of photographs made by Daguerre's process was on display in New York City by late in the year. Visiting it on December 4, 1839, Philip Hone was awed. Almost no one had ever seen a photograph. Everything in the nature of a representation of a human face, or landscape, or a simple still life, was a hand-executed interpretation by an artist. Here now, for the first time, were the same scenes being executed by a boxlike device. Wrote Hone:

> The pictures . . . are extremely beautiful. They consist of views in Paris and exquisite collections of the objects of still life. The manner of producing them constitutes one of the wonders of modern times, and like other miracles, one may almost be excused for disbelieving it without seeing the very process by which it is created. . . . Every object, however minute, is a perfect transcript of the thing itself; the hair of the human head, the gravel of the roadside, the texture of a silk curtain, or the shadow of the smaller leaf reflected upon the wall, are all imprinted as carefully as nature or art has created them in the objects transferred; and those things which are invisible to the naked eye are rendered apparent by the help of a magnifying glass. . . . How greatly ashamed of their ignorance the by-gone generations of mankind ought to be!

The remarkable accuracy of a photograph—we still use the phrase "photographic likeness" today—was what so impressed many. Ezra Dean, for example, reflecting a few years later in *New Things Since I Was a Boy* (1869):

> If yourself you would see, or family all,
>
> On the Photograph man or Ambrotype call;
>
> He will make you a picture, I tell you a fact,
>
> 'Twill be just as you are, entirely exact.

Dean's awe for photography was shared by countless Americans, including the organizers of the Philadelphia Centennial of 1876, the nation's first great celebration of modern technology. One of the major exhibition sites was Photography Hall, a massive structure, nearly the equal of a football field in area. It had accommodations for more than 2,000 exhibitors. That may have been a little too ambitious. On May 20, 1876, ten days after the exposition opened, *Scientific American* lamented that exhibit space was not filling up as quickly as might be liked, and it commented that "there will be an exhibition of photography here such as the world never saw, if there is more enterprise shown in filling the space allotted than there is in subscribing for the stock to build it. In this matter we must do our best, or our friends will beat us." Exhibits of "friends" included "a very elegant and interesting collection sent from Germany" and a "fine collection" then on its way from Vienna.

Photographer Mathew Brady's gallery on Broadway in New York, 1853. Close inspection will reveal what looks bizarrely like a gigantic surveillance camera just over the Brady sign. Actually it's just a big replica of a camera for advertising purposes. (*The Illustrated News,* New York, November 12, 1853)

This, of course, was photography of the old order—the kind that was essentially beyond the scope of the amateur. But with evolution of the photographic process for the professional and serious amateur also went the technical refinement that made possible the craze that came to stay.

Daguerre's method used a silver-coated copper sheet from which an image was developed using mercury vapor. What quickly came to be known as the daguerreotype process produced a surprisingly good image for its time. But there were inherent shortcomings. Posing for a daguerreotype meant sitting perfectly still in front of the camera for a seemingly interminable time. And because the process produced an image directly on a photosensitive plate, without first creating a negative, no additional copies could be made. Nonetheless, from a contemporary point of view, the daguerreotype was a remarkable achievement; and at mid–nineteenth century, Americans in vast numbers hastened to the nearest daguerreotypist to pose. The resulting likeness was apt to be dour in expression, owing largely to the intensity of sitting motionless. But this was a once-in-a-lifetime occasion for many people, and a serious mien was thought more appropriate than a look of levity for the permanence of a photograph.

Similar to the daguerreotype, but cheaper, was the tintype, which was introduced at midcentury and continued in popularity through the nineteenth century. The image was produced on a thin, black iron sheet, hence its popular name.

Meanwhile, William Henry Fox Talbot, a contemporary of Daguerre, was pointing the way to a broader use of photography. Whereas Daguerre had caught the greatest public attention and excited public interest, Talbot was more far-reaching in seeing practical applications. It was Talbot who invented the negative-positive process, and thus the means of making any number of prints of one image. Talbot was also the first to see the potential for photography in publishing. His *Pencil of Nature,* the first volume of which appeared in 1844, was the first book to be photographically illustrated.

In the 1850s a new degree of practicality emerged with the use of silver salts and a syrupy substance known as collodion. A mixture of salts and collodion was used to coat a photographic plate at the time the photograph was to be taken; but since the collodion had to be kept moist during exposure and developing, processing had to be done immediately. A direct positive could be made, as with a daguerreotype; or if a glass plate were used, a negative could be produced, and thus any number of positive prints. There was also a reduction of exposure time to a few seconds. But the photographer still had to take his "darkroom" with him in a wagon or wheelbarrow.

A contemporary magazine article titled "The Wonders of Photography" explained some of the intricacies for the amateur, coincidentally giving the amateur good and sufficient reason for leaving photography to the professional, as a few brief excerpts show:

> The negative is made on clear, crystal glass, first polished and well cleaned with powered rotten-stone or alcohol, coated with a creamy mixture of ether, alcohol, gun-cotton, and sundry bromides and iodides, and dipped into a bath of pure water and nitrate of silver, after remaining in which a few moments, the collodion film becomes highly sensitive to the light, being impregnated with the silver solution, which makes it turn black whenever light is permitted to strike it. This fact may be proved by pouring a little nitrate of silver over a piece of paper and placing a leaf thereon; after exposure to the sun a while, an imprint of the leaf will be found on the paper, showing every vein and pore black, where the light has shone through, white where the substance of the leaf has covered the paper. In the same way are negatives made, and your image is fixed in the sensitized film by the sunbeams as they dance around you while you are sitting for your picture.

The article then had the reader follow into the "mysterious little darkroom" to observe the processing of the negative and marvel as "you shall see your own image come up from the hoary surface and stand out in bold relief before you, an unmistakable likeness, but a negative." And then the making of a print from the negative:

> After fixing, it is again washed, but does not yet assume the proper tone and color. This is attained by another process, called toning, which consists in dipping the print in a solution of chloride of gold and other ingredients. A grand and final bath is now given the print, wherein it is made to whirl around and wash itself for several hours,

by sundry saucy streams of water shooting at it all the time. From this bath it is taken, dried, neatly trimmed, pasted on a card, dried, pressed, polished, and delivered to you.

Caught up in the lure of dancing sunbeams and how they could be made to paint pictures on paper was a young bank clerk named George Eastman in Rochester, New York. He began studying photography in his early twenties, at about the same time (this was the late 1870s) that the wet collodion process was giving way to a new method. It was the dry-plate process, which used a gelatin emulsion for coating the plate in advance of the time of taking the photograph. Since it was no longer necessary to keep the plate moist, the photographer could do his processing when he returned to his own darkroom at home. But there were other significant advantages as well. Heretofore, even if using a glass plate to make a negative from which to print a positive, the resulting positive was exactly the same size as the negative because it was a contact print. This meant the camera had to be at least as large as the image it produced. With the gelatin emulsion process there also came the use of enlargers—printing by projection, rather than by direct contact, on paper also coated with the emulsion. This meant the camera now could be smaller than the print it made—small enough, finally, to be handheld rather than require a tripod. Furthermore, the new plates were much "faster," requiring an exposure time of as little as $\frac{1}{25}$ of a second.

With the change from collodion to dry plate came the potential for mass production of photographic supplies. Silver gelatin emulsion did not require immediate use. Hence, plates could be factory-made and mass distributed, and Eastman saw the potential. Eastman gave up his bank job and began manufacturing dry plates. Then he turned to producing cameras, joining with another Rochester businessman, a camera maker named William H. Walker. They sought to improve on something that had been tried unsuccessfully in Britain: putting the emulsion not on a glass plate but on a strip of film.* In 1885 they introduced a roll-film holder

---

*This first film was a strip of paper coated with a gelatin-bromide emulsion. Once exposed, the emulsion had to be stripped from the paper. In 1889 Eastman introduced transparent nitrocellulose film, which eliminated the stripping operation.

that could be attached to the back of a standard camera in place of the glass plate. By 1886, Eastman had created a camera with the roll-film holder built in. Called the Detective (Eastman only more or less explained that its compact size made it "perfectly adapted to taking groups unobserved"), it went on the market for $45 but was a commercial disaster, partly because of the price but largely because of production delays. No more than fifty were made, and most of these probably never were sold.

But the Detective was merely a step in the evolutionary process. In 1888 came the camera that changed it all—the most practical, compact, easy-to-use device for taking pictures yet developed. At just under 7 inches long and 4 inches square, it was so compact that it struck the *Philadelphia Photographer* magazine as "incredible that so many possibilities should rest within the confines of so tiny a structure, and such an unpretentious one . . . a model of compactness, neatness, and ingenuity." Not only that, its built-in film roller came already stocked with film, enough for 100 photographs. The cost was $25, roughly half the price of the Detective yet still expensive—the equivalent of about $500 today.

JUST PRESS THE BUTTON

But what made this new camera revolutionary was that, for the first time, here was really something for the amateur. No longer was there any need to prepare one's own plates with emulsion and carefully store them for use. And no need for a wagon or wheelbarrow. Or even a tripod. All one had to do, as explained in an early brochure, was:

1. Pull the string [cocking the shutter]
2. Turn the key [advancing the film to a new exposure]
3. Press the button.

And when all 100 shots were taken, simply send the camera back to Eastman in Rochester. The film would be processed and the prints sent to the owner along with the camera, restocked with film. The price of sending the camera back for processing was $10, or ten cents a print.

220   So novel was the camera that it needed a novel name. Eastman

The revolutionary Kodak roll film camera of 1888 as shown in an early advertisement. It could take one hundred photographs and was the simplest camera yet devised (You "press the button—we do the rest."). Once all the shots were taken, the camera was returned to the factory for processing of the film and reloading. But at $25—the equivalent of perhaps $500 today—it was hardly inexpensive. (*Harper's Weekly*, April 27, 1889)

himself, having come to regret the choice of Detective for the last camera, coined a new name—Kodak. It was a unique and arbitrary term, having absolutely no etymological significance. Eastman is said to have once related that it came to him while gazing into a bowl of alphabet soup, but that has been put down as intentionally misleading, a not unexpected product of a prankish nature. Almost certainly untrue is that Kodak was meant to suggest the precise, functional sound of an Eastman shutter snapping open and closed. The coining of the word appears to have been based on nothing more than what Eastman explained in a patent application (in England, where this kind of detail was requisite), that "Kodak" was suitably short, was not given to mispronunciation, and was just as unique as the device it stood for. A 1938 company press release on the origin conceded that, "Philologically, the word 'Kodak' is as meaningless as a child's first 'goo.' "

Business-wise, it was anything but goo. What Eastman coined so caught the spirit of a new era of photography that it became not only a common noun but a verb. Kodakers buying kodaks and going kodaking began the craze that "spread fearfully." Within the first six months, 5,000 Kodaks were sold and the Eastman company was having trouble keeping up with orders. Most significant of all was how the Kodak opened up photography to amateurs. As the *Tribune* observed, "When amateur photography came, it came to stay."

Yet from a later point of view, the first Kodak had its shortcomings. For one thing, a circular image was produced. Subsequent modifications resulted in a rectangular image. For another thing, there was as yet no viewfinder. You simply pointed it, using a v-shape guide, and hoped for the best. And although there was a revolving indicator to show the film had been wound to the next exposure, there was nothing to show specifically which exposure this was and how many of the 100 were left. And certainly no fail-safe to prevent you from clicking the shutter before you wound to the next exposure. President Grover Cleveland discovered this the hard way after returning from a fishing trip with his good friend, actor Joe Jefferson. He had pressed the button (like the Kodak slogan said) a hundred times but never wound the film advance. His first shot was superimposed ninety-nine times over.

Most Kodak owners had the hang of it, though, which was good for Eastman. He concluded from start that it was sales of film, not cameras, that would be the basis of his company's success. But it was continual development of the camera that motivated the buying of film. In 1895 Eastman introduced the Pocket Kodak, which weighed only 6 ounces and measured roughly 2 by 3 by 4 inches. It produced a negative 1½ by 2 inches and cost $5.

The ultimate in amateurism came in 1900 with a $1 camera—

Perhaps even more revolutionary than the roll film camera of 1888 was Kodak's Brownie, introduced in 1900: It opened up photography to children as well as adults. Children becoming owners of Brownies were encouraged in the camera's use by receiving a Kodak booklet on photography and an offer of free membership in the Brownie Camera Club. The name celebrated an elf of folklore whose reputation for kindliness was thought to make the Brownie camera seem especially user-friendly to youngsters. At $1, it was the equivalent of roughly $15 to $20 today. Brownies were made for the United States market until 1970. (*St. Nicholas Magazine,* December 1900. General Research Division, The New York Public Library, Astor, Lenox and Tilden Foundations.)

the Kodak Brownie, a simple box camera, larger and less sophisticated than the Pocket Kodak. It sold for exactly $1 (roughly $15 to $20 today), plus fifteen cents for film, and was aimed at making photographers out of children (hence its name, capitalizing on a celebrated elf whose folklore reputation for kindliness was thought to make the Brownie camera seem especially user-friendly to youngsters). Children becoming owners of Brownies were encouraged in their use by receiving a Kodak booklet on photography and an offer of free membership in the Brownie Camera Club. But the Brownie was calculated to be as simple as possible to use anyway, and there was surely no discouraging people of all ages from becoming Brownie owners. Cameras with the Brownie name continued to be produced by Kodak well past the mid-twentieth century. The last for the U.S. market was made in 1970.

Meanwhile, in December 1891 Kodak had introduced a new series of cameras, with another significant improvement: daylight loading. No longer was a darkroom needed to install a new roll of film. The amateur could do it right out in the park, or on the avenue, or in the backyard—wherever he (and increasingly she) happened to be. And thus it was no longer necessary to send the camera back to Rochester for processing and restocking of film. Film quickly became available almost everywhere. With the ready supply came more and more amateurs to take pictures, generating the craze the *Chicago Tribune* said was "spreading fearfully."

These and other Kodaks still to come and competing models from other manufacturers, along with the ready availability of film and an increasing diversity of accessories, transformed photography from something for the professional to something for everyone. As the Kodak slogan summed it up it, "You press the button, we do the rest." Or as Eastman himself once explained: ". . . the mere mechanical act of taking the picture[,] which anybody can perform, is divorced from all the chemical manipulation of preparing and finishing pictures, which only experts can perform. . . . There is no jugglery about it; photography has simply been brought down to a point where the mechanical work can be entirely separated from the chemical work."

The camera craze struck at the same time as the bicycle craze—the 1890s. George Eastman, who rode a bicycle to the office until he was in his fifties, saw analogy with the 1890s cycling craze and said that, with the Brownie especially, he wanted to reach people "the same way the bicycle has reached them." Bicycle-mania dropped off fast after the coming of the automobile, but cameras have remained an indispensable part of American life.

And it has been virtually the same appeal since the start. Historian Robert Routledge observed in 1890 that "the new art cherishes domestic and friendly feelings by its ever-present transcripts of the familiar faces, keeping fresh the memory of the distant and the dead." Eastman saw that same need as he spoke of amateur photographers' passion for keeping a record "of their everyday life, objects, places or people that interest them in travel, etc." So prolific did amateur picture-takers become (and so common the cameras produced by Eastman) that the term "Kodak freaks" emerged in the early twentieth century to describe those legions of amateurs who, "Wherever they go, and whomever they see, and whatever place they have come to, they have got to have a Kodak along for the purpose of getting pictures."

Inevitably this meant that some of the picture taking was random, and some of those getting "shot" weren't always pleased to be in the picture. In an editorial titled "Kodak Manners," *Ladies' Home Journal* in February 1900 complained that, "It sometimes seems as if the possession of a 'kodak'—applying that term to photographic cameras in general—means the departure of all good breeding from its owner. For it must be confessed that the etiquette of the 'kodaker' has not kept pace with the development of the 'kodak.' It is a difficult point for some people to understand that there are those who have a strong prejudice against being promiscuously 'snapped at' through a camera."

Some of the camera-shy were undoubtedly just new to cameras, and in later times would take the snapping more easily in stride. But there was another form of snapping that posed a more serious problem—one that directly foreshadowed the plight of those who are stalked by the paparazzi of today. As the *Ladies' Home Journal* also observed in 1900:

People whose work or life happens to be of a public nature suffer
224 greatly from this abuse of the "kodak." The wife of an ex-President of

the United States, for instance, has caused it to be frequently made known that she does not desire her children to be made the subjects of promiscuous photographs. And yet these children can scarcely ever venture beyond the confines of their home grounds without having to face some camera leveled at them. And the same is true of the children of a prominent author. Both he and his wife have publicly declared their wish that their children may be recognized as belonging to them, not to the public; yet "kodaks" are leveled at the little ones whenever they appear. It would be discourteous enough to these parents if the pictures were taken solely for the amusement and the private possession of the thoughtless "kodakers." But when the pictures are offered for sale, generally for publication, the thing is unquestionably being carried a little too far.

Photography in the late nineteenth and early twentieth centuries, of course, transcended the amateur and the snapshot. In its totality it has helped transform the quality of life. As Routledge said:

No other of our nineteenth century inventions is at once so beautiful, so precious, so popular, so appreciated as photography. It is exercising a beneficial influence over the social sentiments, the arts, the sciences of the whole world—an influence not the less real because it is wide-spread and unobtrusive. . . . It is lending invaluable aid to almost every science. The astronomer now derives his mathematical data from the photograph; by its aid the architect superintends the erection of distant buildings, the engineer watches over the progress of his designs in remote lands, the medical man amasses records of morbid anatomy, the geologist studies the anatomy of the earth, the ethnologist obtains faithful transcripts of the features of every race.

CHAPTER FOURTEEN

THE WILDFIRE WONDER

RADIO

. . . the rapidity with which the thing has spread has possibly not been equalled in all the centuries of human progress.

—*American Review of Reviews,* January 1923. An article on radio titled "Listening In, Our New National Pastime"

NOTWITHSTANDING all the marvels of consumer technology that had dazzled Americans over the preceding years—from the telegraph of 1844 and the first transatlantic cable ("the greatest triumph that has been achieved for centuries") through turn-of-the-century photography (the "craze that is spreading fearfully")—radio seemed to leap upon the scene in the 1920s. It was as if nothing so wondrous had ever been witnessed. *American Review of Reviews* was only one witness to the phenomenon. Another was the U.S. government in the figure of the secretary of commerce, Herbert Hoover. Since it was his department that regulated radio prior to creation of the Federal Radio Commission in 1927, what he said had the aura of official pronouncement. And what Hoover pronounced, as quoted in *Popular Science* in 1922, was that "the wildfire spread of radio . . . has been much more amazing than any other thing we have seen in our time. One is at a loss in trying to think of any phenomenon to which it can be compared." *Popular Science* had seen it coming (right down to the metaphor) when it advised readers in November 1921: "Wake up to wireless. Do you realize that the use of radio outfits for entertainment in the home is spreading through America like wildfire?"

And this was thought to be only the beginning. *Radio Broadcast* magazine, which came into being in May 1922, a product of Doubleday publishing, declared in its first issue that:

> The movement is probably not even yet at its height; it is still growing in some kind of geometrical progression. There are to-day probably five hundred thousand receiving stations [sets] in the United States. . . . It seems quite likely that before the movement has reached its height, before the market for receiving apparatus becomes approximately saturated, there will be at least five million receiving sets in this country.

Radio Broadcast had no idea how geometric. The 5 million figure for sets in use was reached in just over four years; and in ten years there were more than three times as many as that—more than 18 million households with radio sets—and the height was nowhere near being reached.

Numbers of broadcasting stations are another way of seeing the boom. From the establishing of KDKA in Pittsburgh in 1920 (it claimed the honor of "world's first broadcasting station") through November 1921, the Department of Commerce had granted only 5 broadcasting licenses. Then in December 1921 it issued 23 licenses, followed in 1922 in with 8 in January, 24 in February, 77 in March, 76 in April, 97 in May, 72 in June, and 76 in July. During the spring of 1922, only two years into the process, the Department of Commerce ran out of three-letter combinations (WOR, WJZ, etc.) for station call letters and began issuing only the now-familiar four-letter kind. Meanwhile sales of radio sets and parts reached $60 million in 1922, then $136 million in 1923 and $358 million in 1924.

Numbers of stations and sales of sets are statistics. Behind the statistics were people. As *Radio Broadcast* observed in May 1922: "The rate of increase in the number of people who spend at least a part of their evening in listening in is almost incomprehensible. To those who have recently tried to purchase receiving equipment, some idea of this increase has undoubtedly occurred, as they stood perhaps in the fourth or fifth row at the radio counter waiting their turn only to be told when they finally reached the counter that they might place an order and it would be filled when possible."

Not that radio was new. As "wireless," it was something people had been hearing about for more than twenty years. What happened was that wireless suddenly became radio, essentially as we know it today—a convenient and inexpensive medium of *entertainment*.

Over and above institutional use, the wireless was something for the hobbyist. *Popular Science* estimated nearly half a million "wireless fans" by late 1921. For the most part they were amateurs, including youngsters like Herbert Hoover's son, who (said the elder Hoover) had "gone daft on wireless." Youngsters could read about wireless in newspapers and magazines or get the bug from teen-oriented literature, like *Tom Swift and His Wireless Message* (1911). By 1914 the Boy Scout handbook included detailed instructions for constructing a wireless receiver, including aerial,

TOM SWIFT EXPLAINS THE WIRELESS (1911)

Even though the technical explanations were often rough around the edges, as in this example, many a youngster of the early twentieth century gained a deeper appreciation of new technology reading Tom Swift, *that intrepid young hero of teenage literature. A partial list of titles is a chronicle of developing technology:* Tom Swift and His Airship, *1910;* Tom Swift and His Wizard Camera, *1912;* Tom Swift and His Photo Telephone, *1914;* Tom Swift and His Electric Locomotive, *1922;* Tom Swift and His Airline Express, *1926; and* Tom Swift and His Television Detector, *1933. In the following excerpt from* Tom Swift and His Wireless Message, *1911, Tom is building a wireless station so he can send for help for his fellow castaways and himself, marooned on Earthquake Island.*

"But I can't understand how you are going to do it," said Mrs. Nestor. "I've read about wireless messages, but I can't get it through my head. How is it done, Mr. Swift?"

"The theory is very simple," said the young inventor. "To send a message by wire, over a telegraph system, a battery or dynamo is used. This establishes a current over wires stretched between two points. . . . In telegraphing without wires," went on Tom, "the air is used in place of a metallic conductor, with the help of the earth, which in itself is a big magnet, or a battery, as you choose to regard it. . . . To send a wireless message a current is generated by a dynamo. The current flows along until it gets to the ends of the sending wires, which we have just strung. Then it leaps off into space, so to speak, until it reaches the receiving wires, wherever they may be erected. That is why any wireless receiving station, within a certain radius, can catch any messages that may be flying through the air . . ."

"It's lucky you understand wireless telegraphy, Tom Swift," said Mr. Nestor admiringly, and the others joined in praising the young inventor, until, blushing, he hurried off to make some adjustments to his apparatus.

Victor Appleton, pseud., Tom Swift and His Wireless Message; or, The Castaways of Earthquake Island *(New York: Grosset & Dunlap, 1911) pp. 173–177* for $7.69 (most of which was for headphones). Radio pioneer Lee De Forest told of a father who had written him in 1922 ordering wireless parts for his boys, who were as spellbound with radio as a later generation of youngsters would be with home computers. Said the father:

> I don't know the first thing about wireless; I am just ordering these few things for my boys—hope I have the numbers straight. If every father knew what an interest-holding, instructive and useful thing radio is for a boy or young man, there would be a mast on every roof. My boys talk Radio all day—and dream it all night, I guess. Their mother never wonders where they are or what they are up to. She knows that when they are out of school they are in the radio shack. They certainly get a lot of amusement and good, sound and useful knowledge out of their work. Their radio outfit is the best investment I ever made.

Amateur operators of the early twentieth century, both kids and their elders, were using a *communications* device, not yet an entertainment medium. Institutional use of wireless was largely military and commercial (steamship companies, for example). Amateurs got into it with sending and receiving apparatus that was largely home-constructed out of commercially available parts. Whoever was using it, the language of early wireless was a machine-gun-like exchange of dots and dashes. Generally speaking there was no transmission of human voice, only conversation by code. The vacuum tube, which made possible radio as we know it, was still to be developed. All the wireless could do was use high-voltage electric sparks to generate radio waves in long (dash) and short (dot) bursts.

Most people as of, say, 1910 had had no direct contact with radio. They had heard *of it*, even if only vaguely as personified by Italian inventor Guglielmo Marconi, but they hadn't heard anything transmitted by wireless. And indeed there wasn't much to hear; there were no shows yet as we know them today. Was this some passing scientific fad? Some mere curiosity? After all, the telephone did quite well for letting people communicate, even long-distance now—and by actual voice.

Radio promised something new in being able to communicate without fixed connections between one point and another. A dramatic demonstration came in mid-April 1912 when the sinking of the "unsinkable" ship *Titanic* showed what wireless could do (and perhaps more important, *might* have done) in an emergency. Wireless guided to the scene of the disaster the British ship *Carpathia,* which rescued what survivors there were. And wireless relayed first news of the tragedy to the press, which relayed it to the world.

On the other hand, there is the question of what the wireless might have done to reduce the number of fatalities. The steamship *Californian* was only some 20 miles away when the *Titanic* started going down, but its wireless operator was not on duty.

Nevertheless, there was a new and keener appreciation of the value of wireless at a moment when impressions sank in deeply. Just after the disaster, Marconi was asked about it. He explained modestly enough to a reporter: "I can say only that I am delighted with the part that wireless played in the rescue of passengers from the *Titanic.* But, then, that is one of the things that wireless is for. It has simply done what it was meant to do."

A remarkable thing about early radio was that its essential parts were observable. Basically, you could see what made it work, even if the principle was nebulous. The popularization of wireless began with the discovery, just after the turn of the twentieth century, that certain crystals could detect radio waves. Substances such as silicon, carborundum, and galena (lead ore) were found to work almost magically. This made possible a cheap and reliable form of radio receiver that almost anyone could operate with a little patience. Wireless supply houses offered all that was necessary; or you could buy just the crystal and improvise the rest. A crystal detector set was simple to make. You could use a cardboard tube or even an empty round oatmeal package, and wrap wire around it to make the tuning coil. The condenser could be made from tinfoil. Then a small metal cup or clip for the crystal. You still needed headphones, though, and these didn't lend themselves to being homemade. You were advised to buy these.

Once the set was all together, the trick was to be patient in "tuning in" with a tiny wire, called a cat's whisker. You moved it across the surface of the crystal, looking for the right spot. It was easy to tell. Until you found it, nothing; when you did, as if by magic, voices and music, or whatever was going over the airwaves at that time, came in through your headphones. It must have been a wondrous experience the first time, in that age before radios as they're known today, let alone television. Later a single-tube amplifier could boost audio strength of the signal being received, allowing for reception from a greater distance or letting you connect your crystal set to a simple though still primitive loudspeaker instead of having to use headphones (in which case your family could listen with you).

The invention of the triode vacuum tube by De Forest in 1907—the so-called audion tube—promised a new level of performance. But early tubes were a mixed blessing: They had a tendency toward oscillation and howling and often produced interference in other sets. Pioneer broadcaster Ted Husing recalled the early days as "child radio—an enfant terrible in the beginning—[it] blooped, howled and yowled, often filling the air with a hideous assortment of cacophonous noises, otherwise known as static." *Century Magazine* described interference as ranging from "the hiss of frying bacon" to "the wail of a cat in purgatory." This was after radio began its ascendancy as a mass medium. This was after there was something to hear between the hisses and the yowls. A major breakthrough in radio design was the superheterodyne circuit, introduced in 1924 by Edwin H. Armstrong. It mixed two waves of differing frequencies to generate a third, lower frequency that could be more finely tuned, providing much clearer reception. It also allowed for bringing in weak signals that would otherwise be inaudible. The superheterodyne circuit remains the basic design of almost all radios today.

THE MAKING OF A HOUSEHOLD UTILITY

Development of technology and evolution of broadcasting had been going hand in hand. In fact the idea of the "modern radio set" preceded what there was in the way of modern programs to listen to. The concept was first put forth by David Sarnoff, later president and chairman of Radio Corporation of America, while he was an official of the American Marconi company. For 1920 it was a farseeing proposal for that time and fell on deaf ears. Sarnoff foresaw
232 the future of radio broadcasting and the need for an easy-to-operate

Listening to radio, 1924. A high-necked horn like that on an early phonograph let two or more people listen close-up. Headphones gave better sound quality but could be used by only one person at a time. Soon after this, the cone-type loudspeaker came into use, greatly improving sound quality and making listening a family activity. (Smithsonian Institution)

household appliance that anyone could use. He summed up his concept in a memo to a vice president of Marconi that has become part of radio history:

> I have in mind a plan of development which would make radio a household utility in the same sense as a piano or phonograph. The idea is to bring music into the house by wireless. . . . The receiver can be designed in the form of a simple 'radio music box' and arranged for several different wave lengths, which should be changeable with the throwing of a single switch or pressing of a single button. . . .
>
> [In addition to music, it can be used for] receiving lectures at home, which can be made perfectly audible; also events of national importance can be simultaneously announced and received. Baseball scores can be transmitted in the air by the use of one set installed at the Polo Grounds [in New York]. The same would be true of other cities.
>
> This proposition would be especially interesting to farmers and others living in outlying districts removed from cities. By the purchase of a "radio music box" they could enjoy concerts, lectures, music, recitals, etc., which may be going on in the nearest city within their radius. . . . Should this plan materialize, it would seem reasonable to expect sales of 1,000,000 "radio music boxes" within a period of three years. Roughly estimating the selling price at $75 per set, $75,000,000 can be expected.

Here was what we would later take for granted as radio. It was still a vision when radio was still "wireless." The Marconi com-

pany, clinging to a conception of radio as communication rather than entertainment, was unreceptive. It was only after Sarnoff became an executive at RCA that he was able to sell his idea, and it came into being in 1922 as the Radiola, RCA's first radio in the modern sense—something relatively simple to use, something for the home, something for entertainment and not "ham-radio" communication. Sarnoff's calculation of $75 million in sales in three years was low, however. RCA had $83.5 million in sales between 1922 and 1924.

The rush was on. Westinghouse had its first home radio, the Aeriola Jr., already on sale in June 1921. It was a small crystal set that sold for $25. A more advanced version, the Aeriola Sr., went on sale the next winter. It had a single vacuum tube instead of a crystal. Both Aeriola models as well as the Radiola required use of headphones. Otherwise, according to a brochure for the Aeriola Jr. (and this generally applied to all three):

> Those who seek for extreme simplicity will find Aeriola Jr. ideal.
> Only two adjustments are required: the operation of a single arm
> over a graduated dial, and the occasional simple adjustment of the
> crystal detector. No additional equipment is needed, for the set
> includes all the essentials—a variable tuner, a fixed condenser, a
> supersensitive crystal detector, a high-grade set of head phones,
> antenna outfit, and instructions for installing and operating. The
> receiver in its case, weighs only five pounds.

Here we had essentially the modern radio. But there were still important steps to come. The Aeriolas, the Radiola, and other sets of the early to mid-1920s were battery powered. Early radios worked only on direct current, hence the need for batteries instead of household current, which was generally AC (alternating current). Improvements in radio technology, and especially of the vacuum tube, made plug-in sets possible; and by 1927 sets operating on house current were becoming popular except in rural areas, where battery sets continued in common use because of the absence of electric supply. It was also in 1927 that car radios began to appear.

By the mid-1920s, the cone-type loudspeaker was coming into use, supplanting headphones and an earlier form of speaker, a high-necked horn that looked like what might be found on an early phonograph. The new speakers greatly improved sound; they also made radio listening something for the family rather than for one person at a time using headphones–a huge transition, the significance of which would have full effect with the coming of television. Similarly, the 1920s produced a shift from preoccupation with the technical aspects of radio, particularly what was called DXing–seeking out the most distant station and vying with other operators for distance records. Radio was now mostly entertainment. Radio magazines that in the early 1920s carried mostly technical articles on building and improving sets were filled by the end of the decade with feature articles on up-and-coming radio celebrities.

Largely forgotten today is the idealization that accompanied the coming of radio: glorious goals and lofty ideals, radio as a means of education and dissemination of knowledge, radio even as a cornerstone for peace in the world. There was Secretary of Commerce Hoover insisting that "radio communication is not to be considered as merely a business carried on for private gain, for public advertisement, or for the entertainment of the curious. It is a public concern impressed with the public trust." Lee De Forest in 1922 offered the prediction that "as an educational medium the [radio] broadcast will in time prove second in importance only to the public school."

Yet, practically speaking, how? As wonderful as it was, radio brought with it some fundamental questions. The most basic of all was who paid. If one wanted to read a book or go to a movie or a music hall for entertainment, one expected to pay a price for doing so. Even a newspaper or magazine cost something, although it was full of advertising to cover most of the expense of publication. Radio presented a new dilemma. As *Scientific American* observed in June 1922: "Radio today is a continuous performance. You purchase your ticket in the form of a receiving set . . . and then listen in day in and day out to the music of today, the classics of yesterday, the leaders of the nation, the scientists, the news of the minute, stock quotations, and so on, without further charge of any kind. For such is the radio broadcasting art of today. But what about the broadcasting end? Who foots the bill? Why? Who are the artists and speakers, who volunteer their services? In brief, how long is this going to last?"

Thus the coming of the commercial. The first was aired August 28, 1922, on New York's WEAF, a recently established station of American Telephone and Telegraph. The sponsor was Queensboro Realty Corporation, of Jamaica Heights, New York, which presented a ten-minute talk (at a total cost of $100) about a new real estate development. WEAF and other stations otherwise had been offering various forms of entertainment without the interruption of advertising. A not surprising opponent was *Printer's Ink* magazine, a spokesman for print media that had long existed largely on advertising revenue. *Printer's Ink* declared ". . . we are opposed to the scheme principally because it is against good public policy. We are opposed to it for the same reason that we object to sky writing. People should not be forced to read advertising unless they are so inclined." The radio equivalent of skywriting—the commercial—became a way of life anyway.

A direct effect of commercial sponsorship was to refine the quality of programming. After all, the listener was bound to associate the program with the sponsor, and it was clearly in the sponsor's best interest to make the association a quality one. Ted Husing recalled that "early-day radio programs were often sorry unrehearsed affairs minus any planning. They staggered drunkenly. They had little continuity, no scripts to follow, and only too often the principals failed to show up at air time. But with the discovery of radio as a far-reaching advertising medium, Lucky Strike, Gimbels, the Pennsylvania Railroad, the Reading Railroad, the A&P chain stores and others hopped onto the bandwagon. . . . A program needed more than a man reciting or telling seedy jokes or reading poetry. Music, both jazz and classical, made its bow; situation comedies developed; sportscasts gained headway. Programming was established." De Forest, an idealist, lamented radio salesmen and their commercials as "uncouth tramps, interlopers, who intrude their obnoxious presence into every home, until the tormented listener, awaiting a newscast, or the resumption of a musical number so viciously interrupted, snaps the cut-off switch, and is done for the evening." History, of course, **236** proved his observation wrong. People either accepted commercials or numbed to the "obnoxious presence." In either case they kept tuned. (And once in a while a commercial is as good as, if not better than, the program it accompanies.)

A SEDUCTIVE PRESENCE

As wireless turned into radio, developing the technological and commercial structure necessary to sustain it, it also evolved into the news and entertainment medium we know it as today. This coincided with the transition from a machine-gun exchange of dots and dashes to an instrument for the human voice, and thus sound of any kind. Broadcasting was born. Broadcasting was that seductive presence that drove a husband to write to WEAF in New York in the mid-1920s:

> It is 5:25 P.M.—you have just finished broadcasting; you have practically finished breaking up a happy home. Our set was installed last evening. Today, my wife has not left her chair, listening all day. Our apartment has not been cleaned, the beds are not made, the baby not bathed—and no dinner ready for me.

Another facet of broadcasting was what *Collier's Magazine* had in mind in an article titled "Radio Dreams That Can Come True": a "spreading [of] mutual understanding to all sections of the country, unifying our thoughts, ideals, and purposes, making us a strong and well-knit people." Radio, thought writer Stanley Frost, was uniquely suited to reaching people outside of the cultural, economic, and educational mainstream. As an example of how radio was reaching out to "illiterate or broken people," making them "for the first time in touch with the world about them," Frost reprinted a letter written to WJZ in Newark, New Jersey:

> My husban and I thanks yous all fore the gratiss programas we receved every night and day from WJZ. . . . The Broklin teachers was grand the lecturs was so intresing . . . [the] annonnser must be One grand man the way he tell the stores to the chilren.

As a news and entertainment medium, radio is generally considered to have originated with KDKA in Pittsburgh, which inaugurated regular commercial broadcasting with transmission of

WHAT'S ON RADIO? (1924)

What was it like listening to radio in its earliest days? Here was one day's complete schedule for one of the major stations on the air (WEAF was later known as WNBC in New York). It includes things modern radio (and television) audiences will find familiar, along with an assortment of programs typical of radio in its infancy.

WEAF, New York

Wednesday, October 8, 1924

11:00 A.M.	Minnie Weil, piano; young mother's program.
11:50 A.M.	Market and weather reports.
1:45 P.M.	World Series. New York–Washington baseball game.*
4:00–5:00 P.M.	Davis Orchestra.
6:00 P.M.	Waldorf-Astoria dinner music
7:30 P.M.	Emma Burkhardt, contralto; Isador Drimer, violin.
7:40 P.M.	Carrie Brookins, piano.
7:50 P.M.	"Why the Holstein Appeals to Me as a Dairy Cow," by C. F. Bigler.
8:00 P.M.	Emma Burkhardt, contralto; Isador Drimer, violin.
8:10 P.M.	Carrie Brookins, piano.
8:20 P.M.	"What Makes a Good Investment?" by H. K. Hutchins.
8:30 P.M.	Florence Chalmers, cello.
8:40 P.M.	Emma Burkhardt, soprano.
8:50 P.M.	Florence Chalmers, cello.
9:00–10:00 P.M.	Empire State Orchestra.

The first live play-by-play broadcast of a baseball game was by KDKA, Pittsburgh, August 5, 1921.

presidential election returns in 1920. What became KDKA started out in 1916 in the garage of Dr. Frank Conrad, in the Pittsburgh suburb of Wilkinsburg, Pennsylvania. Conrad, assistant chief engineer for Westinghouse, used a small experimental transmitter to go on the air as 8XK. In ordinary circumstances, use of a private transmitter was prohibited during the war, but Conrad did wireless work for the Navy and was allowed to continue using his own transmitter. Following the war he hit on the idea of playing phonograph records on the air. Then his sons got into the act, rounding up neighborhood talent to sing and play instruments. People with wireless—there weren't a great many but they were pretty spirited about it—began listening in, and Conrad, to oblige them, had to set up a regular schedule: two hours of music every Sunday and Wednesday night. The audience widened after the Joseph Horne Department Store in Pittsburgh began advertising wireless sets with which to tune in Conrad's program. Then an official of Westinghouse, knowing Conrad and seeing the ad, wondered why Westinghouse didn't get into radio broadcasting as a way of promoting sales of its own receivers. So the company, after asking Conrad to set up a more powerful transmitter at the plant, applied for and received a license to broadcast as KDKA, which henceforth claimed the distinction of being "the world's first broadcasting station."

Approval came just before the presidential election of 1920. This gave KDKA the opportunity to cover major national news as a way of inaugurating regular commercial broadcasting. A telephone link was set up between the *Pittsburgh Post* and a rooftop radio shack at Westinghouse. From a microphone there, on November 2, 1920, Leo H. Rosenberg, a young publicist for the company, read returns for more than four hours, his presentation interspersed with music from a hand-cranked phonograph. Periodically, Rosenberg would explain to listeners who and what they were hearing and ask them to send a postcard to Westinghouse advising as to where they were tuned in. Hundreds of cards arrived from throughout the country.

News quickly became a major offering of broadcast radio, although, for the time being, radio would not of itself be the news-gathering organization in the sense that the modern networks are. News was usually supplied by a local newspaper; and in fact, the local paper, about as often as not, owned the radio station.

The 1920s, the first decade of radio broadcasting, happened to have some good news material for listeners. The year 1925, for example, brought with it one of the most celebrated court cases of the century, the Scopes trial, or so-called monkey trial, at which a young science teacher named John Scopes was charged with teaching Darwin's theory of evolution in violation of state law. The case drew national attention when the renowned criminal attorney, Clarence Darrow, volunteered in Scopes's defense, countering William Jennings Bryan, who handled the prosecution. The *Chicago Tribune,* at a cost of a thousand dollars a day, arranged for an open telephone line to Dayton, Tennessee, where the trial was held, so a steady stream of live reports could be carried over its radio station, WGN. Its reporter, Quin Ryan, used a microphone that stood near the counsels' tables.

Two years later there was Lindbergh's first solo flight across the Atlantic. Since he carried no radio equipment, Lindbergh left an anxious public in suspense after his departure from Roosevelt Field, on New York's Long Island. Radio station CHNS in

How exciting was it to be part of the *radio* revolution? In 1923, on her family's farm near Butler, New Jersey, Maud Muller—content with old-time technique, a horse, to do the hard work—rigged up an antenna and battery-powered receiver so she could make hay while the radio played. (Library of Congress)

Halifax provided the first word, more than eleven hours after the takeoff: Lindbergh was sighted over Cape Race, Newfoundland, but the weather was poor. The Halifax report was immediately relayed by stations around America. Finally there came a short-wave report by Radio Paris that a lone monoplane, almost certainly the "Lone Eagle," had just been spotted by a ship in Cherbourg harbor; and soon after that the news that Lindbergh had landed safely in Paris after thirty-three and a half hours in the air. This was back when newspapers published "extras" for major breaking news, a tradition now virtually extinct. Yet even in 1927 the thrill of hearing a street-corner newsboy bellowing "extra, extra," and being able immediately to *"read* all about it" was diminished by the fact that many Americans could, and did, *hear* all about it first by radio.

A mainstay of early radio was music. It was the simplest of all forms of entertainment to air when using phonograph records. All that was needed was to pull the victrola up to the microphone and put on a record. Even live music was relatively easy to present; given the existing level of fidelity, a small brass band was hard to distinguish from a symphony orchestra. And in fact it was grand opera that was radio's first announced-in-advance program. Lee De Forest in January 1910 sought to show that radio was more than dots and dashes by arranging for a live broadcast from New York's Metropolitan Opera House. The presentation was that perennial twin-bill, *Cavalleria Rusticana* and *I Pagliacci,* made all the more memorable by the singing of the legendary Enrico Caruso. That Caruso's "golden melody" actually could be heard by wireless made all the more distressing the "painful electric hiccoughing" (quoting the *New York Herald*) that accompanied his performance. The interference, over and above the acoustical clutter that everyone expected, was the work of an early hacker of sorts, who cut in with his transmitter tuned to the same frequency as the broadcast. The *Herald* gave the broadcast a lukewarm response with the headline OPERA WAVELETS WANDER WEARILY BY WIRELESS.*

---

*It was not until a performance of *Hansel and Gretel* on December 25, 1931, that live broadcasts began on a regular basis at the Metropolitan Opera.

As important as news was, and as reliable a holder of audiences as was the live music that became a staple of early radio, what made this new medium unique was its diverse programming—basically the same sort of fare that addicts countless listeners of radio and television today. Here was something new in American life. Popularity of the top-rated shows tended to dictate what people did when. Never before were people all over the country joined in doing the same thing at the same time, as was the case when a really popular program was on. Comedy, drawing heavily at first on comedians trained in vaudeville, usually had the largest audiences, but dramatic shows were also very popular. Comedy was especially a hit during the Depression-era 1930s, when many people could afford to do little except sit at home and listen to the radio and the comic relief it offered from the drudgery of daily life. Said *Broadcasting Magazine* in 1933: "Hard times have added millions of persons to the radio audience. You can get Eddie Cantor on the air for nothing. It costs you 50 cents or more to get him at the theater."

A classic among radio programs was *Amos 'n' Andy*—two white comedians, Freeman Gosden and Charles Correll, impersonating two black characters. It began as *Sam 'n' Henry,* a local show in Chicago in 1926, became *Amos 'n' Andy* in 1928, and a year later went nationwide on the NBC network. Within another year it was the most listened-to show on radio. At the height of its popularity it was on daily from 7:00 to 7:15 P.M. Eastern Standard Time and was so popular that some stores and restaurants aired it over public address systems rather than risk having customers stay home and listen, so as not to miss an episode. Many movie theaters scheduled features to end just prior to 7:00 P.M. or start after 7:15. As the Depression set in, narrowing to a precious few what life offered in the way of diversions, millions who could at least afford a radio and a roof to go over it sat captivated in front of it nightly at seven. One Sunday in 1933 a minister announced that he would preach on the Book of Amos the following Sunday and was delighted to find the church filled. His congregation, of course, **242** thought he meant the radio Amos, not the biblical one. The program continued into the 1950s, becoming the *Amos 'n' Andy Music Hall,* and then went down and out on television.

Other favorites of the so-called Golden Age of Radio—the mid-1920s through the early 1950s—included comedians like Jack Benny, Fred Allen, Bob Hope, and Eddie Cantor; situation comedies like *Fibber McGee and Molly,* and *Duffy's Tavern;* dramatic shows and mysteries like *Inner Sanctum, The Lone Ranger,* and *Gangbusters;* soap operas like *The Guiding Light* and *One Man's Family;* and musical offerings by such band leaders as Glenn Miller, Tommy Dorsey, Duke Ellington, and Guy Lombardo.

How much impact did radio have? If there was any doubt about its hold on listeners, it was dispelled Halloween Eve 1938 with the broadcast of a dramatic production titled *The War of the Worlds* by the Mercury Theater, directed by Orson Welles. Although there were brief announcements to the effect that the program was fiction, countless people either did not take them seriously, or tuned in late and missed them, or were otherwise caught up in the drama. The result was mass hysteria of an unprecedented kind.

The drama simulated a regular radio program, including "live" segments of popular music played by a hotel orchestra. This was interrupted by news bulletins, the thrust of which was that America was being invaded by Martians. The actual point of invasion was Grovers Mill, New Jersey, near Princeton. A "reporter at the scene" gave a spine-tingling account of how a creature from another world had just landed and could send out rays that caused barns, automobiles, and woods to burst into flames. Then there were accounts of landings elsewhere in the United States, including the nation's capital.

Was it simply theatrical realism or were Martians actually invading America? By some estimates, as many as a million Americans were palpably frightened. Some people required medical treatment for shock and hysteria. Many got in their cars and took to the highways, just so they could get from wherever they were to somewhere, anywhere, else. Others rushed into the streets. On one block in Newark, New Jersey, more than twenty families ran out with wet handkerchiefs and towels over their heads. Around the country police stations and newspaper offices were flooded with calls; the *New York Times* office alone counted 875 rings of the telephone. People called priests wanting to make confessions. In the state of Washington, there was a power failure; residents were sure it was linked to the "invasion." Here and there people insisted they really had spotted Martians.

Welles next day held a press conference to say that no harm was meant, but public reaction was generally that the program went too far in taking an unsuspecting public for granted. Within three weeks, there were more than 12,000 newspaper stories relating to the presentation, analyzing and assessing the power that radio had come to wield. A net result was that the broadcasting industry made a taboo of fictionalized news bulletins and strove to keep a clear demarcation between news and non-news programming.

More important, in retrospect, is the *War of the Worlds* episode as a manifestation of the great hold that radio had come to have on American life. It would become even more all-encompassing with another form of broadcasting that was in its infancy in 1938—television.

Was there anyone who didn't like radio? Probably, but their numbers must have been few, and whatever they may have offered in dissent was drowned out by the accolades. There is one whose protest was perhaps a surprising exception—John Philip Sousa, the legendary bandmaster and composer of marches ("The Stars and Stripes Forever," and on and on).

Sousa's objection was simple: "The rapport between performer and audience is invaluable and can be fully attained only through actual vision. I have refrained from broadcasting for this very reason; I am reluctant to lose the warm personal touch with my audience." The same, of course, applied to phonograph records, and Sousa at first was just as distrustful of mechanically reproduced music as he was of music broadcast to listeners out of his presence. He relented on recordings and made a number of them with his band. But for years he absolutely refused to perform over the air. Finally in 1929, at the age of seventy-four, he gave in. His concert on a Monday night in May, from a studio of WEAF in New York, was carried by a coast-to-coast hookup of thirty-seven stations of the National Broadcasting Company and heard by millions.

What made him change his mind, Sousa later explained, as quoted by a newspaper account, was that "thousands of letters requested that he choose radio so music lovers might hear his band and music via [radio] loudspeakers throughout the nation." In an interview after his nationwide band concert, Sousa confessed he was only doing what he had long enjoyed hearing others doing—talking, singing, performing on the air. "I feared that over the radio any concert would be sort of ground out or cut and dried, without this intangible thing called personality. I was wrong. I admit it. I, personally, was just as much interested in playing before a microphone as before any visible audience of my experience. I actually felt the presence, the criticism, the approval of unseen millions as we played. I have been and will continue to be immensely benefited by radio broadcasting, for I shall continue to enjoy listening in and to play for the vast audience out beyond the microphone."

CHAPTER FIFTEEN

ADDING SIGHT TO SOUND

TELEVISION

"Now we add radio sight to sound."
–David Sarnoff, 1939

WITH THOSE WORDS, still as haunting with historic promise as they seemed then, RCA president David Sarnoff marked a broadcasting milestone on Thursday, April 20, 1939: In dedicating the just completed RCA Building at the still-to-open New York World's Fair, he announced the effective beginning of regularly scheduled telecasting. The setting was symbolic. The fair was a gigantic affirmation of Tomorrow, although the clouds of war that were the morrow's forecast would delay the fullest realization of the promise. Sarnoff, a member of the planning committee for the fair, saw its symbolism as the perfect opportunity for launching the communications medium of Tomorrow, not even waiting for the fair officially to open.

A picture added to radio's sound had been a dream since the earliest days of wireless; and even as far back as the late 1870s, there were futuristic glimpses of television-like devices inspired by the telephone (see illustrations, page 248). By 1939 the dream became a moving picture on a small screen. It was roughly like looking at a small black-and-white photograph coming to life.

But it was a dream-come-to-life for only a very few. The audience that first day of the television broadcasting era consisted primarily of a hundred or so guests of RCA who had gathered in front of television sets at the RCA Building in Radio City, some 8 miles from the fair. What they got to see, besides Sarnoff and an assortment of other speakers, including television pioneer Vladimir Zworykin, was an inside look at the fair prior to its April 30 opening. The camera panned down the Avenue of Patriots, giving viewers an exciting peek at the fair's two most notable landmarks, the Perisphere and Trylon. But since the fair was still not completed, the camera's eye also caught hundreds of workmen feverishly intent at doing the completing. They lined up at curbside to spend their lunch hour watching the television cameramen do their work. "The laborers in white overalls added contrast and stood out distinctly in the crowd," wrote a *New York Times* reporter. Then a bugle blew, and the Stars and Stripes was shown

VISIONS OF TELEVISION. Improvising on emerging technology of the nineteenth century, notably the telephone and photography, George Dumaurier, a leading British illustrator of the day, dreamed up this "electric camera-obscura" for the *Punch Almanac for 1879*. Was it a preview of television? Reynaud's projecting praxinoscope of 1882 was a sophisticated magic lantern capable of showing moving images. Did this also sense a predilection for watching things on the screen?

as it ascended to signal ceremonies dedicating one structure so far finished, the RCA Building. "Every detail was distinct," said the same reporter of the scene at the fair, "even the fleecy nature of the clouds."

By later standards of broadcast journalism, it was hardly exhilarating coverage. But it was television. "The public [such as it was] was delighted," said the *Saturday Evening Post* . . . "flesh and blood celebrities appeared and talked by television." Next day, however, the fare was down to "ancient newsreel stuff such as Sponge Fishing in Florida, which nearly everybody would give twenty-five or thirty cents not to know about." "Merely an expensive and impractical toy," reflected a writer in *The New Yorker* a little later.

But the fascination had taken root. By the time the fair officially opened on April 30, 1939, there were an estimated 100 to 200 receivers in use, and a thousand people tuned in. President Franklin D. Roosevelt, the first president to appear on broadcast television, delivered the opening presentation, in which he took notice of television as preparing to "take Americans sight-seeing by radio."

For the time, the sight-seeing would be offered only three to **248** five days a week. There would be studio-based programs like plays, scenes from operas, singers, puppets, and kitchen demonstrations (usually salads, since the lights made it too hot to cook anything), and that indispensable of early television, the feature film, westerns especially. Short subjects, travelogues, government documentaries, and cartoons rounded out the schedule. But what was often the most exciting to watch was what came from the NBC mobile unit that roamed from public event to boxing match to parade to football game, even eyeing celebrities arriving at the world premiere of *Gone With the Wind* at New York's Capitol Theater—the kind of action that television was perfect for. The mobile unit consisted of two large buses, one a studio-on-wheels, the other a mobile transmitter. The two buses, prominently marked as to purpose, were on the road every broadcasting day and served not only to provide remote coverage but also to proclaim the increasing presence of television in everyday life.

Yet the presence was not immediately to be measured by the number of watchers. By one estimate, only a few dozen sets were sold as a result of the inauguration of television transmission at the World's Fair, adding to the handful otherwise in private use. A slow start? Perhaps in comparison to radio in the early 1920s, but a television set was substantially more expensive. And in light of a scarcity of what to watch on television compared with the abundance of what to listen to on radio meant that to own a television set was to own a very costly novelty.

The promise, nonetheless, was there. It is "a new art so important in its implications that it is bound to affect all society," Sarnoff said that first day of telecasting at the World's Fair. "Television will become an important factor in American economic life."

Understatements, in retrospect. In 1939 television was just beginning the turn from the visionary to the practical. The mechanics of it had only recently been

An advertisement for an RCA Victor television set, 1939. The image on the video screen was reflected in a mirror in the folding top of the cabinet. (Smithsonian Institution)

WHAT'S ON TELEVISION?

Television programming began on a regular basis with NBC's coverage of the New York World's Fair in April 1939. A year later, this is what could be seen on NBC in New York. Except for occasional specials, programs were scheduled only for Wednesday through Sunday.

W2XBS
New York City (NBC)
Week of March 25–March 31, 1940

Wednesday, March 27

3:30 P.M.	Film, "Aesop's Fables"
3:40–4:40 P.M.	Feature film, "Fighting Trooper," with Kermit Maynard
6:45–7:00 P.M.	News
8:30 P.M.	"See Hear!" A Visual Digest of the Month
9:30–9:45 P.M.	Esso Reporter

Thursday, March 2

3:30 P.M.	Film, "Florida's Golden Harvest"
3:50 P.M.	Film, "Yankee Doodle Goes to Town"
4:20–4:30 P.M.	"Natchez," American Express Company film
6:45–7:00 P.M.	News
8:30–9:30 P.M.	Feature film, "Happiness C.O.D.," with Donald Meek

Friday, March 29

3:30–4:40 P.M.	Feature film, "Thanks for Listening," with Pinky Tomlin
6:45–7:00 P.M.	News
8:30–9:30 P.M.	"A Fine Place to Visit," celebrating opening of new store of Finkenberg's Sons Inc.

Saturday, March 30

3:30–5:00 P.M.	Baseball Game: Fordham vs. St. Peter's
7:30–8:00 P.M.	Art for Your Sake
8:30 P.M.	Carveth Wells and his travel films;
	Pauline Comanor, cartoonist
	Variety
9:30–9:45 P.M.	Television for You

Sunday, March 31

3:30–4:30 P.M.	Feature film, "Man in the Mirror," with Edward Everett Horton and Genevieve Tobin
8:45–10:30 P.M.	Finnish Track Meet at Madison Square Garden

HERE'S WHAT VIEWERS THOUGHT

There was yet no independent ratings system for television in 1940. NBC compiled its own ratings using postcard responses from viewers. Among shows broadcast during the period of March 27–31, 1940, the top-rated was Carveth Wells, followed by the track meet at Madison Square Garden and the Saturday night variety show. Least liked was the American Express short, "Natchez." British-born explorer and adventurer Carveth Wells was a highly popular lecturer of his day. His program on March 30 was titled "Tamest Africa, or Debunking Big Game Hunting."

Sources: National Broadcasting Company, Television's First Year (New York, 1940) (reprint of program and ratings); New York Times, *March 24, 1940 (additional details), Feb. 17, 1957 (Carveth Wells obituary).*

resolved. Getting to the point of actually broadcasting—other than experimentally—had not been simple. Television transmission involved technical hurdles that were never in the way of radio's quick rise to becoming a nearly indispensable part of daily life.

Concerted attempts at creating television as we know it began in the 1920s in the form of experimentation with mechanical systems, an approach proposed as early as 1884 by the German physicist Paul Nipkow. Nipkow sought to transmit images by telegraph wire by first scanning them with a spinning perforated disk. Now there were several scanning disk systems being developed, notably by John Logie Baird in England and Charles Francis Jenkins in the United States. The latter's work was announced by *Popular Science* in 1924 as "radio-vision . . . a contrivance . . . for instantly viewing far-away events." The following year Jenkins demonstrated his system in Washington. It was the first working television system.

But mechanical television was cumbersome, awkward, and incapable of producing a sharp picture. As a 1931 newspaper account observed, "One of the problems of television has been to eliminate the moving mechanical parts, especially the whirring scanning disk and its associated motor. . . . such parts must be eliminated before television [is] ready for home use as a simplified, foolproof machine as easily operated as a [radio] broadcast receiver."

Foolproof, more or less, was all-electronic television, which did away with the scanning disk and in the process produced a much sharper picture. One such system, using an image dissector tube, was devised by a young inventor named Philo T. Farnsworth. Another system using an electronic camera paired with an electronic receiving set was developed by Vladimir Zworykin, working for Radio Corporation of America (RCA). Eventually, after obtaining a license from Farnsworth, RCA combined the two systems.

Electronic, as opposed to mechanical, television also meant considerably greater flexibility as to how and what could be televised. Thus began the turn from futuristic to practical. During the 1920s and 1930s, as radio soared in popularity, people heard about television and could use their imagination as to what that radio on

the table would be like with a screen and a moving picture in the middle of it. But television still had a futuristic tinge to it. Hollywood, its rival in years to come, took delight in the status quo. Hinting at an insidious side to the new medium was a 1935 Bela Lugosi film that centered on the killing of a professor without a trace. The killer used a demonstration of television as his cover. Thus the title, *Murder by Television.* (In due time, of course, television did nearly murder movies.)

After years of experimenting, the practical side of television— the right kind of camera, the right kind of receiver—had finally been worked out. But television was no instant successor to radio. Radios were fairly inexpensive or could be made with parts from the radio store for a few dollars. Furthermore, the airwaves were alive with radio programs from morning to night, and sometimes through the night, with diversity that included something for almost everyone.

Television receivers were another matter entirely. Although TV sets in kit form did become available, they were also considerably more expensive than home-built radios and more difficult to construct. And factory-made sets, as almost all were, carried price tags like those on automobiles. To have watched a television screen in 1939, as Sarnoff was telling you that technology was adding sight to sound, would have required, on your part, a receiver costing anywhere from $200 to $1,000. A brand-new Ford or Chevrolet could be had for $660. A television set was far beyond the means of most people. And here is what you would have gotten for $200: merely an attachment with a 4- by 5-inch picture to hook up to an existing radio. For $1,000, it was a self-contained console with a picture 7 by 10 inches (black and white, of course). People who could afford television got the sheer delight of being the first to have something wondrously new, which presumably made up for the fact that those hundreds of dollars provided only a skimpy selection of programs to choose from.

But television ultimately was aimed not at the relative few who could afford to purchase the earliest sets but at a mass audience who would buy once the price came down. What, in fact, would these prospective "average" viewers think? RCA in 1939 set out to determine that by using a test market. It needed an average town— not too large, not too small, people not too wealthy, not too **253** poor—within range of NBC's television signal in New York City yet far enough away to represent the kind of reception the "average" town would get once television broadcasting was in full swing. RCA decided on Newburgh, New York (population 30,000), 54 miles up the Hudson River from NBC's transmitter on the Empire State Building.

Here, in the fall of 1939, RCA began a two-month campaign to encourage the purchase of television sets by reducing prices a third. Newspaper ads appeared in Newburgh as well as nearby Poughkeepsie and Middletown. According to *Business Week*, they "quoted no prices, but built up consumer interest. Then those dealers who were cooperating in the program made up lists of their best prospects and went out to give demonstrations in homes. This 'pick-and-choose' selling is at variance to the 'walk-in-the-store' radio selling methods usually used. It proved surprisingly successful." Once dealer and customer got to prices, there was good reason for the success. Sets usually selling for $600 could be had for $395. Receivers that listed at $450 were marked down to $295 and those for $199.50 to $135.

The result was the sale of some 100 sets by the end of November. In the opinion of a business writer for the *New York Times:* "The fact that the Newburgh public in two months bought 100 sets as against sales of only 1,000 in the entire New York area since May indicates very graphically that prices have been one of the chief factors in the slow sales, according to observers." The writer gave as another reason for the pickup in sales an increase in quality and quantity of programs broadcast by NBC plus the expectation that CBS would be on the air with regular telecasting by early 1940, doubling what there was to watch. Subsequently, by one estimate, the number of sets in use rose to between 400 and 500. NBC estimated the total of television receivers in homes in the New York metropolitan area at 3,000, as of April 30, 1940. In addition, it said, there were about 150 receivers in taverns, restaurants, schools, theater lobbies, and stores. The total New York area viewing *audience* as of mid-1940 was placed at 15,000. By this time, NBC had produced more than 600 cumulative hours of televiewing.

Television in 1940 was showing its potential in an area where it has had some of its greatest impact—the political process. Covering the Republican national convention in 1940, *New York Times* radio-television correspondent Orrin E. Dunlap Jr. saw what was coming:

> Even in 1928, the politicians confessed that radio had to a great extent taken over and revolutionized politics. . . . The microphone as a mouthpiece of the nation now has binocular-like eyes. Radio has forced candidates to speak for themselves directly to the people, not through party leaders. Now, they are put on display from head to foot. How they comb their hair, how they smile and how they loop their necktie become new factors in politics.

Despite gradually increasing sales, television was largely a novelty for most people. Sets were still primitive by modern standards. Less expensive ones could only tune in three channels, a form of built-in obsolescence. Picture quality was considered about equal to a good newspaper halftone but only under favorable conditions of transmission and reception. "But these conditions are seldom achieved, and considerable detail is lost when large scenes are televised," said *Consumer Reports* in June 1939. Overall the consumer watchdog had mostly cold water to throw: "As an instrument of common, everyday use, for the great majority of people, television still belongs to the somewhat distant future. Even the claims currently made for the invention are premature by several years. . . . Consumers Union suggests, therefore, that unless you are interested in experimentation, you avoid an investment in television for at least another year."

TELEVISION IN TELEVISIONVILLE

Yet the excitement—the sense of euphoria of riding the leading wave of some thrilling new age—covered a multitude of defects. When TV came to town, as it did in Newburgh, it came to stay.

Not for everyone at once, of course. For most people in Newburgh, all there was to see of television at the outset was a curious contraption—"freakish looking . . . might be a huge necktie rack"—that began sprouting on roofs of homes around town. People caught on quickly. A television antenna.

Besides its intended function of gathering in waves of transmitted sound and video, the antenna was found to be gathering in cousins, brothers-in-law, aunts and uncles, nephews, nieces, and friends one never knew one had. One man, in the early days of Newburgh television, complained that "My brother-in-law thinks my house is a movie theater. He calls up to see what's on, comes over frankly to watch the telecast; when it's over he just gets up and walks out without even saying good night."

The night of a major boxing match it was said you could spot the television houses by counting the cars parked out front. TV dealer Hyman Shapiro, who sold most of the sets in the area, said he personally had thirty-five people in his living room for a Joe Louis fight but was "not sure yet which ones were invited." Wrestling also was a regular favorite. From a technical viewpoint, it was relatively easy to televise, and so became a staple of the early TV diet.

Frank R. Dutcher, of Balmville Road, estimated the televiewing capacity of his small cottage at thirty persons, including standees in the kitchen. The Dutchers' home was one of several in Newburgh visited by James L. Fly, chairman of the Federal Communications Commission, for an in-person look at how the new medium was working in the home. Mrs. Dutcher quoted him as saying, "This is going to kill the movies."

Children generally were less enthusiastic, largely because there was little of interest to them. Sports, western movies, and the Quiz Kids were okay with kids but represented only a small part of a schedule that was small to start with. Probably typical of many was the eleven-year-old who inquired of his father, "Any movies on tonight, Dad?" "No movies tonight, son." "Can I go play?" In coming years, with an ever-broadening variety of programming geared to children, the challenge would be to get the kids to go play instead of being glued to the set.

Summing up the "Town That Tested Television" in *Better Homes & Gardens,* writer Hal Borland asked, "What has television done to Newburgh home life? Several families say it has strengthened home ties, that home is the entertainment center once more. Youngsters bring their friends in, instead of going out. Parents like to stay at home, particularly when there are special telecasts." As for reading: "Does television replace one's reading? One professional man says yes. He used to read for relaxation; now he watches television. Others say no."

Homes got most of the attention in Newburgh's test of early television, but there were also sets in taverns, bars, cafés, restaurants, and other places of amusement and socializing. John Guzorsky had TV at his eatery, called Your Lunch. He and some of his patrons liked horse races and had been known to place a bet or two. It quickly dawned on Guzorsky, once he had television installed, that he would know the winner just ahead of his friend, the bookmaker, who had to wait until the judges posted the numbers to see who won. On the afternoon of the opening at New York's Belmont Park, which was televised, Guzorsky called the bookie in six straight races, each time a few split seconds before the posting, and six straight times picked the winner. The bookie pleaded to know the secret. "Television," explained Guzorsky. Satisfied merely with beating the system, he then returned his winnings.

Overall the consensus was that Newburgh, "Televisionville of America . . . loves television" (quoting the *Saturday Evening Post*). Though it seems tinged with the apocryphal, the *Post* solemnly quoted one Newburgher as saying, "You can take my wife or my automobile, but not my television set."

What people were watching in Newburgh in 1939–1940, however, was not yet commercial television as it exists today. Nor was it television of a technical quality on a par with today's. The limited broadcasting supplied by NBC in New York and similar broadcasting in other markets—General Electric in Schenectady later in 1939, Zenith Corporation in Chicago in 1940—was carried out while regulation remained in a gray area. The FCC had temporarily banned use of commercials and left engineering standards unspecified. Finally in May 1941, the FCC authorized commercial television to go into effect on July 1, 1941. With this authorization came uniform engineering standards, notably a picture of 525 scanning lines, substantially improving picture quality. In addition, FM was now used for transmission of sound. (A set manufactured in accordance with the new standard could still be used today with only a minor adjustment.) As with radio, having sponsors had the effect of upgrading the quality of programming, since a sponsor naturally wants to be identified with something of distinction. As of July 1941, New York had three TV stations on the air—WCBW, operated by CBS, and W2XWV, of Dumont Laboratories, in addition to NBC. Nationwide, more than twenty stations went on the air.

Meanwhile, in 1939, another televisionville was getting its antennas up and its pencils out. This one was in Schenectady, New York, home of General Electric, which had its station, WRGB, Schenectady, in operation November 6, 1939, broadcasting to roughly 300 households in the Albany-Troy-Schenectady area. Here was another systematic attempt to find out what people thought about television and what it had to offer—even before commercial standards were set. WRGB mailed out weekly schedules to set owners, and with each included a reply card for audience comments. Of the 300 owners of television sets, twenty-five to forty viewers regularly returned ratings. In addition, the station periodically sent out special questionnaires. In 1945, these various surveys resulted in a five-year evaluation of viewer likes and dislikes. And here were the principal results:

Highest rated of live entertainment was light opera (Gilbert and Sullivan's *Trial by Jury* being the favorite), followed by puppet shows and news. At the other end of the scale were art, religion, and public service programs. Sports placed sixth on the list of twenty-three types of programming, just ahead of grand opera and just behind dramatic productions. In addition to live shows, there were motion pictures, including feature films, documentaries, and travelogues.

Obviously television has changed. Opera, light or otherwise, has long since disappeared from major network scheduling, although it can still be seen on public broadcasting. But the entire range of programming reflected simpler technology, so that direct comparisons with modern-day television must be made with care. Opera, light or grand, was relatively easy to present because there was generally no attempt to show the panorama of an entire operatic stage but rather to focus on one or a few singers. Sports, according to one contemporary account, largely consisted of "instruction in game fundamentals rather than telecasts of contests or matches." However, once a month in 1944, the WRGB studio was turned into a sports arena for boxing or wrestling matches. In **258** addition, boxing and wrestling were occasionally televised at New

From the late 1940s through the mid-1950s, Tuesday night at eight was owned by Milton Berle, often called "Mr. Television." His NBC show, echoing old-time vaudeville, was probably the most popular show of the early days. It was said that Berle sold more television sets than any advertising campaign. (Smithsonian Institution)

York City's Madison Square Garden and relayed to the studio for broadcast.

This was television in its infancy—little steps. Yet there were signs of what was to come. A handbook of television programming published by General Electric in 1945, incorporating results of these various surveys, commented in one case that "the high percentage of people who correctly identified the sponsor indicates the impact of television" and, in another case, "The high percentage of returns indicates the wide interest in television among set owners." Impact—the story of television in one word.

Yet as of 1945 there were fewer than 7,000 television sets in the entire country and only nine stations (besides Schenectady, three in New York City, two each in Chicago and Hollywood, and one in Philadelphia) then on the air. World War II, which ended in the summer of 1945, had severely restricted growth. There was a wartime ban on the manufacture of sets and the construction of new stations. That ban was lifted in October 1945, and finally the industry could begin to gear up for a mass market. At almost the same time, there was a technical advance of great consequence.

One reason for the limited kind of programming WRGB offered was the relatively primitive camera then in use. When it was demonstrated in 1925, a camera invented by Vladimir

259

The sign says "Radio Mart," but it was a television set in the window of this store in Washington, D.C., that attracted these onlookers for the World Series in 1949. For many Americans, their first experience with television was watching on the sidewalk. Passersby stopped, often at length, to watch the news, a baseball game, or some popular program at a TV store window. As the price came down, and more and more people got television sets of their own, window-watching disappeared from the American scene. (National Archives)

Zworykin was the first all-electronic system, eventually replacing a mechanical spinning-disk system. But even an improved version was satisfactory only for relatively close-up work. By 1945 the so-called iconoscope was itself obsolete. Its successor, the image orthicon camera, was 100 times sharper and had a much greater depth of field. Now, it was not only possible to present indoor productions showing an entire stage but outdoor events like football or baseball games.

With the broader programming made possible by the image orthicon camera and with the lifting of the ban on new stations and manufacture of sets, television began to soar in popularity. In five years, at midcentury, the number of sets in use had gone from fewer than 7,000 to more than 3,250,000. Still, radio dominated. Some 42 million homes had at least one radio, and half had more than one. And there were four times as many automobile radios as television sets. TV was still expensive. The average cost of a new set was

$300, one-fifth the cost of a two-door 1949 Chevrolet automobile ($1,501). The cheapest TV, at $100, had only a 3-inch screen.

Yet while set owners could be expressed as a finite number, there was no way of knowing the number of *viewers*. As in Newburgh, New York, in 1939, those who bought television sets suddenly found they had more friends than they realized—friends who liked to drop by for a visit, say, when Milton Berle was about to go on (see photograph, below). There was also a phenomenon of the late 1940s and early 1950s that might be called window-watching. Department stores and radio-television shops throughout the country not only had sets in their windows but had them on. Passersby stopped, often at great length, to watch the news, or a baseball game, or some popular program. For countless Americans in the late 1940s, this was the extent of their TV viewing. As the novelty wore off and the price came down, and more and more people got sets of their own, window-watching disappeared from the American scene.

By the early 1950s, in the judgment of one contemporary observer, television was joining the radio, the bathtub, and the automobile as a standard of American life.

The American family and the American family pastime, Washington, D.C., 1957. (Library of Congress, Prints & Photographs Division, *U.S. News & World Report* Magazine Collection)

EPILOGUE

IN A SENSE, there is no ending to this book. New technologies are continually unfolding, and new thresholds looming into view. Even as this was being written, new wonders were antiquating merely recent ones.

How fast are things changing? A couple of years ago, it was a matter of getting "wired." To be wired to the Internet was to be connected—to be in the forefront of technological innovation. *Data Communications International* in 1995 said, "Build a better Web site, and the wired will beat a path to your door." Libraries, not always noted for being cutting-edge, were advised by *Library Manager* that same year "to adjust quickly to . . . all the new, more informal, 'wired' ways [for] sharing information." "Wired," in this new sense, was duly added to the 1997 edition of the *Oxford Dictionary of New Words*.

A few years later (just after the 1996 edition of the *Oxford English Reference Dictionary* decreed the noun "wireless" archaic) it was wireless that was sweeping to popularity. Not the old wildfire wonder, of course. This was the Internet in the palm of your hand, something that was virtually science fiction a decade earlier.

Web-enabled cell phones began coming on the market in 2000. Although the screen was small, and the applications somewhat limited, wireless Web could be used for such purposes as e-mail, brief news items, travel information, and stock quotes.

Interactive television—allowing viewers to interact with the show they are watching as well as to personalize what is on the screen—was another new technology dating to the year 2000.

Digital photography, high-definition television (HDTV), digital video discs (DVD), and other refinements of existing technology continue to offer exiting new prospects.

Miniaturization points toward the possibility of making a Web-connected cell phone of the present look as big as a telephone booth of old by comparison.

What wonders are still to come? What indeed?

> The realization of so marvelous a device cannot fail to stimulate speculation as to where such wonders will stop. . . . What next?

. . . as *Popular Science Monthly* said in March 1878 about a wondrous new contrivance called the telephone.

SOURCE NOTES

PROLOGUE

(Sources here are specific to Prologue and not otherwise cited in source notes)

Douglas, *Listening In,* 73 (quote, "It is not the substance of communication"); *Elisha,* "More Wonderful Than the Telegraph," 4–8 (George and Thomas's visit to the telegraph office, early 1850s), *Frank Leslie's Illustrated Newspaper,* Sept. 18, 1858 (details, service at Trinity Church); Museum Village, Monroe, N.Y. (instruction card for Terriff's Perfect Washer, c. 1850); *New York Times,* Sept. 2, 1858 (account of city celebration of transatlantic cable, "wondrous event of a wondrous age," "display such as even New York has never witnessed"; note: chief among those at "Reception of Heroes" was Cyrus Field), July 6, 1932 (brief item identifying Knudsen as "Norwegian scientist [who] demonstrated long-distance typesetting by wireless"); Pool, *Social Impact of the Telephone,* 50 (Emerson quotation); *Popular Science Monthly,* April 1878 ("acoustical marvel of the century"); *Scientific American,* Oct. 31, 1908 (Knudsen Wireless Typewriter); *Statistical Abstract of the United States,* 2000, 568 (more than 80 million Americans); *Time,* April 10, 2000, "Will Anyone Ever Run a 3 Minute Mile?" (four-minute mile statistics).

TRANSPORTATION

INTRODUCTION

American Review of Reviews, Aug. 1927 ("Air-Shy America"); Haskins, *Canajoharie-Catskill Railroad* (wreck of 1840).

ANNIHILATING TIME AND SPACE

American Railroad Journal, "Changes Wrought by Steam," Sept. 15, 1841 ("The mere introduction as an agent of power," "The transforming power of steam,"); *Baltimore American,* May 24, 1830, as quoted in Brown, *History of the First Locomotives,* 98 ("the extraordinary rate of fifteen miles per hour"), n.d., as quoted in *Niles' Register,* April 25, 1835 ("the day is not distant when travellers"); Brown, *History of the First Locomotives,* passim, 176 ("This locomotive, the 'De Witt Clinton' "); *Charleston Courier,* Dec. 29, 1830 ("We flew on the wings of the wind"), as quoted in Brown, *History of the First Locomotives,* 151; J. Henry Clark, *Sight and Hearing,* New York,

1856, as quoted in Zboray, q.v. ("Observe the passengers in the train");
[Ezra Dean], "New Things Since I Was a Boy!" [1869], Smithsonian
Institution Archives, Warshaw Collection, "Inventions," Box 1; Douglas,
All Aboard, passim, 42–43 (travel conditions on early railroads); Fletcher,
Lionel (first Lionel locomotive); Shea, *All in the Game,* 151–52, (Smashed-
Up Locomotive, Blown-Up Steamer); *Forrester's Pictorial Miscellany,* 282
("The progress of railroad building"); Freeman, *Yesterday's Toys,* 118 (early
steam locomotives, "the blow-off catch could be turned off"); Nathaniel
Hawthorne, *Passages from the American Note-Books,* New York, 1893, 369
("Four or five long cars"); Historical and Philosophical Society of Ohio,
Bulletin, vol. 6, Oct. 1948, "Western Travels" (John W. Baker, "6 AM left
home in the Cars"); Ierley, *National Road,* 115 (Mary Reed Eastman, "We
left Columbus yesterday"), 138 (Matilda Houstoun, "It was impossible, for
one moment"); Klamkin, *Railroadiana,* 238 (first self-propelled locomotive, 1856); McClintock, *Toys in America,* 374–75 (electric trains); *Maryland
Historical Magazine,* vol. 49, Sept. 1954, "Travel Extracts from the Journal
of Alexander Randall, 1830–1831," Richard H. Randall, ed. ("I again traveled on the Rail Road"); *Michigan History,* vol. 43, March 1959, "Michigan
Journal, 1836" (John M. Gordon, "We left Albany in the cars"); *Niles'
Register,* April 23, 1831 ("rail roads, we think, associated with steam"), June
27, 1835 ("The time will come when people will travel"), as quoted in
Ward, *Railroads and the American Character,* 111 ("To see more clearly,"
"Science has conquered space"); Stover, *American Railroads,* passim, 31
(quoting Davy Crockett, "I can only judge"); Stover, *History of the Baltimore
and Ohio,* 35 (first use of *Tom Thumb*); Taylor, *Transportation Revolution,* passim, 141–46 (speeds of various forms of transportation, 1830s); Thoreau
("We do not ride") as quoted in Ceruzzi, *Modern Computing,* 312; *University
of Rochester Library Bulletin,* vol. 4, winter 1949 (Frederica Broke, "Being the
first time I ever travelled"); Ward, *Railroads and the Character of America,*
36–37 (opposition to railroads, quoting Lanman "dragons of mightier
power," quoting Thoreau "when I hear the iron horse"), 110–12 (railroads
and concepts of time and space); Withuhn, *Rails Across America,* introduction (impact of railroads generally), 17 (quoting Daniel J. Boorstin, *The
Americans,* 104, Weld, engine darting "with rocket-like impetuosity");
Ronald J. Zboray, "The Railroad, the Community and the Book,"
Southwest Review, Aug. 1986 (railroads and increase in correspondence
1840–1860, and dissemination of books and periodicals; quoting J. Harry
Clark "Observe the passengers").

Adoption of Standard Time: *Chicago Tribune,* Nov. 18, 19, 1883 (details of
adoption of standard time); Corliss, Carlton J., *The Day of Two Noons*
(Washington: Association of American Railroads, 1952), excerpted in
Botkin, *Railroad Folklore,* 514–18 (adoption of standard time generally,
time discrepancies Philadelphia/New York/Baltimore and west and south
266 of Chicago, quoting *Chicago Tribune,* March 1, 1853, "The clock in

Sherwood and Waiteley's"); Harriet Martineau, *Society in America,* London, 1837, vol. 2, 206 (Americans are "very imaginative in respect of the hour"); *New York Times,* Nov. 13, 1883, "Notes from Washington" (attorney general's opinion on standard time); O'Malley, *Keeping Watch,* 87–95 (time balls, the telegraph and other influences on standardization of time); Zboray, *supra* (quoting Thoreau, the trains "come and go").

Railroads and the Telegraph: Erie Railroad, *Erie Railroad,* 9 (first use of telegraph for dispatching trains); Ringwalt, *Development of Transportation,* 164 (use of telegraph by Erie Railroad, 1850); Stover, *American Railroads,* 38 (use of telegraph by Erie, including date).

TRAVELING, NOT BEING TRAVELED

Boston Advertiser, Dec. 27, 1878 ("Mounted on his 52-inch wheel") as quoted in the *New York Times,* Dec. 28, 1878, "The Winged Wheel"; Leek, *Bicycle,* 88 (Coney Island and Pasadena cycleways); *Lippincott's* magazine, Nov. 1879, "The Bicycle, and Riding It" (fastest speeds as of 1879, comparative data for velocipede and bicycle of 1879, "Rinks and schools multiplied," "Being free from objections"); New York Central Rail Road, *Time Table of Passenger Trains,* Dec. 1868 (railroad times and distances quoted); *New York Times,* Dec. 7, 1868 ("There is no man living who can say"), Jan. 27, 1869 ("too limited to accommodate"), Nov. 7, 1874, "The Bicycle" ("A form of amusement"), Dec. 6, 1878, "Bicycle Races in Boston"; Pratt, *American Bicycler,* 67–73 (accessories of 1879, "a very useful device," "desirable for night riding"); Time-Life, *Fabulous Century: 1870–1900,* 119 ("I found a whole philosophy of life"), 120 (numbers of riders, 1896); U.S. Census Bureau, *Historical Statistics,* 696 (bicycle production, 1899–1909); Willard, *Wheel,* 38 ("that blessed woman question"), 38–39 ("We saw that the physical development"), 75 ("the most remarkable motor yet devised").

LOVE AT FIRST SIGHT

A uniquely good source here was James J. Flink's *America Adopts the Automobile, 1895–1910* (MIT Press), as will be apparent from the numerous source references. *American Monthly Review of Reviews,* June 1900, Cleveland Moffett, "Automobiles for the Average Man" ("of late the average man has been stirred"); Case, *Ford Smiles* (excerpt quoted); *Country Life in America,* Feb. 1909, C. O. Morris, "The Cause of Automobile Accidents," as quoted in Flink, *America Adopts,* 225 ("new drivers are making their debut"); Flink, *America Adopts,* 166–74 (auto registration), 174–78 (licensing of drivers), 179–90 (regulating speed), 213–16 (insurance), 225–31 (driver training, mechanical expertise); Flink, *Automobile Age,* 155 (first mall, Country Club Plaza), 161 (first drive-in fast-food, Hailey's Pig Stand); Flink, *Car Culture,* 20 (quoting *Automobile,* "the unprecedented and well nigh incredible"), 22 (425 Oldsmobiles produced in 1901); *Harper's Weekly,* Nov. 18, 1899, "Status of the Horse" ("As the companion of man"); *Horseless Age,* Aug. 21, 1901, as quoted in Flink, *America Adopts,* 225–26 ("the owner just sits down and trembles"); Kane, *Famous First Facts,* 386 (first auto accident, first fatality); Mall of America, Bloomington, Minn., management office (by telephone, "12,750 parking spaces"); Maxim, *Horseless Carriage Days,* 121 ("One of the major difficulties in 1897"), 131–33 ("It is a highly significant thing"), 132 ("I have taught a large number"), 132 ("Is the gasoline motor car"); Mecredy, *Motor Book,* 100–101 ("Steep hills should never be descended," "Corners constitute a very serious danger"); *Motor Age,* Dec. 7, 1899, as quoted in Flink, *America Adopts,* 181 ("The people wanted it"); *Motor World,* 1901, as quoted in Sears, *American Heritage History of the Automobile,* 87 ("To take control of this materialized energy"); *Munsey's Magazine,* May 1903, "Impressions by the Way" ("It is my understanding that the product"); *New York Times,* Nov. 11, 1900, "Great Motor Show Ended" (details of final day of 1900 New York Auto Show, quotes "It is the Horse Show, indeed," "Nearly every man, woman, and child that visited"); *Outlook,* July 25, 1908, "Concerning Automobiling" ("The automobile has become"), Aug. 15, 1908, "Letters" ("It has been my lot"), Dec. 31, 1910, "The Cost of Motoring by a Man of Moderate Means" ("The price of the car, the cost of maintenance"); Post, M., *A Woman's Summer,* 14–15 ("After an hour devoted to waiting"); Rae, *Road and Car,* 57 (auto output 1914 exceeds wagons and carriages), 59 (report of Hoover-appointed commission cited: "It is probable that no invention"); Ramsey, *Veil, Duster and Tire Iron,* 10–12 (procedures for starting generally, "The driver occupied the front seat"), 11 ("I was born mechanical"); Scharchburg, *Carriages Without Horses,* 77–81 (first Duryea car, quotations from *Springfield Union*); *Scientific American,* May 26, 1906, as quoted in Flink, *America Adopts,* 225 ("manufacturers of popular cars have estimated"); Sears, *American Heritage History of the Automobile,* 52 (Edison quote, "cars and trucks in every large city run with motors"), 82 (120 pieces of music 1905–07); *Scientific American,* "An Automobile School," May 6, 1906 (automobile schools); U.S. Census Bureau, *Historical Statistics,* 200 (wholesale prices indexes), 716 (motor vehicle sales and registration figures, 1900–1929); White, *Second Tree,* 36–37 ("Then, whistling as though thinking"); *World's Work,* June 1903, Henry Norman, "Can I Afford an Automobile" (data in box, "What It Cost to Operate"). The toy auto c. 1895 referred to in the caption for the 1900 toy auto was manufactured by Morton E. Converse, Winchendon, Mass., and is in the toy collection of the Strong Museum, Rochester, N.Y. (ID No. 77.7453). "$650 as representing about twenty-five percent of a typical doctor's annual income" is from

the Smithsonian Institution (exhibit of a 1903 Oldsmobile).

LOOKING HEAVENWARD

Balloons and Dirigibles: *Albany Evening Journal,* July 5, 1859 (quoting *Albany Morning Express,* July 4, as to details of voyage of *Atlantic,* sightings over Fort Wayne, Sandusky, Cleveland, and quotes "created no little excitement," "Trans-Continental Air Voyage," and reception in Adams "exceeding celebration of Atlantic Cable"); Blanchard, *Journal of My Forty-Fifth Ascension* (Blanchard's flight, Philadelphia, 1793); *Buffalo Courier,* July 4, 1859, as quoted in *Full Particulars* (sighting of *Atlantic* over Buffalo and Niagara Falls); Cohen, I. Bernard, "Benjamin Franklin and Aeronautics," *Journal of the Franklin Institute,* Aug. 1941 (Franklin generally, including substantiation of "new-born baby" quote); Crouch, *Eagle Aloft,* 248–56 (flight of the *Atlantic* generally), 248 (in the neighborhood of $30,000), 254 (established record that lasted until 1910); *Dictionary of American Biography* (Wise's aborted balloon trip to Europe and death by drowning); *Dunlap's American Daily Advertiser,* Jan. 10, 1793 ("when it began to rise"), as quoted in Penn Mutual, *The First Air Voyage,* 13; *Exhibition of Early Children's Books* (accounts of balloon flight in children's books generally); *Full Particulars of the Greatest Aerial Voyage* (account of Wise's voyage of 1859 generally, including entire text quoted); Glines, *Lighter-Than-Air,* 60–66 (flight of the *Atlantic*), 61 (quoting Wise, "It is established now beyond a doubt"); Hazen, *Symbolic Primer,* as quoted in *Exhibition of Early Children's Books* [note: 1829 edition of *Symbolic Primer* has a shorter, simpler definition]; Ierley, *A Place in History,* 105–10 (Aero Carnival generally, Fort "aerial age"); *Literary Digest,* July 4, 1925, "Aboard the Airship 'Los Angeles' to Porto Rico and Back" (resembling "more than anything else"); *Living Age,* Aug. 15, 1925, Walter Scherz, "In Three Days to America" ("Our most modern method"); Lowe, *Air-Ship New York,* 6 (3,000 balloon ascensions by 8,000 persons), 12 (details of *City of New York*); *Mother Goose Melodies,* Boston, 1881, as quoted in *Exhibition of Early Children's Books* (text quoted); *National Magazine,* Jan. 1853, "Balloons and Ballooning"; *New York Times,* Oct. 5, 1924, "Greatest Zeppelin Sails" (preview of ZR-3); *New York World,* May 26, 1909 (Aero Carnival generally, "evidence of tremendous interest"); *Newark [N.J.] Evening News,* May 26, 1909 (Aero Carnival, "Everything looked propitious"); Penn Mutual, *The First Air Voyage,* (details of Blanchard's flight, Philadelphia, 1793, including distance and landing site); *St. Louis Democrat,* July 2, 1859, as quoted in *Full Particulars; Swift, First Lessons,* 104 ("Do accidents ever happen?"), 105 (parachutes); *Talisman: A Tale for Boys,* as quoted in *Exhibition of Early Children's Books; Third Chapter of Accidents,* as quoted in *Exhibition of Early Children's Books; Wisconsin Magazine of History,* (vol. 49) winter 1965–1966, Louis P. Lochner, "Aboard the Airship Hindenburg: Louis P. Lochner's Diary of Its Maiden Flight to the United States" ("Jules Verne come true" and subsequent quotes); Wise, *System of Aeronautics* ("the genius of our favorably gifted country").

Machines with Wings: *Air Facts and Feats,* New York, 1974 (first DC-3 flight); Allen, *Airline Builders,* 126–27, 133–34 (Boeing 247, DC-2, DC-3), 170–71 (formation of various airlines); *American Review of Reviews,* Aug. 1927, "Air-Shy America"; Botting, *Giant Airships,* passim (dirigibles generally); *Collier's,* April 2, 1927, William G. Shepherd, "Good Roads in the Sky" (beacons for night airmail flight); Crouch, *Bishop's Boys,* 56–57 (toy helicopter, O. Wright "Our first interest began") 270–73 (Lorin Wright as press agent, press response to telegram about flights of Dec. 17, 1903), 397–99 (details of successful demonstration of Wright Flyer for U.S. Army at Fort Myer, Va., July 1909); *Everybody's Magazine,* Maximilian Foster, "The Highway of the Air," Jan. 1909 (quoting Wright "No flying machine will ever fly," quoting Bell "The aerodrome has at a stroke," "Wright climbed into his seat"); Hatfield, *Aeroplane Scrap Book,* 218 (1933 ad for Boeing 247); Howard, *Wilbur and Orville,* 138–45 (press coverage of first successful flights at Kitty Hawk, Dec. 1903); *Living Age,* "Balloons and Voyages in the Air," Aug. 21, 1875 ("There are many students of aerial locomotion"); *New York Herald,* Dec. 19, 1903, "Wright Brothers Experimenting with Flying Machine"; *New York Times,* July 8, 1929, July 10, 1929 (transcontinental air-train); *New York World,* May 26, 1909 (estimate of 50,000 at Aero Carnival, which may well have been exaggerated since Joseph Pulitzer's *World* presumably had some part in its planning; the Pulitzer Building in New York was the turnaround point for flights originating at the show); *Overland Monthly and Out West Magazine,* July 1928, Mrs. Frederick H. Colburn, "A Trip in a De Luxe Tri-Motor Airplane" (quotes attributed); St. John, *Things a Boy Should Know About Wireless* (advertisement for St. John's "Electric Air Ship" game); *Scientific American,* Jan. 1927, "Learning to Use Our Wings"; Walsh, *Kitty Hawk,* 152–57 (press coverage of first successful flights at Kitty Hawk, Dec. 1903); *Wisconsin Magazine of History,* winter 1965–1966, Louis P. Lochner, "Aboard the Airship Hindenburg: Louis P. Lochner's Diary of Its Maiden Flight to the United States" ("My first experience in an American plane"). The National Archives photograph of the U.S.S. *Akron* c. 1932 is from General Records of the Department of the Navy, 1798–1947 (80-G-458713).

COMMUNICATIONS

INTRODUCTION

Elisha, c. 1850, copy at American Antiquarian Society (telegraph wires **270** seemed like "cobwebs in the air").

Auchincloss, *Hone & Strong Diaries,* 175 ("Everybody all agog"); *Baltimore Patriot & Commercial Gazette,* April 30, 1844 (opening date of Whig convention), May 25, 1844 ("Morse's Electro Magnetic Telegraph now connects"), May 28, 1844 (bulletins posted in Rotunda, crowd numbered several hundred), June 6, 1844 ("We are requested to state"), June 10, 1844 ("The telegraph will be in operation this afternoon"), June 15, 1844 (detailed account of how telegraph worked); Bremer ("remarkable that in all directions"), as quoted in Turner, *Rediscovering America,* 39; Crouthamel, *Bennett's New York Herald,* 44–46 (early news gathering and early application of telegraph by newspapers generally), 45 ("Once this extraordinary invention"), 46 (post office obsolete); Forrester, *Pictorial Miscellany,* "The Magnetic Telegraph," 27–34, 27 ("I propose to give my little readers"), 33 (anecdote about the fellow waiting for a letter to go by); Hone, *Diary,* 773–74 ("Magnetic Telegraph. Strange and wonderful discovery"); *International Directory of Company Histories,* 17, 345, "New Valley Corporation" (history of Western Union, its predecessor); Lee, *Daily Newspaper in America,* 527 (rates of manual transmission by telegraph); Mabee, *American Leonardo,* 275–79 (reporting of Democratic convention by telegraph, May 1844), 278 ("Polk is unanimously nom.," quoting recollections of Ezra Cornell in Albert W. Smith, *Ezra Cornell* [1934], 42–44); *Milwaukee Sentinel* ("At nine o'clock yesterday morning"), quoted in Hone, *Diary,* 851–52; *National Intelligencer,* Washington, May 29, 1844 ("mingled delight and wonder"); *New York Herald,* May 30, 1844 ("Little else is done here"), Oct. 24, 1845 (Bennett: "supersede the Post Office"), Aug. 6, 1858 ("Triumph of Science," "London within a flash of New York," "send an electric thrill," roundup of events celebrating completion of cable), Aug. 9, 1858 ("It is interesting to notice"); *New York Times,* Aug. 7, 1858 ("The transmission of matter"), Aug. 9, 1858 ("The Atlantic Telegraph is felt to be . . . The irrepressible outburst"), Aug. 17, 1858 (message from queen to president); Papers of Samuel F. B. Morse, Library of Congress, vol. 17 (reel #3), Vail to Morse, June 3, 1844 ("Every thing went well last week"); Philadelphia *Evening Journal* ("This is the greatest triumph"), quoted in *New York Times,* Aug. 6, 1858; Prime, *Life of Morse,* 501–2 (anecdote about young girl, "You will then send me"); Richards, *Village Life,* 101 (Auburn, N.Y., "There was a celebration in town"); Taylor, *Transportation Revolution,* 150 (postage of 3 cents, 1851), 152 (early uses of telegraph including chess games, telegram rates in 1850s).

Weather Forecasting: *American Almanac,* Boston, 1838, 73, "Prognostics of the Weather" (folk wisdom as to the weather, bees and ants, bats flitting, "An evening red and morning gray"); *Galaxy,* Dec. 1871, "Weather Prognostics by the People" (availability of weather forecasts to the press);

Historical and Philosophical Society of Ohio, *Bulletin,* July 1949, "National Weather Service Origins" (early weather reporting generally); *New York Times,* Dec. 10, 1870 ("only served to indicate," "When this service has been in operation," details of weather forecasting in early 1870s generally), Nov. 20, 1871 (forecast issued Dec. 19, 1871); Smithsonian Institution, *Annual Report,* 1892, 89–93, "The Meteorological Work of the Smithsonian Institution" (Smithsonian role in weather forecasting).

THE FIRST COMMUNICATIONS HIGHWAY

Boettinger, *Telephone Book,* 98 (telephone called voice telegraph in England), 106 (origin of telephone numbers); *Boston Daily Globe,* Feb. 13, 1877 (details of Salem lecture, "Professor Bell asked Mr. Watson"), April 5, 1877 ("Professor A. Graham Bell, the inventor"); *Boston Transcript,* Feb. 1, 1877 ("Let us hope that the day"), as quoted in *New York Times,* Feb. 3, 1877; *Boston Traveller* ("telegraphing voices"), as quoted in *New York Times,* July 23, 1876; Bruce, *Bell,* 218–19 (Salem lecture, London *Athenaeum, La Nature:* "Le Télégraphe Parlant"); *Chicago Tribune,* Nov. 8, 1885, as quoted in *New York Times,* Nov. 9 (costs of telephone use in selected cities); Bernard S. Finn, "Alexander Graham Bell's Experiments with the Variable-Resistance Transmitter," *Smithsonian Journal of History,* vol. 1, no. 4, winter 1966, 7–8 (account of Bell and Watson on March 10, 1876, including quotation "Mr. Watson—Come here"); Fischer, *America Calling,* 67 (early emphasis on marketing telephone to business, with residential use secondary), 75 (trend toward sociable use of telephone by 1920s), 78–79 (early concerns about frivolous use of telephone for conversation, especially for inappropriate or dangerous discussions), 255 (phones in one-fourth of households in 1909, quoting AT&T ad, 1909, "highway of communication"); Freeman, *Yesterday's Toys,* 100 (toy telephones); Grosvenor, *Bell,* 94, 174 (women as telephone operators), 122 (70,000 phones in late 1879, American Bell with 130,000 phones in 1881), 128 (early long-distance service); Hill, *Modern History of New Haven,* 211–15 (early telephone service in New Haven), 212–13 ("Making a connection with a subscriber"); *International Directory of Company Histories,* VI, 338 ("carriage bolts, teapot lids," early history of New Haven District Telephone); Kane, *Famous First Facts,* 591 (first pay phone); McClintock, *Toys in America,* 369 (toy telephones electrified in early twentieth century); Metropolitan Telephone and Telegraph Co., New York, "Subscribers' List," 1884, Smithsonian Archives, Warshaw Collection, "Telephone," Box 7 (as cited); *New York Times,* Feb. 8, 1877 ("Last Rose of Summer" sung by telegraph), March 4, 1877 ("It looks as if we're upon the verge"; note: original reads "as if we were upon" but the context of paragraph as a whole, and use of the present tense after this phrase, makes "we were" a probable typographical error and "we're" the original intent), May 20, 1877 ("The beginner needs a little practice," Chickering Hall and the stereopticon), July 23, 1905 ("The up-to-date barber's chair"), Dec. 23, 1906 (Mark Twain, "When I lived up in Hartford"), Aug. 4, 1922 (telephones silent for Bell's funeral); Pool, *Social Impact of the Telephone,* 15–16 (Hubbard and $100,000 offer to Western Union, Orton's decline, "What use could company make"), 17 (31 million telegrams a year, 214,000 miles of wire c. 1877), 28 (early telephone use largely business and commercial), 32 (81,000 pay phones in 1902), 131 (tenfold increase in telephones 1904–1914, change from flat rate to message rate reducing cost for small user, same accomplished in New York City 1896, quoting *McClure's* "Until [1900] telephone a luxury"); *Popular Science,* Nov. 1921 ("Nearly every home in America"); *Scientific American,* Oct. 29, 1892 ("It is a remarkable achievement," New York–Chicago telephone line statistics); Rhodes, *Visions of Technology,* 106 (Carter Glass resolution on dial phones); Smith, *Anatomy,* 24 (Boston banker by name, numbers of customers June to November 1877); Spofford, *American Almanac,* 1884 (120 million "communications by telephone" per year as of Jan. 1, 1883; note: Editor Ainsworth Spofford was librarian of Congress); *Statistical Abstract of the United States,* 1889, 257 (telephone statistics, Jan. 1, 1890); Watson, *Exploring Life,* 78 ("Mr. Watson, come here," "He forgot the accident"), 94–95 ("The common attitude toward anything new").

Cell Phones: *Engineering Magazine,* July 1901, as quoted in *Century Magazine,* March 1902, "Marconi and His Transatlantic Signal" ("if a person wanted to call a friend"); *Forbes,* April 23, 1984, "Car phones that really work" ($3,000 including installation, hundreds per month in charges, 2,000 subscribers in New York and 30-minute wait for dial tone, early cellular phone as four pieces of hardware, prediction of up to 1.5 million cell phone users by 1990, "If he knew how long it has taken to develop"); *Fortune,* Aug. 24, 1992, Andrew Kupfer, "Phones That Will Work Anywhere" ("With it, you'll be reachable"); Kane, *Famous First Facts,* 590 (experiment mobile phone in New York 1910); *New York Daily News,* June 6, 2000, edit. (quoting *New England Journal of Medicine,* 85 million cell phone users, restrictions on cell phones while driving in England, Germany, et al.); *New York Times,* Dec. 17, 1981, edit. (appeal of early cell phone largely to business), March 4, 1982 (FCC go-ahead for cellular service); *Newsweek,* July 9, 1984 ("Hello? Hello? Cruuuunch!," "dialing while driving"); Verizon Wireless ad, New York metropolitan area, Nov. 2, 2000 (cell phone purchase for $39.99 plus monthly access of $29.99).

A NEW NECESSITY OF CIVILIZATION

Beeching, *Century of the Typewriter,* 34–35 (the typewriter as a liberating force for women), 39–40 (origin of the QWERTY keyboard), 40 (*Cosmopolitan Shorthander*), 40–41 (McGurrin and Taub), note: Beeching was director of the British Typewriter Museum; *Education* magazine, June 1891, 631 ("The Typewriter makes it possible"), 632 ("There is no doubt these machines," "Not that it is probable every one who learns"), 633 ("Were it possible I would have every pupil"); June 1892, 622 ("The machine itself has had"), 623 ("The typewriter has become a necessity"), 628 (over 200,000 on the market, typewriters in more than 200 New England schools); Hammond Typewriter, *What Folks Say* (quotes and towns cited, c.1888); Herkimer Historical Society, *Story,* passim; 74 (J. P. Johns), 76 (Philadelphia Centennial), 81 (first typing school, D. L. Scott-Browne); *Illustrated Phonographic World,* November 1893 (Remington ad providing sales and production statistics, 1873–1892), June 1894 ("The Typewriter One Hundred Years Hence," a look ahead to 1994), April 1895 (1,990 typewriters in use by federal government); Cynthia Monaco, "The Difficult Birth of the Typewriter," *American Heritage of Invention & Technology,* Spring/Summer, 1988; *Nature,* May 18, 1876 ("The method of inking is excellent"); *Scientific American,* Jan. 22, 1876 ("The machine in appearance somewhat resembles"); Zellers, *The Typewriter,* 12–14 (early Remingtons; note: Zellers was vice president of Remington Rand, Inc.), 13 (Kentucky mountaineer, Philadelphia Centennial), 14 (Remington Model No. 2).

"YOU SHOULD GET ONE"

Aurora General Advertiser, Philadelphia, Oct. 6, 1803 ("Neat Mahogany portable Polygraph," "I have neither spared labour or expence"); Bedini, *Jefferson* (a uniquely helpful work on the early history of this subject), 10–21 (details of copying press generally), 17–18 (Jefferson-Madison correspondence), 19 (Washington and his copying press), 34 (footnote, Peale's painter's quadrant), 38 (Brunel), 90 (Jefferson, copying presses for consuls abroad), 193–94 (Bushnell's Copying Book, Langley); Brodie, *Jefferson,* 22 (18,000 letters); Cutler, *Life, Journals,* 269 (Cutler's visit to Franklin); A. B. Dick Company, "The Edison Mimeograph," 1889, Warshaw Collection, Smithsonian Institution Archives (details of Edison mimeograph); [A. B. Dick Company], "The Story of Stencil Duplication" [1935], New York Public Library (electric pen, early mimeographs generally, first rotary machine); Autocopyist Co., New York, "The Black Autocopyist," c. 1895, Warshaw Collection, Smithsonian Institution Archives (50,000 autocopyist machines in use by merchants, agents, etc.); Boyd, *Papers,* 6, 373 ("Copying Machine for Mr. Jefferson," 1784); *Chicago Advance,* June 6, 1895 (Bamford), as quoted in the *Oxford English Dictionary* ("mimeograph"); Fleming, *Man from Monticello,* 326 ("the finest invention of the present age"); *International Directory of Company Histories,* "Xerox Corporation" (history of Xerox); *Knight's New Mechanical Dictionary,* 220 (copygraph, gelatin process); *Memoir, Correspondence of Jefferson,* 4, 33 ("Mr. Hawkins of Frankford"); *New York Times,* Oct. 23, 1948 ("Even an unskilled person," "a system has been discovered," "ink jumps into place"); Peale, *Peale and His World,* 151–52 (Hawkins); *Technology Review,* Sept./Oct. 1998, 96, "The Original Duplicator" (Chester Carlson, Xerox 914 as first push-button, plain-paper copier); *The Voice,* New York, Sept. 19, 1889 (Mahoney quote).

DROPPING ON TARGET

Business Week, Aug. 3, 1987; *Encyclopaedia Britannica,* 1998, "Telecom-munications" (Bain, Blakewell); *New York Times,* Nov. 24, 1907 ("Photographs by Telegraph," "If pictures can be flashed" [an account of a demonstration by Dr. Arthur Korn of the University of Munich]), May 6, 1988, "Coast-to-Coast in 20 Seconds" (brief history of fax machine, 1988 boom in faxes, prices generally, "Law firms are placing them"), Dec. 21, 1988 (sending junk mail by fax), June 10, 1989 (Russell Baker, "The fax is just the latest"), March 19, 1991 (bicycle messengers), Dec. 22, 1991 (leg-islation regulating junk faxes); *Time,* Aug. 31, 1987.

DOING WHAT CAME NATURALLY

Better Homes and Gardens, Feb. 1976 (institution of the Universal Product Code); *Business Week,* April 16, 1979, "Personal Business" (San Francisco area, lease time on computers for $2.25, hosting birthday par-ties); Ceruzzi, *History of Computing,* 203 (computer development generally, Dartmouth, Kemeny as math chairman); Consumer Reports, *I'll Buy That,* 127 (Apple II, inc. cost), 128 (Honeywell 1969, $10,600); *Current Literature,* "Calculating Machines," April 1900 (vol. 28, p. 53); De Forest, *Wireless in the Home,* 4–6 ("The young man or boy who takes it up as a hobby"); Eames, *Computer Perspective,* 12–13 (Babbage), 19 (Jacquard, programmed musical instruments of eighteenth century); *Education Digest,* March 1973, Warren J. Koch, "Basic Facts about Using the Computer in Instruction" (National Association of Secondary School Principals 1971), Feb. 1977, Sylvia Charp and H. H. Altschuler, "A Decade of Usage of Computers for Instructional Purposes" (Philadelphia 1966–1976); *Electrical Engineer* (London), Sept. 11, 1891 (Hollerith tabulators bought by Canada and Austria); *Electrical Engineer* (New York), Nov. 11, 1891 ("This apparatus works unerringly"); Evans, *Making of the Micro,* 54 (Hollerith generally, tab-ulators for Czarist Russia); F. A. O. Schwarz, New York, N. Y., "Schwarz Toy Bazaar," catalog, 1962 ("Analog Computer" and "Brainiac Laboratory"); Herz, *Joystick Nation,* 17 (*Pac-Man, Space Invaders,* reference to *New England Journal of Medicine*); Herman Miller Co., *Ideas,* April 1978 [Henry Ford Museum Research Center], 1 ("Word processing is the big buzzword right now"); *Library Journal,* March 15, 1976 (computerization of libraries, including Library of Congress); Loftus, *Mind at Play,* 4 (games as principal use of home computer, 1983), 7 (social acceptance of *Pong*);

McCall's, Oct. 1979, "Computers on Campus Are Multiplying" (Dartmouth in 1979, Kemeny quote, "one third of 30,000 high schools" in 1979); *Mechanix Illustrated,* Oct. 1977, 48 (original price of calculators), 49 (computers on sale by Macy's, Montgomery Ward); *New York Herald Tribune,* Nov. 5, 1952, "Poll Forecasts Lagged Behind Actual Results" (polls relating to 1952 presidential election); *New York Times,* Feb. 15, 1946 ("One of the war's top secrets," "a series of cards in which holes are punched," "digital counter. Basically it does nothing more"), Nov. 7, 1952 (ABC use of blackboard for 1952 election coverage); Aug. 25, 1977, Richard W. Langer, "Computers Find a Home" (computers 1977 generally, Singer sewing machine, Amana range, Radio Shack Personal Electronic Transactor); *Newsweek,* Nov. 17, 1952 (television election coverage generally, NBC's Monrobot); Oct. 30, 1972 (popularity of *Odyssey,* quote "It keeps kids quiet"), Nov. 10, 1973 (popularity of *Pong*), March 9, 1981, "Classroom Computers," 88 (five-year-old in Dallas, "See how easy"), Feb. 22, 1982, "How to Work the Thing" (Elizabeth Peer, "Aw, com'on . . ."), Dec. 27, 1982, "The Great Computer Frenzy" ("Even parents who know nothing"); Palfreman, *Dream Machine,* 67–69 (CBS and use of UNIVAC for 1952 election coverage, Collingwood quote: "I don't know . . . I think that UNIVAC is probably an honest machine"); *Popular Mechanics,* Ivan Berger, "Home Sweet Computerized Home," Sept. 1976 (computers in 1976 generally, up to 15,000 PCs in use); *Science Digest,* Jan. 1973, William Seil, "How the Real 'Hal' Computers Will Change Your Life Before 2001" (Hal, *2001: A Space Odyssey*), May 1978, Ted Nelson, "Computers in the Home" ("The computer is a machine that brings out the kid in all of us"), Nov. 1982, "Computer Kids" ("Kids have no fear," "A kid's whole life is set up," "Kids aren't mad when asked"); *Scientific American,* Aug. 30, 1890 (details of 1890 Census, "an interesting alliance," male clerks 32,000 and women 47,000 cards tabulated per day), April 19, 1902 ("The machine has been adapted"), Oct. 26, 1895 (telephone newspaper); Shurkin, *Engines,* 73 (Hollerith quote, "I was travelling in the West"), 79 (toilet seats wired to dynamo); *Statistical Abstract of the United States,* 1993, 165 (percentages of schools using computers for instruction, 1981–1991), 2000, 568 (more than 80 million Americans); *Time,* May 22, 1972 (Magnavox, introduction of *Odyssey*); Timex Computer Corp., *User Manual, TS-1000,* 1982 ("You shouldn't be afraid of the computer"); Tomlinson, *Cyclopaedia,* "Calculating Machines," 270 ("A most valuable feature intended to be introduced," "printer" for Babbage's calculating machine); Turkle, *Second Self,* 13 ("Computers call up strong feelings"); *U.S. News & World Report,* July 19, 1976 ("out of public view," "Every corner of society," "the size of a half-stick of gum").

The Internet: *Access Magazine,* March 26, 2000, "Wired for the Future" (estimate of 72.1 percent of teens vs. 55.7 of general population online by

2003, estimate of 28 percent of high school students vs. 16 percent of adults online 20 or more hours a week, quotes "I think the Internet will be the basis," "The Internet will replace phones"); *Atlantic Monthly,* Feb. 1889, Philip G. Hubert Jr., "The New Talking Machines" ("I really see no reason"); *Business Week,* Oct. 4, 1999 (e-mail volume surpassed hand-delivered mail in 1998, to reach 8 billion messages a day by 2002, quote "Get It? Got it," quoting James Billington "The letter is an artifact"), May 8, 2000, Roger O. Crockett, "How to Bridge America's Digital Divide" (households online vs. household income, Maine proposal to give every junior-senior high school student a PC), June 5, 2000 (Stanford University survey generally, including quotes "Internet promises profound effects," "a powerful isolating technology"), Campbell-Kelly, *Computer,* 283 (growth of Internet 1991–1996, 300,000 to 10 million), 285–86, 300 (H. G. Wells, including quote, "The time is close at hand"); *Editor and Publisher,* March 2, 1912, "No Telephone News" (demise of Newark's Telephone Herald, charge of five cents a day); *Fortune,* Oct. 30, 2000, "Dot-Coms: What Have We Learned?" (decline of dot-com stocks generally); *Grand Larousse universel,* "Robida" (brief biography); Israel, *Edison: A Life,* 148–49 (Puskas as Edison's agent in Europe); *Literary Digest,* March 16, 1912, "An American Telephone Newspaper" (suspension of service of Newark Telephone Herald, financial difficulties generally; story is mostly a reprint of *Technical World,* q.v.); *Living Age,* Boston, "A Telephone Newspaper," Aug. 8, 1903 (Telefon-Hirmondo, "Probably there are few who would be so rash"); *New York Times,* May 20, 1877, "The Speaking Telephone" ("It is a rainy morning"), March 24, 1925 (obituary of Manly M. Gillam, which makes no mention of the Telephone Herald, further evidence of its short span; Gillam is connected to the enterprise by *Technical World,* q.v.); *New Choices,* Oct. 1999, Peter Meyer, "The Wild Wired World of E-Mail" (space shuttle *Endeavor,* quoting retired bookstore owner, "Practically all my friends"); Pool, *Social Impact,* 53 (phonograph fixed to Telefon-Hirmondo "in such a way that the first sound"), 54 (Telefon-Hirmondo still inoperation in 1918), 55 (Electrophone Company, only 600 subscribers), 56 (quoting the *Electrician,* "we are getting perilously near the idea"); *Popular Science,* March 2000, "It's an Internet World" (survey showing 53 percent think society too dependent on computers, quoting Center for Energy and Climate Solutions as to environmental impact of Internet); Rhodes, *Visions of Technology,* 336 (quotations of the sixth and seventh graders, 1983, as to expectations of computers, as recorded by Nancy Kreinberg and Elizabeth K. Stage); Robida, *Le Vingtième Siècle,* Quatrième Partie: *La Vie électrique* (Robida's conception of Internet-like devices); *Scientific American,* Oct. 26, 1895, quoting *New York Sun* ("The telephone newspaper has 6,000"); *Technical World Magazine,* Feb. 1912, "Telephone Newspaper—A Marvel" (Telephone Herald generally, M. M. Gillam, Telefon-Hirmondo and number of subscribers, charge of 18 florins, Emperor Franz Josef, typical day's programming, "There is no transmitter for the subscriber"); *Time Almanac, 2001,* 583 (more than 92 million Internet users); *U.S. News & World Report,* May 1, 2000, Fred Vogelstein and Janet Rae-Dupree, "East dot com, easy dot go" (stock prices cited, Internet stocks down 50 percent, decline in dot-com stocks generally).

ENTERTAINMENT

INTRODUCTION

Josephson, *Edison,* 427 (quoting Edison, "the greatest musical instrument"); Thomas A. Edison, Inc., booklet, *Edison and Music,* Orange, N.J., 1919 ("his favorite invention").

A SUCCESSION OF WONDERS

American Review of Reviews, June 1900 (Aeolian ad as quoted); *Atlantic Monthly,* July 1867, "The Piano in the United States" (125 pianos a day in 1867, "When we consider, that every hotel," "Cold, glittering, and dumb"); Braden, *Leisure and Entertainment,* "Home Music," 110–13 (pianos and player pianos generally), 111–12 (affordability of piano for middle class, 1890s); *De Natuur,* 1883, 12 ("To make these moving figures visible"); Fostle, *Steinway Saga,* 448 (player piano peak of popularity in mid-1920s, sales of 200,000 in 1923), 455 (40 percent decline in piano sales 1927–1929); *Frank Leslie's Illustrated Newspaper,* Nov. 23, 1872 (illustration of rooftop stereopticon for election results in New York); *Grove's New Dictionary of Music,* "Player Piano" (history of, generally; reprint of 1900 ad for Orchestrelle Co. player piano: "With its aid any number of your household"); Jenkins, *Two Points of View,* 7–8 (stereo views produced by E. Anthony by 1859, popularity of stereoscope generally); McAllister, *Stereopticons,* 10–11 (magic lanterns, Civil War slides), 48 (stereopticon, used to produce dissolving views); Milton Bradley Co., *Milton Bradley,* 15–16 (Checkered Game of Life), Work and Play, 35 (zoetrope, "In this instrument"); *Oxford English Dictionary,* "Magic Lantern" (1696, a magic lantern was a "small Optical Macheen"), "Zoetrope" ("newly invented" as of 1867); *Parlour Magic,* preface, 75–76 (laughing gas); Roehl, *Player Piano Treasury* (player pianos generally, contemporary cartoon with caption ". . . great foot for music"); Shea, *All in the Game,* 46–52 (Milton Bradley's Game of Life), among illustrations, no page number (myriopticon); Time-Life Books, *This Fabulous Century,* 1870–1900, 184–85 (million pianos in 1899). The 1940s zoetrope referred to (caption, 1880s zoetrope illustration) is a zoetrope dated 1945, Mastercraft Toy Co., New York, at the Strong Museum, Rochester, N.Y. (ID No. 84.3100).

WHERE'S THE BAND?

Atlantic Monthly, Feb. 1889, Philip G. Hubert Jr., "The New Talking Machines" ("When it comes to music"); *Boston Transcript,* June 17, 1872 (World's Peace Jubilee Music Festival, 20,000 voices, orchestra of 1,000); Conot, *Streak of Luck,* 315–19 (Edison phonograph generally, early twentieth century, Blue Amberol); Heyn, *Century of Wonders,* 88 (quoting early ad, "a machine that not only talks"), 90 (Nightingale, Sullivan: "For myself I can only say," reaction of dogs to early phonographs), 91 (German toy in 1889), 92 ("Years ago . . . the parlor organ"); Israel, *Edison,* 147 (quoting *North American Review* as to Edison's perceived uses of phonograph, *Daily Graphic:* "this is my baby and I expect it to grow up"); Josephson, *Edison,* 162–63 (basic development of phonograph, "Mary Had a Little Lamb," quoting Edison: "I designed a little machine," "I was never so taken aback"), 172–73 (Edison Speaking Phonograph Co. generally, $1,800 in royalties, a "burlesque or parody of the human voice"), 326 (Gladstone, Browning, and Sullivan), 332 (Berliner, gramophone), 425–27 (Edison phonograph production generally, 1906–1914); *New York Times,* May 13, 1888 (Electric Club, "the most ingenious thing ever worked out of the human brain"); *Popular Science Monthly,* March 1878 ("If words may be converted into electricity"), April 1878 ("simple as a grindstone . . . simple as a coffee-mill"); *Scientific American,* Nov. 17, 1877 ("Imagine an opera or an oratorio"), Dec. 22, 1877 ("Mr. Edison recently came into this office," "We have already pointed out the startling possibility"), March 9, 1901 ("When the phonograph first made its appearance"); Siefert, Marsha, "The Audience at Home: The Early Recording Industry and the Marketing of Musical Taste," *Sage Annual Reviews of Communication Research,* vol. 22, Sage Publications, Thousand Oaks, 1994 ("opera at home," Victor vs. Edison generally); Wachhorst, *Edison,* 19 (origin of "Wizard of Menlo Park"), 20 (Methodist bishop and his biblical names), 20–21 (demonstration at National Academy of Sciences, for Congress, and for President Hayes). The caption for the 1888 photograph of a weary Edison with his improved phonograph after a straight seventy-two hours of work is based on Wachhorst, *Edison,* 45.

THE CRAZE THAT STAYED

Ackerman, *Eastman,* 20–22 ("The negative is made"), 75–76 (origin of "Kodak"), 78 ("Pull the string"), 78 ("the mere mechanical act," "There is no jugglery"), 83 (daylight loading); Auchincloss, *Hone & Strong Diaries,* 81 ("I went this morning by invitation"); Beaumont, *History of Photography,* 89 (Kodak roll-film cameras, transition from paper to nitrocellulose film); Brayer, *Eastman,* 60–72 (Eastman, early development of photography and Kodak cameras generally), 63–64 (origin of "Kodak"), 152 (Eastman's use of bicycle to go to work), 162–63 (Pocket Kodak), 204–5 (Brownie camera), 205, ("the same way the bicycle has reached them"), 205 ("Kodak freak," "Wherever they go"; both the term and quotation are from the transcript of a court trial, *People v. Gillette,* 1905); *Chicago Tribune,* n.d., 1891, cited in Ackerman, *Eastman,* 83 ("The craze is spreading fearfully"); Dean, *New Things,* 5 ("If yourself you would see"); *Ladies' Home Journal,* Feb. 1900, "Kodak Manners" ("It sometimes seems as if the possession of a 'kodak,' " "People whose work of life"); Routledge, *Discoveries and Inventions,* 504 ("No other of our nineteenth century inventions," "The new art cherishes"); *Scientific American,* May 20, 1876 ("there will be an exhibition of photography here").

THE WILDFIRE WONDER

An Aeriola Home, brochure, n.d. [Smithsonian Archives, Warshaw Collection, "Radios," Box 1, "RCA"] ("Those who seek for extreme simplicity," details of Aeriola generally); Barnouw, *Tower in Babel,* 68 (quoting Horne department store ad), 71–72 ("The impact was immediate"), 91 (numbers of licenses, 1921–22), 100 (Commerce Dept. runs out of three-letter station call letters), 210 (in 1927 AC-powered radio sets becoming common, first car radios on market), *Golden Web,* 5–6 (*Amos 'n' Andy* on radio, minister preaching on Amos), 87–89 *(War of the Worlds),* 126–297 (*Amos 'n' Andy* on television); Bliss, *Now the News,* 3 (Sarnoff and the *Titanic*), 7–8 (origins of KDKA), 19–20 (broadcasting of Scopes trial and Lindbergh's flight); Boy Scouts of America, *Official Handbook for Boys,* 11th ed., New York, 1914, 246 (cost of building homemade wireless receiver); Braden, *Leisure and Entertainment,* 117–20 (radio generally); *Broadcasting Magazine,* 1933, as quoted in Braden, *Leisure,* 119 ("Hard times have added millions"); Buxton, *Big Broadcast,* 13–14 *(Amos 'n' Andy);* De Forest, *Wireless in the Home,* 6 ("I don't know the first thing"); De Forest, *Father of Radio,* 444 ("Herbert Hoover, while Secretary," "second in importance to public school"), 445 ("uncouth tramps, interlopers"); Douglas, *Inventing Broadcasting,* 303 (radio sales 1922–1924), 306 (reference to *Collier's* article, "Radio Dreams," including quote, "My husban and I thanks yous"), *Listening In,* 58–59 (technology of crystal receivers), 78 (radio magazines, transition from technical to celebrity articles during 1920s), 165 (reactions to *War of the Worlds*); Dunlap, *Communications,* 36 (making of homemade crystal set), 38 ("It is 5:25 P.M.," quoting *Commercial Broadcasting Pioneer: The WEAF Experiment,* Harvard University Press, 1946, p. 90); Husing, *Bloops, Howls,* 53 ("child radio–an *enfant terrible*"), 55–56 ("Early-day radio programs were often"); Kane, *Famous First Facts,* 118 (first radio commercial); *Literary Digest,* "Astonishing Growth of the Radiotelephone," April 15, 1922; Nachman, *Raised on Radio,* passim (early radio), 18 (Hoover: own son "daft on wireless"); *New York Herald,* Jan. 14, 1910 ("Opera Wavelets Wander"); *New York Times,* April 16, 1912, "Wireless Inventor's View" (Marconi, "I can say only

that I am delighted"); May 7, 1929, "Sousa Makes Radio Debut"; May 12,

1929, "Sousa Confesses Why Radio Won" ("thousands of letters requested," "I feared that over the radio"), Oct. 31, Nov. 1, 1938 (reaction to *War of the Worlds*); *Popular Science,* Nov. 1921 ("Up to the instant," half million wireless fans); *Printer's Ink,* 1923, as quoted in Rhodes, *Visions of Technology,* 71 ("we are opposed to the scheme"); *Radio Broadcast,* May 1922 ("The movement is probably not even," "The rate of increase in the number of people"); Radio Corporation of America, *First 25 Years,* 20 (details of Radiola, which here is said to have come out in 1921; Bliss, *Now the News,* 6, 8, 480*n*, is more convincing in saying it was 1922), 21 (Sarnoff: "I have in mind a plan," Radiola generally, $83.5 million in sales); Sousa, *Marching Along,* 357 ("The rapport between performer and audience"); U.S. Census Bureau, *Historical Statistics of the United States,* 796 (number of radio stations operating early 1920s, number of households with radio 1922–1932).

ADDING SIGHT TO SOUND

Barnouw, *History of Broadcasting,* vol. 2, *The Golden Web,* 125–28 (Sarnoff and 1939 World's Fair, early television fare including "usually salads, since the lights made it too hot to cook"); *Better Homes and Gardens,* Sept. 1940, "What You Can Expect of Television This Coming Year" (Newburgh as "television town"), Oct. 1946, Hal Borland, "The Town That Tested Television" (estimate of "between 400 and 500 sets," Hyman Shapiro, "freakish looking . . . huge necktie racks," "My brother-in-law thinks my house is a movie theater," "Any movies on tonight, Dad?"); *Business Week,* as quoted in *Newburgh News,* Nov. 30, 1939 ("quoted no prices but built consumer interest"); Castleman, *Watching TV,* 6 (Jenkins, first working system, 1925), 20 (7,000 sets in 1945, wartime ban on sets and stations, image orthicon camera); *Consumer Reports,* June 1939, "Television" ("only three channels," "As an instrument of common, everyday use"), July 1949 ("The television set is on its way"); Dupuy, *Television Show Business,* 204–7 (WRGB generally), 207 ("the high percentage who identified the sponsor," "The high percentage of returns"); Heyn, *Century of Wonders,* 210 ("radio-vision"), 215 (cheapest TV, 1949); Nash, *Motion Picture Guide,* 2048 *(Murder by Television);* National Broadcasting Co., *Television's First Year* (relevant statistics, NBC television, 1939–40; time on air for W2XBS was 601 hours, April 30, 1939 to April 30, 1940); *New York Times,* Nov. 24, 1907 (first transmission of photo by wire), April 26, 1931 ("One of the problems of television"), April 21, 1939 (TV coverage of the World's Fair, Sarnoff: "Now we add radio sight to sound," "The laborers in white overalls"), May 1, 1939, as reported by Orrin E. Dunlap Jr. (opening of World's Fair, "take Americans sight-seeing by radio"), Nov. 29, 1939 ("The fact that Newburgh bought 100 sets"), June 30, 1940, Dunlap, "Seeing Democracy at Work" ("Even in 1928, the politicians confessed"), April 25, May 3, July 1, Aug. 3, 1941 (authorization of commercial television by FCC), Dec. 23, 1945 (obituary of Arthur Korn), Jan. 20, 1949 (price of 1949 Chevrolet); *The New Yorker*, July 27, 1940, "The Age of Television" ("an expensive and impractical toy"); *Saturday Evening Post*, Sept. 28, 1940, Alva Johnston, "Trouble in Television" ("The public was delighted . . . ancient newsreel stuff," Frank R. Dutcher, Guzorsky and the races), March 9, March 16, March 23, 1946, "Television: Boom or Bubble?"; *Science Digest*, Nov. 1940, "Programs for Television"; *World Almanac*, 1950, 755 (number and value of radio and television sets in use). The National Archives photograph of Washingtonians watching the World Series on a storefront television screen in 1949 is from "Street Scenes—Washington, DC" and is #49-13976 (Still Pictures Branch).

EPILOGUE

Oxford Dictionary of New Words, 1997 ed., 350, "wired" (quoting *Library Manager* and *Data Communications International*).

BIBLIOGRAPHY

Abbate, Janet. *Inventing the Internet.* Cambridge, Mass.: MIT Press, 1999.

A. B. Dick Company. *The Edison Mimeograph.* (Pamph.) Chicago, 1889.

[A. B. Dick Company]. *The Story of Stencil Duplication.* (Pamph.) [Chicago, 1935].

Ackerman, Carl W. *George Eastman.* Boston: Houghton Mifflin, 1930.

Allen, Oliver E., and the editors of Time-Life Books. *The Airline Builders.* Alexandria, Va.: Time-Life Books, 1981.

Andrews, Jane. *Ten Boys Who Lived on the Road from Long Ago to Now.* Boston, 1893.

Appleton, Victor, pseud. *Tom Swift and His Wireless Message; or, The Castaways of Earthquake Island.* New York: Grosset & Dunlap, 1911.

Asimov, Isaac. *How Did We Find Out about Computers?* New York: Walker, 1984.

Auchincloss, Louis, ed. *The Hone & Strong Diaries of Old New York.* New York: Abbeville Press, 1989.

Austrian, Geoffrey D. *Herman Hollerith: Forgotten Giant of Information Processing.* New York: Columbia University Press, 1982.

Auto Fun: Pictures and Comments from "Life." New York: Crowell, 1905.

Bacon, George Washington, and William George Larkins. *Bacon's Descriptive Handbook of America.* London, 1866.

Bagdade, Susan, and Al Bagdade. *Collector's Guide to American Toy Trains.* Radnor, Pa.: Wallace-Homestead, 1990.

Baigell, Matthew. *Thomas Cole.* New York: Watson-Guptill, 1985.

Baldwin, Neil. *Edison: Inventing the Century.* New York: Hyperion, 1995.

Barnes, Lovisa Ellen. *How to Become Expert in Typewriting.* St. Louis, Mo., 1890.

Barnouw, Erik. *A History of Broadcasting in the United States.* New York: Oxford University Press. Vol. 1, *A Tower in Babel: A History of Broadcasting in the United States to 1933,* 1966. Vol. 2, *The Golden Web: A History of Broadcasting in the United States, 1933 to 1953,* 1968.

Bedini, Silvio A. *Thomas Jefferson and His Copying Machine.* Charlottesville, Va.: University Press of Virginia, 1984.

Beeching, Wilfred A. *The Century of the Typewriter.* New York: St. Martin's Press, 1974.

Bishop, J. Leander. *A History of American Manufacturers from 1608 to 1860.* 3d ed. Philadelphia, 1868. Reprinted, New York: A. M. Kelly, 1966.

[Blanchard, J.-P.]. *Journal of My Forty-Fifth Ascension, Being the First Performed in America, on the Ninth of January, 1793.* Philadelphia, 1793.

Bliss, Edward Jr. *Now the News: The Story of Broadcast Journalism.* New York: Columbia University Press, 1991.

Blondheim, Menahem. *News Over the Wires: The Telegraph and the Flow of Public Information in America, 1844–1897.* Cambridge, Mass.: Harvard University Press, 1994.

Boettinger, H. M. *The Telephone Book: Bell, Watson, Vail and American Life, 1876–1976.* Croton-on-Hudson, N.Y.: Riverwood Publishers, 1977.

Boorstin, Daniel J. *The Americans: The National Experience.* New York: Random House, 1965.

Botkin, B. A., and Alvin F. Harlow, eds. *A Treasury of Railroad Folklore.* New York: Crown, 1953.

Botting, Douglas, and the editors of Time-Life Books. *The Giant Airships.* Alexandria, Va.: Time-Life Books, 1989.

Boyd, Julian P., ed. *The Papers of Thomas Jefferson.* Princeton, N.J.: Princeton University Press, 1950–.

Braden, Donna R. *Leisure and Entertainment in America.* Dearborn, Mich.: Henry Ford Museum and Greenfield Village, 1988.

Brayer, Elizabeth. *George Eastman: A Biography.* Baltimore: Johns Hopkins University Press, 1996.

Briggs, Charles F. *The Story of the Telegraph.* New York, 1858.

Brodie, Fawn M. *Thomas Jefferson: An Intimate History.* New York: Norton, 1974.

Brown, William H. *The History of the First Locomotives in America: From Original Documents and the Testimony of Living Witnesses.* New York, 1874.

Bruce, Robert V. *Bell: Alexander Graham Bell and the Conquest of Solitude.* Boston: Little, Brown, 1973.

Brun, Philippe. *Albert Robida, 1848–1926: sa vie, son oeuvre.* [Paris], Editions Promodis, c. 1984.

Buckingham, J. S. *America: Historical, Statistic, and Descriptive.* London, 1841.

Buxton, Frank, and Bill Owen. *The Big Broadcast, 1920–1950.* New York: Viking, 1972.

Byrn, Edward W. *The Progress of Invention in the Nineteenth Century.* New York, 1900.

Campbell-Kelly, Martin, and William Aspray. *Computer: A History of the Information Machine.* New York: Basic Books, 1996.

Case, Carleton B. *Ford Smiles: All the Best Current Jokes about a Rattling Good Car.* [Chicago: Shrewesbury Pub. Co., c. 1917].

Castleman, Harry, and Walter J. Podrazik. *Watching TV: Four Decades of American Television.* New York: McGraw-Hill, 1982.

Ceruzzi, Paul E. *A History of Modern Computing.* Cambridge, Mass.: MIT Press, 1998.

Cist, Charles. *The Cincinnati Miscellany.* Cincinnati, 1845; reprint, Arno Press, 1971.

Clark, Ronald W. *The Scientific Breakthrough: The Impact of Modern Invention.* New York: Putnam's, 1974.

Clemente, Peter C. *State of the Net: The New Frontier.* New York: McGraw-Hill, 1998.

Cleveland, Frederick A., and Fred Wilbur Powell. *Railroad Promotion and Capitalization in the United States.* New York: Longmans, Green, 1909.

Coe, Lewis. *The Telegraph: A History of Morse's Invention and Its Predecessors in the United States.* Jefferson, N.C.: McFarland, 1993.

Consumer Reports. *I'll Buy That! 50 Small Wonders and Big Deals That Revolutionized the Lives of Consumers: A 50-Year Retrospective by the Editors of Consumer Reports.* Mount Vernon, N.Y.: Consumers Union, 1986.

Conot, Robert. *A Streak of Luck: The Life and Legend of Thomas Alva Edison.* New York: Seaview Books, 1979.

Crouch, Tom D. *The Bishop's Boys: A Life of Wilbur and Orville Wright.* New York: Norton, 1989.

——. *The Eagle Aloft: Two Centuries of the Balloon in America.* Washington, D.C.: Smithsonian Institution Press, 1983.

Crouthamel, James L. *Bennett's New York Herald and the Rise of the Popular Press.* Syracuse, N.Y.: Syracuse University Press, 1989.

Cutler, William Parker. *Life, Journals, and Correspondence of Rev. Manasseh Cutler.* Reprint of original 1888 edition. Athens, Ohio: Ohio University Press, 1987.

Danly, Susan, and Leo Marx, eds., *The Railroad in American Art: Representations of Technological Change.* Cambridge, Mass.: MIT Press, 1988.

[Dean, Ezra]. *New Things Since I Was a Boy! 1808–1869.* Auburn, [N.Y.?], 1869. [Smithsonian Institution, Archives Center, Warshaw Collection, "Inventions"].

De Forest, Lee. *Father of Radio: The Autobiography of Lee de Forest.* Chicago: Wilcox & Follet, 1950.

——. *The Wireless in the Home.* New York: De Forest Radio Telephone and Telegraph Company, 1922.

Derrick, Samuel Melanchthon. *Centennial History of South Carolina Railroad.* Columbia, S.C.: The State Company, 1930.

De Vries, Leonard. *Victorian Inventions.* New York: American Heritage Press, 1971.

Dickinson, H. W. *James Watt, Craftsman & Engineer.* Cambridge, Eng.: University Press, 1936.

Doolittle, James Rood. *The Romance of the Automobile Industry.* New York: Klebold Press, 1916.

Douglas, George H. *All Aboard: The Railroad in American Life.* New York: Smithmark, 1996.

Douglas, Susan J. *Inventing American Broadcasting, 1899–1922.* Baltimore: Johns Hopkins University Press, 1987.

——. *Listening In: Radio and the American Imagination.* New York: Times Books, 1999.

Dunlap, Orrin E., Jr. *Communications in Space: From Marconi to Man on the Moon.* New York: Harper & Row, 1970.

Dupuy, Judy. *Television Show Business: A Handbook of Television Programming and Production, Based on Five Years of Operation of General Electric's Television Station, WRGB, Schenectady, New York.* [Schenectady], General Electric, 1945.

Duryea, J. Frank. *America's First Automobile.* Springfield, Mass.: Donald M. Macauly, 1942.

Dwight, Theodore. *Things As They Are; or Notes of a Traveler.* New York, 1834.

Dyke, A. L. *The Anatomy of the Automobile.* 1st rev. ed. St. Louis, Mo.: A. L. Dyke, 1908.

——. *Dyke's Automobile and Gasoline Engine Encyclopedia.* 12th ed. St. Louis, Mo., 1920.

Eames, Charles and Ray, Office of. *A Computer Perspective: Background to the Computer Age.* Cambridge, Mass.: Harvard University Press, 1990.

Edwards, Frank. *My First 10,000,000 Sponsors.* New York: Ballantine, 1956.

Elisha, and Other Books for Children. New York, c. 1850s. [A collection of eight tracts, each of 16 pages, published by the American Tract Society. Copy at American Antiquarian Society is cataloged as being "not before 1848?"].

Erie Railroad Company. *Erie Railroad: Its Beginnings, 1851.* [New York: Erie Railroad Co., 1951?].

Evans, Christopher. *The Making of the Micro: A History of the Computer.* New York: Van Nostrand Reinhold, 1981.

Exhibition of Early American Children's Books of Aeronautical Interest, Dime Novels about Flying Machines, Aviation Fiction for Boys and Girls from the

Bella C. Landau Aeronautical Collection. New York: Institute of the Aeronautical Sciences, 1942.

Filson Young, A. B. *The Complete Motorist.* New York: McClure, Phillips & Co., 1904.

Fireside Philosophy, or Familiar Talks about Common Things. New York, 1861.

Fischer, Claude S. *America Calling: A Social History of the Telephone to 1940.* Berkeley, Calif.: University of California Press, 1992.

Fisher, David E., and Marshall Jon Fisher. *Tube: The Invention of Television.* Washington, D.C.: Counterpoint, 1996.

Fleming, Thomas. *The Man from Monticello.* New York: Morrow, 1969.

Fletcher, Denise Cross. *Lionel All in One.* Clearwater, Fla.: Trains 'n Things, 1979.

Flink, James J. *America Adopts the Automobile, 1895–1910.* Cambridge, Mass.: MIT Press, 1970.

——. *The Automobile Age.* Cambridge, Mass.: MIT Press, 1988.

——. *The Car Culture.* Cambridge, Mass.: MIT Press, 1975.

Forrester, Mark, ed. *Forrester's Pictorial Miscellany for Boys and Girls.* Boston, 1854.

Fostle, D. W. *The Steinway Saga: An American Dynasty.* New York: Scribner, 1995.

Freeman, G. L., and R. S. Freeman. *Yesterday's Toys.* Watkins Glen, N.Y.: Century House, 1962.

Full Particulars of the Greatest Aerial Voyage on Record. New York, [1859].

General Electric Co. *Electronics—A New Science for the World.* Schenectady, N.Y.: General Electric Co., 1942.

Gibson, Charles R. *Wireless Telegraphy.* London: Seeley, Service, 1914.

Giscard d'Estaing, Valérie-Anne. *World Almanac Book of Inventions.* New York: World Almanac, 1985.

Gladding, Effie Price. *Across the Continent by the Lincoln Highway.* New York: Brentano's, 1915.

Glines, C. V., ed. *Lighter-Than-Air Flight.* New York: Franklin Watts, 1965.

Goodfriend, Joyce D. *The Published Diaries and Letters of American Women: An Annotated Bibliography.* Boston: G. K. Hall, 1987.

Grosvenor, Edwin S., and Morgan Wesson: *Alexander Graham Bell: The Life and Times of the Man Who Invented the Telephone.* New York: Abrams, 1997.

Hall, N. John. *Trollope: A Biography.* Oxford, Eng.: Oxford University Press, 1991.

Hammond Typewriter Corp. *What Folks Say of the Hammond Typewriter.* [New York, c. 1888].

Hargrove, Jim. *Computer Wars.* Chicago: Children's Press, 1985.

Harlow, Alvin F. *Old Wires and New Waves: The History of the Telegraph, Telephone, and Wireless.* New York, London: Appleton-Century, 1936.

Harris, Jay S., ed., in association with the editors of TV Guide Magazine. *TV Guide: The First 25 Years.* New York: Simon & Schuster, 1978.

Haskins, Vernon. *The Canajoharie-Catskill Railroad, 1832–1840.* East Durham, N.Y.: Durham Center Museum, 1967.

Hatfield, D. D., comp. *Aeroplane Scrap Book Number 1: Historical Data and Reproductions.* Inglewood, Calif.: Northrop University Press, 1976.

Hazen, Edward. *The Symbolic Primer.* Hartford, Conn., 1829.

Herkimer County Historical Society. *The Story of the Typewriter.* Herkimer, N.Y.: Herkimer County Historical Society, 1923.

Herz, J. C. *Joystick Nation: How Videogames Ate Our Quarters, Won Our Hearts, and Rewired Our Minds.* Boston: Little, Brown, 1997.

Heyn, Ernest V. *A Century of Wonders: 100 Years of Popular Science.* Garden City, N.Y.: Doubleday, 1972.

Hill, Everett G. *A Modern History of New Haven.* New York and Chicago: S. J. Clarke, 1918.

Hiscox, Gardner D. *Horseless Vehicles, Automobiles, Motor Cycles.* New York: Norman W. Henley & Co., 1900.

Hoke, Donald. *Ingenious Yankees: The Rise of the American System of Manufactures in the Private Sector.* New York: Columbia University Press, 1990.

Hone, Philip. *The Diary of Philip Hone, 1828–1851.* Allan Nevins, ed. New York: Dodd, Mead, 1936.

Howard, Fred. *Wilbur and Orville: A Biography of the Wright Brothers.* New York: Knopf, 1987.

Hubbard, Freeman. *Encyclopedia of North American Railroading: 150 Years of Railroading in the United States and Canada.* New York: McGraw-Hill, 1981.

Hungerford, Edward. *Men of Erie.* New York: Random House, 1946.

Husing, Ted. *My Eyes Are in My Heart.* New York: Bernard Geis/Random House, 1959.

Ierley, Merritt. *The Comforts of Home: The American House and the Evolution of Modern Convenience.* New York: Clarkson Potter, 1999.

——. *A Place in History: North Arlington, New Jersey, A Centennial Chronicle of the Birthplace of Steam Power in America.* North Arlington: North Arlington Public Library, 1994.

——. *Traveling the National Road: Across the Centuries on America's First Highway.* Woodstock, N.Y.: Overlook Press, 1990.

International Directory of Company Histories. Chicago, St. James Press, 1988. Place of publication varies with successive volumes.

Israel, Paul. *Edison: A Life of Invention.* New York: Wiley, 1998.

Jenkins, Harold F. *Two Points of View: The History of the Parlor Stereoscope.* Elmira, N.Y.: World in Color Productions, 1957.

Jensen, Oliver. *The American Heritage History of Railroads in America.* New York: American Heritage, 1975.

Josephson, Matthew. *Edison: A Biography.* New York: McGraw-Hill, 1959.

Kane, Joseph Nathan. *Famous First Facts.* 5th ed. New York: H. W. Wilson, 1997.

Klamkin, Charles. *Railroadiana: The Collector's Guide to Railroad Memorabilia.* New York: Funk & Wagnalls, 1976.

Knight, Edward H. *Knight's American Mechanical Dictionary.* New York, 1876.

——. *Knight's New Mechanical Dictionary.* Boston, 1884.

Knowles & Maxim. *The Real Pen-Work Self-Instructor in Penmanship.* Pittsfield, Mass., 1881.

Lacey, Robert. *Ford: The Men and the Machine.* Boston: Little, Brown, 1986.

Lee, Alfred McClung. *The Daily Newspaper in America.* New York: Macmillan, 1947.

Leek, Stephen, and Sybil Leek. *The Bicycle—That Curious Invention.* Nashville, Tenn.: Thomas Nelson, 1973.

Leonard, L. W. *The Literary and Scientific Class Book.* Keene, N.H., 1826.

Little Charley's Christmas Amusements. Philadelphia, 1852, 1858.

Little Charley's Picture Home Book. Philadelphia, 1857.

Littman, Mark S., ed. *A Statistical Portrait of the United States: Social Conditions and Trends.* Lanham, Md.: Bernan Press, 1998.

Loftus, Geoffrey R., and Elizabeth F. Loftus. *Mind at Play: The Psychology of Video Games.* New York: Basic Books, 1983.

[Lowe, T. S. C.]. *The Air-Ship City of New York.* New York, 1859.

Lynd, Robert S., and Helen Merrell Lynd. *Middletown: A Study in Contemporary American Culture.* New York: Harcourt Brace, 1929.

Mabee, Carleton. *The American Leonardo: A Life of Samuel F. B. Morse.* New York, Knopf, 1943.

Mackenzie, Catherine. *Alexander Graham Bell: The Man Who Contracted Space.* Boston and New York: Houghton Mifflin, 1928.

Magic, Pretended Miracles, and Remarkable Natural Phenomena. Philadelphia: American Sunday-School Union, c. 1846.

Marland, E. A. *Early Electrical Communication.* London: Abelard-Schuman, 1964.

Martineau, Harriet. *Society in America*. London, 1837.

Maxim, Hiram Percy. *Horseless Carriage Days*. New York: Harper, 1937.

McAllister, T. H. *Catalogue and Price List of Stereopticons, Dissolving Views, Apparatus, Magic Lanterns, and Artistically Colored Photographic Views*. New York, [1870].

McClintock, Inez, and Marshall McClintock. *Toys in America*. Washington: Public Affairs Press, 1961.

McFarland, Marvin W., ed. *The Papers of Wilbur and Orville Wright*. New York: McGraw-Hill, 1953.

Mecredy, R. J. *The Motor Book*. London and New York: John Lane, 1903.

Memoir, Correspondence and Miscellanies, from the Papers of Thomas Jefferson. Boston, 1830.

Milton Bradley Co. *Milton Bradley, a Successful Man*. Springfield, Mass.: Milton Bradley Co., 1910.

——. *Work and Play: Annual of Home Amusements and Social Sports*. Springfield, Mass.: Milton Bradley Co., 1872.

Morse, Edward Lind, ed. *Samuel F. B. Morse: His Letters and Journals*. Boston and New York: Houghton Mifflin, 1914.

Moschovitis, Christos J. P., et al. *History of the Internet*. Santa Barbara, Calif.: ABC-CLIO, 1999.

Mott, Frank Luther. *American Journalism: A History, 1690–1960*. 3d ed. New York: Macmillan, 1962.

Nachman, Gerald. *Raised on Radio*. New York: Pantheon, 1998.

Nash, Jay Robert, and Stanley Ralph Ross. *The Motion Picture Guide*. Chicago: CineBooks, 1985–.

National Broadcasting Company. *Television's First Year*. [New York, 1940].

National Geographic Special Publications Division. *Those Inventive Americans*. Washington, D.C.: National Geographic, 1971.

Newhall, Beaumont. *The History of Photography*. Rev. ed. New York: Museum of Modern Art, 1964; 1971.

Noble, Louis Legrand. *The Life and Works of Thomas Cole*. Cambridge, Mass.: Harvard University Press, 1964.

Noyce, Elisha. *The Boy's Book of Industrial Information*. New York, 1859.

O'Brien, Richard. *The Story of American Toys*. New York: Abbeville, 1990.

Oliver, Smith Hempstone, and Donald H. Berkebile. *Wheels and Wheeling: The Smithsonian Cycle Collection*. Washington, D.C.: Smithsonian Press, 1974.

O'Malley, Michael. *Keeping Watch: A History of American Time*. New York: Viking, 1990.

Page, Arthur W. *The Bell Telephone System*. New York: Harper Bros., 1941.

Palfreman, Jon, and Doron Swade. *The Dream Machine: Exploring the Computer Age*. London: BBC Books, 1991.

Parlour Magic. Philadelphia, 1838.

Payson, Dunton & Scribner. *Manual of Penmanship*. New York, 1872.

Peale, Charles Willson. *Charles Willson Peale and His World*. Edgar P. Richardson, Brooke Hindle, Lillian B. Miller, eds. New York: Abrams, 1983.

Penn Mutual Life Insurance Company. *The First Air Voyage in America*. Philadelphia, 1943.

Pool, Ithiel de Sola. *Forecasting the Telephone: A Retrospective Technology Assessment*. Norwood, N.J.: ABLEX, 1983.

——, ed. *The Social Impact of the Telephone*. Cambridge, Mass.: MIT Press, 1977.

Poole, Steven. *Trigger Happy: Videogames and the Entertainment Revolution*. New York: Arcade Pub., 2000.

Porter, Luther Henry. *Wheels and Wheeling: An Indispensable Handbook for Cyclists*. Boston, 1892.

Post, Emily. *By Motor to the Golden State*. New York: Appleton, 1916.

Post, Mary D. *A Woman's Summer in a Motor Car*. New York: Privately printed, 1907.

Pratt, Charles E. *The American Bicycler: A Manual for the Observer, the Learner, and the Expert*. Boston, 1879.

Prime, Samuel Irenaeus. *The Life of Samuel F. B. Morse*. New York, 1875.

Radio Corporation of America. *The First 25 Years of RCA*. New York, 1944.

Rae, John B. *The Road and the Car in American Life*. Cambridge, Mass.: MIT Press, 1971.

Ramsey, Alice Huyler. *Veil, Duster and Tire Iron*. Covina, Calif., 1961.

Rhoads, B. Eric. *Blast from the Past: A Pictorial History of Radio's First 75 Years*. West Palm Beach, Fla.: Streamline Publishing, 1996.

Rhodes, Frederick Leland. *Beginnings of Telephony*. New York, London: Harper & Bros., 1929.

Rhodes, Richard, ed. *Visions of Technology: A Century of Vital Debate About Machines, Systems and the Human World*. New York: Simon & Schuster, 1999.

Richards, Caroline Cowles. *Village Life in America, 1852–1872*. New York: Holt, 1913.

Richards, George Tilghman. *History and Development of Typewriters*. London, Science Museum, 1964.

Ringwalt, J. L. *The Development of Transportation Systems in the United States*. Philadelphia, 1888.

[Robida, Albert]. *Le Vingtième Siècle par A. Robida.* Paris, [1883?].

Roehl, Harvey N. *Player Piano Treasury: A Scrapbook History of the Mechanical Piano in America.* New York: Vestal Press, 1961.

Routledge, Robert. *Discoveries and Inventions of the Nineteenth Century.* 9th ed., London, New York: G. Routledge, rev. and partly rewritten, 1891. Reprint, Crescent Books, 1989.

St. John, Thomas M. *How Two Boys Made Their Own Electrical Apparatus.* New York, 1898.

——. *Real Electric Toy-Making for Boys.* New York, 1905.

——. *Things a Boy Should Know About Wireless.* New York, 1910.

Scharchburg, Richard P. *Carriages Without Horses: J. Frank Duryea and the Birth of the American Automobile Industry.* Warrendale, Pa.: Society of Automotive Engineers, 1993.

Schroeder, Joseph J., Jr. *The Wonderful World of Toys, Games & Dolls, 1860–1930.* Northfield, Ill.: Digest Books, 1971.

Sears, Stephen W. *The American Heritage History of the Automobile in America.* New York: American Heritage, 1977.

Shea, James J., as told to Charles Mercer. *It's All in the Game* [biography of Milton Bradley]. New York: Putnam, 1960.

Sherwood, M. E. W. [Mary Elizabeth Wilson]. *Home Amusements.* New York, 1881.

Shiers, George. *Early Television: A Bibliographic Guide to 1940.* New York: Garland, 1997.

Shurkin, Joel. *Engines of the Mind: A History of the Computer.* New York: Norton, 1984.

Smith, Albert E. *Two Reels and a Crank.* Garden City, N.Y.: Doubleday, 1952.

Smith, George David. *The Anatomy of a Business Strategy: Bell, Western Electric, and the Origins of the American Telephone Industry.* Baltimore and London: Johns Hopkins University Press, 1985.

Smith, Mark, and Naomi Black. *America on Wheels: Tales and Trivia of the Automobile.* New York: Morrow, 1986.

Smithsonian Institution. *The Smithsonian Collection of Newspaper Comics.* Washington, D.C.: Smithsonian Institution Press and H. N. Abrams.

Solved; or the Sunday Evening Problem. New York, 1895.

Sousa, John Philip. *Marching Along.* Westerville, Ohio: Integrity Press, 1994; reprint of original 1928 edition.

Spofford, Ainsworth R., ed. *American Almanac and Treasury of Facts, Statistical, Financial, and Political.* New York and Washington, D.C., 1878–1889.

Steinberg, Cobbett S. *TV Facts.* New York: Facts on File, 1980.

Stern, Ellen, and Emily Gwathmey. *Once Upon a Telephone: An Illustrated Social History.* New York: Harcourt Brace, 1994.

Stover, John F. *American Railroads.* 2d ed. Chicago: University of Chicago Press, 1997.

——. *History of the Baltimore and Ohio Railroad.* West Lafayette, Ind.: Purdue University Press, 1987.

Swift, Mary A. *First Lessons on Natural Philosophy, for Children.* Hartford, Conn., 1849.

Taylor, George Rogers. *The Transportation Revolution, 1815–1860 (Volume IV, The Economic History of the United States).* New York: Holt, Rinehart and Winston, 1951.

Thompson, Robert Luther. *Wiring a Continent: The History of the Telegraph Industry in the United States 1832–1866.* Princeton, N.J.: Princeton University Press, 1947.

Time-Life Books. *Toys and Games: Imaginative Playthings from America's Past.* Alexandria, Va.: Time-Life Books, 1991.

Tomlinson, Charles. *Cyclopaedia of Useful Arts, Mechanical and Chemical, Manufactures, Mining and Engineering.* London, 1868.

The Traveller; Or Wonders of Art. New York, 1847.

Turkle, Sherry. *Life on the Screen: Identity in the Age of the Internet.* New York: Simon & Schuster, 1995.

——. *The Second Self: Computers and the Human Spirit.* New York: Simon & Schuster, 1984.

Turner, Frederick. *Rediscovering America: John Muir in His Time and Ours.* New York: Viking, 1985.

U.S. Census Bureau. *Historical Statistics of the United States, Colonial Times to 1970.* Washington, D.C., 1975.

Wachhorst, Wyn. *Thomas Alva Edison: An American Myth.* Cambridge, Mass.: MIT Press, 1981.

Waitley, Douglas. *The Roads We Traveled: An Amusing History of the Automobile.* New York: Julian Messner, 1979.

Walsh, John Evangelist. *One Day at Kitty Hawk: The Untold Story of the Wright Brothers and the Airplane.* New York: Crowell, 1975.

Ward, James A. *Railroads and the Character of America, 1820–1887.* Knoxville, Tenn.: University of Tennessee Press, 1986.

Watson, Thomas A. *Exploring Life: The Autobiography of Thomas A. Watson.* New York: Appleton, 1926.

Watt, James. *The Origin and Progress of the Mechanical Inventions of James Watt.* By James Muirhead. London, 1854.

White, E. B. *The Second Tree from the Corner.* New York: Harper, 1954.

Whitton, Blair. *Toys.* New York: Knopf, 1984.

Willard, Frances E. *A Wheel Within a Wheel: How I Learned to Ride the Bicycle.* New York, 1895.

Wise, John. *A System of Aeronautics.* Philadelphia, 1850.

Withuhn, William L., ed. *Rails Across America: A History of Railroads in North America.* New York: Smithmark, 1993.

Zellers, John A. *The Typewriter: A Short History on Its 75th Anniversary, 1873–1948.* New York: Newcomen Society of England, American Branch, 1948.

INDEX

Page numbers in *italic* type indicate illustrations.

ABOUT THE AUTHOR

Merritt Ierley, a social historian, is the author of eight books relating to American history and technology, including the recently published *The Comforts of Home: The American House and the Evolution of Modern Convenience* (Clarkson Potter, 1999). Other books include *Open House: A Guided Tour of the American Home, Traveling the National Road,* and *With Charity for All: Welfare and Society, Ancient Times to the Present.* He was the recipient of grants from the Alfred P. Sloan Foundation for this book and for *The Comforts of Home.* He is an alumnus of the College of William and Mary and Gill St. Bernard's School, Gladstone, New Jersey.